CW01216657

TOGETHER STANDING TALL

Gill Books
Hume Avenue
Park West
Dublin 12

www.gillbooks.ie

Gill Books is an imprint of M.H. Gill and Co.

© John Scally 2024

978 18045 8054 7

Designed by Bartek Janczak

Layout by Niamh McArdle

Edited by Ruairí Ó Brógáin

Proofread by Paula Elmore

Printed and bound by L.E.G.O. SpA, Italy

This book is typeset in Minion Pro and Mr Eaves.

The paper used in this book comes from the wood pulp of sustainably managed forests.

All rights reserved.
No part of this publication may be copied, reproduced or transmitted in any form or by any means, without written permission of the publishers.

All images courtesy of INPHO, with the exception of 18 (© PA Images / Alamy Stock Photo), 32L (© piemags/ww2archive / Alamy Stock Photo) and 212L (© Pictorial Press Ltd / Alamy Stock Photo).

Author's note: Unless otherwise stated, all quotations are taken from interviews conducted by the author.

A CIP catalogue record for this book is available from the British Library.

5 4 3 2 1

TOGETHER STANDING TALL

150 YEARS OF IRISH RUGBY

JOHN SCALLY

GILL BOOKS

To the many heroic men and women who gave so much so often as volunteers, supporters, coaches, players, referees, mums, dads and administrators to Irish rugby over the last 150 years – with wonderment, gratitude and amazement.

Without you, the story of Irish rugby could not be written.

The story of Irish rugby is one that begins at the heart of the community.

The Irish Rugby Football Union proudly celebrates the 150th year of our inaugural international match against England in February 1875, but the game was played at local levels for many years before that historic game.

One hundred and fifty years later, Ireland now stands proudly as a leader in the international game and our high-performance system is seen as best in class. It is important that we always acknowledge our past and the people whose foresight and vision over many years have brought us to this special time in our history.

The Irish Rugby Football Union is today a modern, inclusive and diverse organisation. Our values of respect, inclusivity, integrity, excellence and fun underpin all we do. These values have been handed down through the generations and remain at the heart and core of our game.

From the bedrock of clubs to schools and across all four provinces, countless volunteers, referees, administrators, players and coaches have helped cultivate and foster the passion for the game. While tangible on-field success is the ultimate goal, participation is the fuel that drives the love of the game.

The sense of fun, engagement and passion that is found in every corner of the island helps the game grow. This book is a testament to that passion; it's a story about people and the recounting of the IRFU's history in this landmark year is a timely reminder that rugby is a game for all, male and female, young and old. In an ever-changing world we remain conscious of change in society and how people live their lives. The book is also a story of evolution and change and is a reminder that the one certainty in life is that change is inevitable.

To my colleagues on the IRFU 150 Working Group, who have worked behind the scenes over the last 18 months, thank you for your hard work.

I would like to thank our publishers Gill for their professionalism and dedication to the project. To author John Scally, whose diligence and passion has captured the essence of the game and its wider impact across Irish society and to Billy Stickland, and the team at Inpho, whose photography brings the story to life, congratulations to you all on a job well done.

I hope that you, the reader, enjoy the book and thank you for your ongoing support of Irish rugby.

Yours in rugby,

DECLAN MADDEN
IRFU PRESIDENT, 2024/25

Paul O'Connell wins a line-out at Twickenham, 2015.

FOREWORD

It was the honour of my life to have played for Ireland. The only thing that could have trumped it was when I was fortunate enough to captain my country.

As these pages document, the story of Irish rugby is a rich and fascinating one. The last 150 years have brought many great moments and it is a welcome opportunity to look back on so many games that put a smile on the face of the nation. It is a timely reminder too of the many great players, male and female, who have worn the green jersey with such distinction.

The rugby landscape has changed dramatically over the last 150 years, reflecting the many profound changes in Irish society. As a father of a daughter myself, I am especially pleased to see that the women's game has become so prominent and that girls and women are rightfully taking centre stage in Irish rugby. The success of mini rugby all across the country has been pivotal in that respect.

Irish rugby celebrates its 150th anniversary in a healthy state. This has not happened by accident. It is the result of a lot of hard work by a great many people. The recent success of Irish rugby is built on a number of component parts: a great schools system; an underage structure that is the envy of many countries; fantastic clubs who have given us so many great players; and of course our highly admired provincial system.

In recent years as part of Andy Farrell's backroom staff I have seen how those building blocks contribute so positively to Irish rugby.

PAUL O'CONNELL

CONTENTS

Introduction 1

Part One: Standing on the Shoulders of Giants 3

    1: The Kick-Off (1874–1947) 5

    2: Magic Moments (1948–77) 23

    3: Crowning Glory (1978–95) 53

    4: True Professionals (1995–2008) 85

    5: Shoulder to Shoulder (2009–24) 103

    6: All in the Game 139

Part Two: Pillars of the Irish Rugby Community 165

    7: The Four Proud Provinces 167

    8: In the Club 195

    9: Bricks in the Rugby Wall 211

    10: The Best Is Yet to Come 229

Extra Time 235

Index 236

The Irish team in front of the old stand at Lansdowne Road, 2006.

INTRODUCTION

On 8 September 2023 the Rugby World Cup began. That day both the *Irish Times* and the *Irish Independent* devoted their editorials to the tournament and Ireland's prospects in it. It was just one indication of the central place rugby had assumed not just in Irish sport but in the life of the nation as a whole.

As would be expected, *The Late Late Toy Show* was the most viewed show in Ireland that year. However, what was somewhat surprising was that the other four of the five most-watched programmes were Irish rugby international matches.

The staggering surge in popularity of rugby in recent years was reflected in the massive support for the team during that World Cup. The hype reached a climax when Ireland cemented their status as the number one side in world rugby as they edged an enthralling and bruising tussle with defending world champions South Africa at the Stade de France, winning 13–8 in a tense Pool B match.

The nation held its breath as the boys in green lost a pulsating contest in the quarter-final to the All Blacks. Despite the disappointment of the loss, *Liveline* listeners voted for Ireland's achievements in the Rugby World Cup as their moment of the year in 2023.

*

For much of its history rugby was a man's game, but all that has changed utterly. On Valentine's Day in 1993 the Irish women's team played their first international against Scotland at Raeburn Place in Edinburgh. Women have moved from the periphery to the centre of Irish rugby, and their involvement has elevated the sport in the nation's affections.

The second half of the twentieth century was largely barren for Irish rugby apart from Munster's unforgettable win over the All Blacks in 1978 and Ireland's Triple Crown victories in 1982 and 1985. Everybody loves a winner and over the past 25 years the Irish national side and our provinces have enjoyed unprecedented success. The cumulative effect of the catalogue of success enjoyed by both the provincial and the national sides is the emergence of a huge fan base for the game throughout the country.

The popularity of the sport at the time of the 2023 World Cup was a far cry from when, nearly 150 years before, in 1875, Ireland played England in their first rugby international. In the early amateur years of Irish rugby, things were very different from the professionalism of recent years. A case in point is that of John Macaulay, a lock-forward who worked as a miller's agent. He got married just to get leave of absence to play for Ireland against England in 1887. The things we do for love.

*

This is a story not just of great players and personalities, classic victories and thrilling contests but of what happened off the field. As we shall see again and again in these pages, family – literal and metaphorical – is the tie that binds Irish rugby together.

For 150 years rugby has been a rare fixed point in a fast-changing Ireland. These years have been momentous but have not been without their troubles. But even when the storm clouds gathered, Irish rugby prevailed, and a vibrant game lay in the sunshine when the tempest was past.

The first part of this book looks back over the 150-year journey of the game in Ireland. The rugby past did not take place in a vacuum but against the backdrop of complex social, economic, political and cultural forces. We shall see how Irish rugby survived many trials and tribulations and also, through its production of so many great players, how it went on to enjoy remarkable success.

The new popularity of rugby in Ireland is no accident. The second part of this book considers the four great pillars of the success of Irish rugby: the provinces, the clubs, the schools and the underage structure.

As we shall discover, the story of Irish rugby is an epic tale of guts, grit and glory.

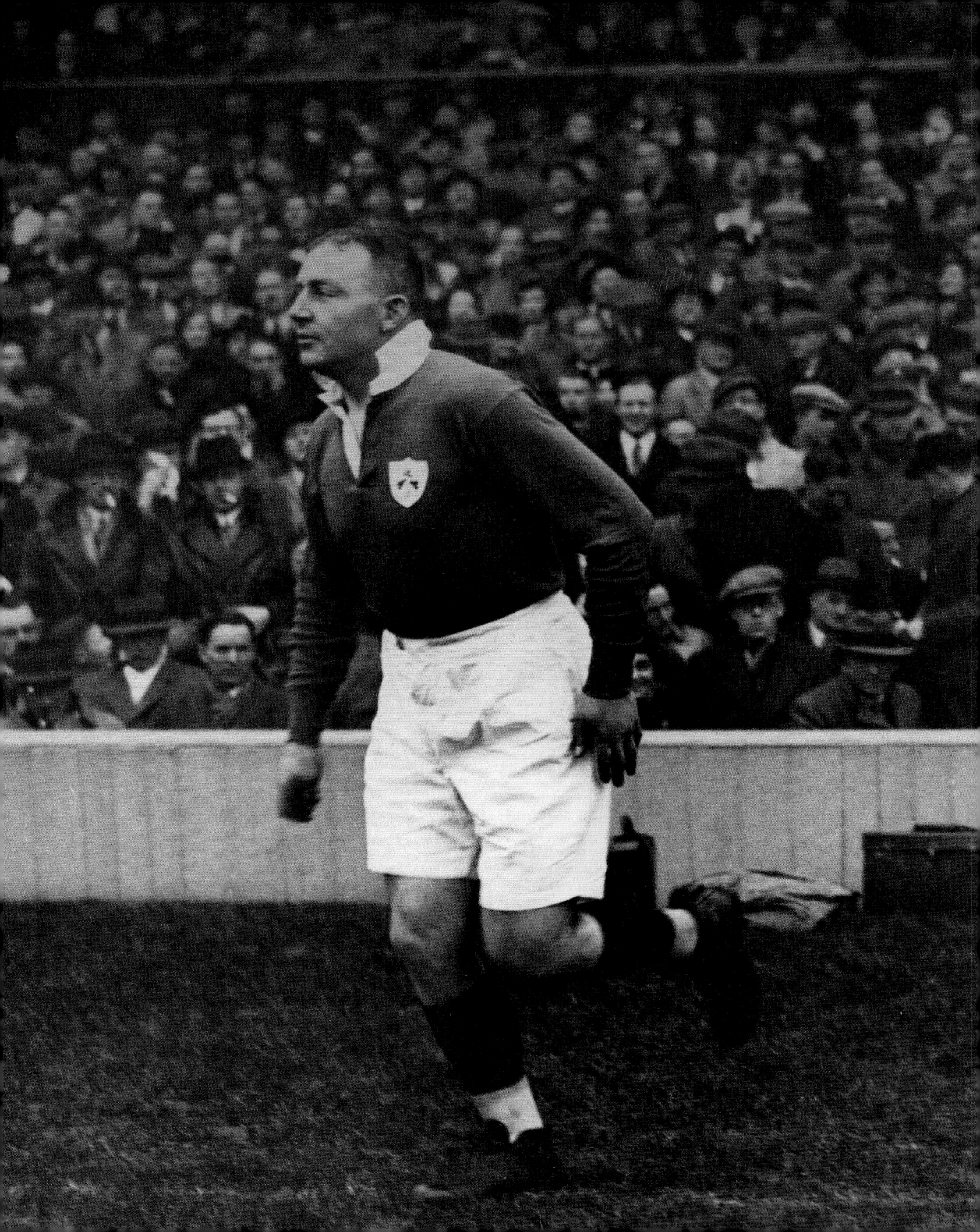

PART ONE:

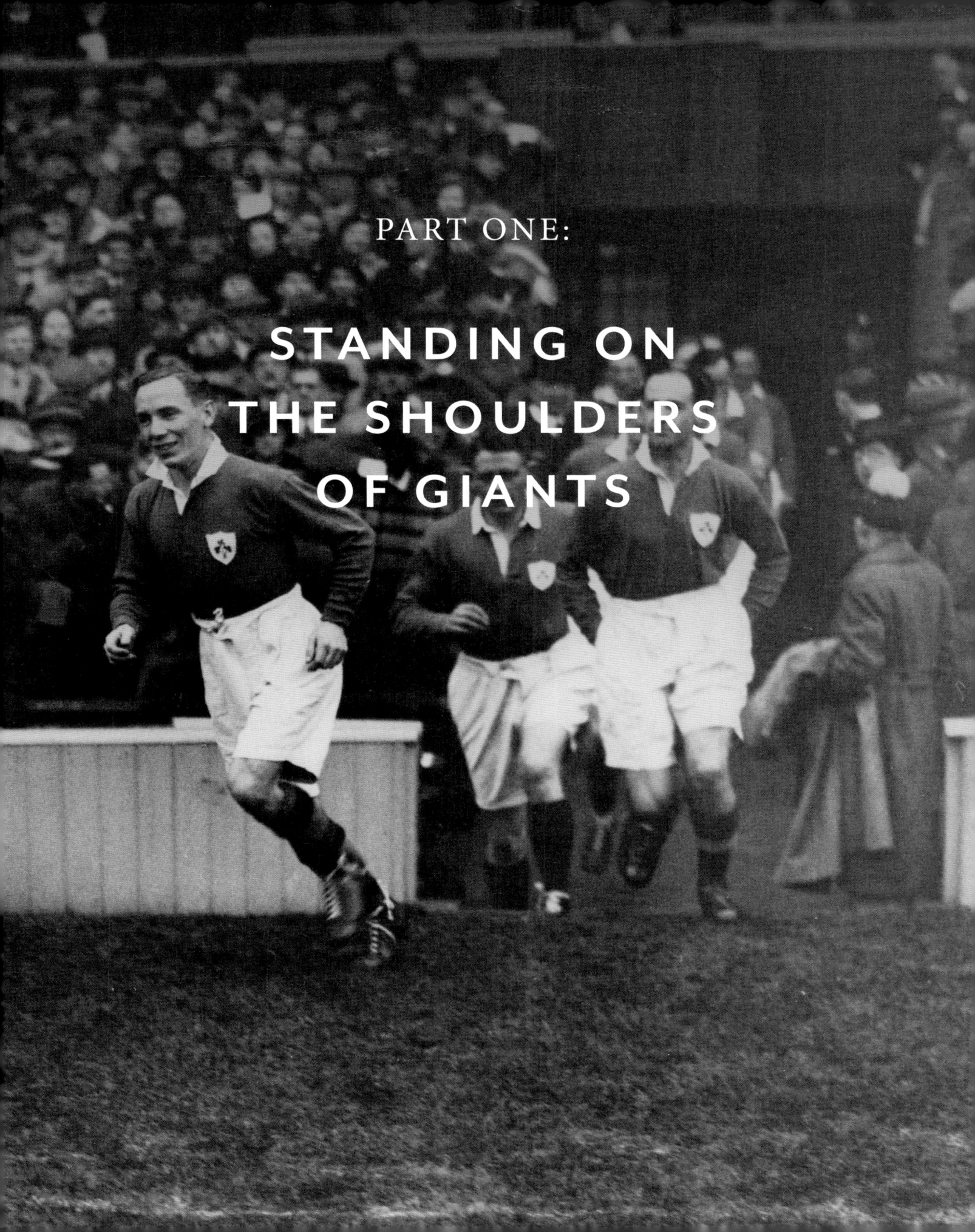

STANDING ON THE SHOULDERS OF GIANTS

The first Ireland international squad, 1875.

1

THE KICK-OFF
(1874–1947)

Every epic tale needs a great founding story.

This chapter provides the background to the emergence of rugby as a core part of the Irish sporting landscape over its first 70 years in the country – including the massive disruption of two world wars. To understand the origins of the story, it is necessary to appreciate the context – or more accurately the web of contexts.

Rugby's spread to Ireland can be traced directly to England. According to legend, the game began in 1823 when William Webb Ellis, a schoolboy in Rugby School, caught a ball and ran with it. The game became popular in some of the most prestigious schools in England.

A number of the sons of wealthy Irish families were educated in Britain, and when they continued their education at universities back home in Ireland, they brought a great love of the oval-shaped ball with them. It was in these academies that the Irish rugby story emerged.

CLUB TOGETHER

Founded in 1592, Trinity College, Dublin, is Ireland's oldest university. It also has the distinction of having the country's oldest rugby club, Dublin University Football Club, founded about 1854. (The Guy's Hospital Football Club, representing the medics of Guy's Hospital in London, is accepted by the Rugby Football Union and *Guinness World Records* as being the oldest rugby club in the world, with a foundation date of 1843.)

Trinity's connection with rugby was no accident. It was the consequence of young Irishmen returning from English public schools to study there. Back home at university they shared their love for the game with new disciples.

Another important step in the history of Irish rugby came in 1872 when the rugby club of Queen's College, Cork (later University College Cork (UCC)), was formed. UCC Rugby was the first sports club in the college and has defined the look of sports in UCC through its iconic skull-and-crossbones emblem, which has been seen since about 1880.

These two universities had a huge multiplier effect on the spread of the game around the country.

The example of Co. Kerry illustrates the larger story. Today, Kerry is synonymous with Gaelic football, but in the early years of the GAA, rugby rivalled it as Kerry's pre-eminent sport. The ancient game of caid had been popular among the Kerry population for countless generations. Rugby's spread into the Kingdom was facilitated by the characteristics it shared with caid. Both involved a group of players seeking possession of the ball before passing it to faster players on the wings, who ran with ball in hand. As a result of these similarities, the same 10 players would line out both for the Killorglin Rugby Club in February 1888 and for the Laune Rangers Gaelic football team in the 1890 county championship.

Rugby soon got its tentacles into the larger towns of Co. Kerry. Tralee Rugby Club was established in 1882 and competed in the inaugural Munster Senior Cup in 1886. Their star out-half, Dr John Hayes, had been introduced to rugby as a student in Trinity, and as they did in Britain, university graduates, once they moved home, brought with them knowledge and love of the game.

A further catalyst in the spread of the game was the presence of foreign companies, such as the Anglo-American Cable Company, in areas like Valencia Island from the 1860s. British employees acquainted with rugby introduced it to the islanders, who formed a local club.

By 1890 other clubs had been formed, and many of these are still in existence today. As well as UCC, these include Wanderers (founded in 1869), Lansdowne (1873), Dungannon (1873), Co. Carlow (1873), Ballinasloe (1875), NIFC (now merged with Collegians to form Belfast Harlequins)(1868) and Queen's University (1869).

A TALE OF TWO UNIONS

From 1874 to 1879 there were two rugby unions, and a fledgling rugby bureaucracy emerged. The Irish Football Union had jurisdiction over clubs in Leinster, Munster and parts of Ulster, and the Northern Football Union of Ireland controlled the Belfast area.

Developments from across the water again shaped the trajectory of Irish rugby. A meeting of Dublin University Football Club was held in 1874 to organise a match between Ireland and England, at which a letter from the secretary of the English Rugby Union (formed in 1871) suggesting dates for the game the following February was read. The other clubs were alerted and selected their attendees. This gathering took place in the Grafton Street premises of the sports supplier John Lawrence, editor of the distinguished *Handbook of Cricket in Ireland*. Dublin University, Wanderers, Lansdowne, Bray, Engineers, Portora Royal School, Dungannon Royal School and Monaghan were represented, many delegates of the other clubs also being Trinity members. However, the most prominent of the Belfast clubs, North of Ireland FC (NIFC), was not represented at this gathering.

Afterwards a circular was issued to the clubs and to the media, acknowledging the role that the Rugby Union had as the representative organisation in England and seeking support for the embryonic Irish Football Union. The circular proposed interprovincial and North v. South fixtures and a February date for the forthcoming fixture with England.

Before this game took place, a meeting was held in Belfast in January at which a Northern Football Union was formed for 'lovers of football in Belfast and neighbourhood', according to the notice convening its inaugural meeting. It was agreed to offer 'physical assistance' to Ireland in the forthcoming international, and a Belfast v. Dublin challenge was arranged for later in the season.

When the first international was played against England, on 15 February 1875, the teams were 20-a-side, and the Irish team included 12 players from Leinster and 8 from Ulster. The team was selected in Trinity College and featured 9 Trinity scholars, including the captain, George Stack. As a show of support the new Irish team was granted the shamrock for use as its emblem by Dublin University Football Club, which took up the college crest as a replacement.

The Irish team on that momentous day, in a 0–7 loss against England at Kennington Oval in London before three thousand spectators, was:

BACKS

E. Galbraith	Dublin University
R.B. Walkington	NIFC

THREE-QUARTER-BACKS

E. McIlwaine	NIFC
R. Galbraith	Dublin University

HALF-BACKS

A.P. Cronyn	Dublin University
G.H. Stack (capt.)	Dublin University
R. Bell	NIFC

FORWARDS

J. Allen	Wanderers
G. Andrews	NIFC
W. Ash	NIFC
M. Barlow	Wanderers
B. Casement	Dublin University
A. Combe	NIFC
W. Gaffikin	Windsor
J. Myles	Dublin University
H.L. Cox	Dublin University
F.T. Hewson	Wanderers
J. MacDonald	Methodist College
J. Magennis	Dublin University
H.D. Walsh	Dublin University

The first 15-a-side match was in 1877 in a defeat to Scotland. The first Munster players were chosen in 1879. Another milestone came in the same year, when the two unions agreed to amalgamate as the Irish Rugby Football Union (IRFU) for the whole country. Clubs formed before this date were entitled to retain the designation 'football club', whereas those formed after the formation of the IRFU were called 'rugby football club'.

Branches were to be formed in Leinster, Munster and Ulster. The IRFU was to be run by a council of 18, made up of six from each province. The council was to meet annually.

In 1885, 26 clubs were affiliated to the IRFU, of which 10 were in Ulster, 9 in Leinster and 7 in Munster. The Connacht branch was formed in 1886.

Ireland had competed in the Home Nations Championship (known today as the Six Nations) since 1883. Finally, after

12 defeats, Ireland experienced the thrill of beating the big neighbour when they defeated England in 1887 in front of five thousand people in Lansdowne Road. The stadium was founded in 1872 when Henry Wallace Dunlop acquired from the Earl of Pembroke a lease of land near Lansdowne Road railway station and developed a ground with facilities for athletics, tennis, cricket, croquet, archery and rugby. Its patrons included the Lord Chancellor, members of the nobility, members of Parliament and several British Army officers. Now, 150 years later, it remains the 'theatre of dreams' for young rugby players, albeit under its new name, the Aviva Stadium.

In victory or defeat the Irish team knew how to celebrate. In 1890, after the official dinner for the Ireland and Wales match, the high spirits of the players attracted the attention of the police, who stopped the party and summonsed the players to attend Dublin District Court the following Monday morning.

There was further cause for celebration when Ireland won the Triple Crown in both 1894 and 1899. Ireland's match against Wales at Stradey Park was memorable because of an incident involving William James Bancroft, the first superstar of Welsh rugby. Because there were no barriers around the pitch, the crowd lined up along the touchline. The referee was forced to delay the match for half an hour while police and officials attempted to force the crowd back. During the second half Bancroft attempted one of his trademark testing runs to tire out the opposition but was caught by Mick and Jack, Ireland's Ryan brothers of Rockwell College, who tackled him and dumped him over the touchline and into the crowd. Bancroft landed awkwardly and fractured several ribs, forcing him to retire from the match. Bancroft would retire with 33 successive caps and was the world record cap holder. This was the only game he didn't finish.

When the century ended, England had three Triple Crowns, Scotland and Ireland had two and Wales had one.

Ireland vs England, 1886.

Ireland vs New Zealand, 1905.

So, after a poor start, Ireland were punching above their weight by the turn of the century.

And stars were emerging: Larry Bulger was capped eight times as a winger between 1896 and 1898. He played four Test matches for the British and Irish Lions in their 1896 tour of South Africa, where he became the first Irishman to score a try against South Africa and the first Irish player to score a try for the Lions. His older brother Michael was also capped for Ireland.

The All Blacks team visited Dublin in November 1905 during their first tour of Britain and Ireland, and to meet the exceptional interest the IRFU made the game the first all-ticket rugby international in history. Ireland played only seven forwards, imitating the method New Zealand then had of playing a 'rover' – a forward who could double as a second scrum-half. The outcome was a defeat to New Zealand on a scoreline of 0–15.

That All Blacks team, then known as the Originals because they were the first New Zealand team to tour outside Australasia, were captained by a Co. Donegal native, Dave Gallaher. When Letterkenny Rugby Football Club opened its Dave Gallaher Memorial Park in 2005, the ceremony was attended by that year's touring All Black squad, who also visited Gallaher's birthplace in Ramelton.

THE KICK-OFF (1874–1947) | 9

On 20 March 1909 Ireland played France for the first time, winning 19–8. This was Ireland's biggest victory yet in international rugby and their highest points tally, which included a record five tries.

On 30 November 1912 South Africa met Ireland at Lansdowne Road for the first time, the 1906 tour game having been played at Ravenhill in Belfast. Ireland, with seven new caps, were overwhelmed by a record margin of 38–0, with the Springboks scoring ten tries.

HOSPITAL PASS

Sociology is the key to understanding the development of rugby in Ireland. It was a game for the upper and middle classes – though, as we shall see in our examination of the centrality of the clubs, Limerick has been a notable exception in this respect. It is therefore hardly surprising that doctors feature so prominently in the story of Irish rugby.

He may have won only five caps between 1879 and 1881, and scored only one drop goal, yet the contribution of Dr John Christopher Bagot to Irish rugby is significant. In his final appearance in the green shirt his drop goal in the dying minutes of a victory over Scotland in 1881 secured Ireland's first international victory after 10 defeats.

When Dr William Cox Neville captained Ireland against England in 1879, he became one of a select few players to captain on his or her debut international. The Dundalk native was the first elected president of the IRFU.

Dr Tommy Smyth became the first Irish player to captain the Lions on the tour to South Africa in 1910.

Dr Paddy Stokes is one of only eight players to be capped both before and after the First World War – winning 12 caps in total.

Dr Thomas Wallace achieved the unique honour of captaining two different countries at rugby. Firstly, he captained Ireland in 1920 while working in Wales. Then, in light of his distinguished service to Cardiff club rugby, he captained a Wales XV in an unofficial match against the English Civil Service FC.

Dr Tom Crean (not to be confused with the famous explorer) played an important part in Ireland's historic first Championship and Triple Crown win in 1894 and toured South Africa with the 1896 Lions. In 1881, at the age of 18, he won the first of his medals for bravery when he was awarded the Royal Humane Society's medal for saving a life at sea. In 1901, working as a surgeon in the Boer War in South Africa, he won a Victoria Cross when he successfully tended the wounds of two soldiers and a fellow officer under heavy enemy fire. He was wounded in the stomach and arm during these encounters and was invalided back to England, where he made a full recovery.

The large number of doctors playing rugby led to the formation of a Dublin Hospitals Football Union in 1881 and the running of the Dublin Hospitals Cup to this day. The inaugural final took place in Lansdowne Road in March 1882, with the Meath Hospital defeating Sir Patrick Dun's Hospital. In 1905–6 the Cork Charity Cup was launched with the aim of providing funds for the Cork hospitals.

THE DRACULA CONNECTION

Another noteworthy feature of Irish rugby is the number of internationals who also excelled in other sports. Frank Stoker, a distant relative of Bram Stoker, creator of Dracula, has a unique place in sporting history. In rugby he was capped five times for Ireland, between 1886 and 1891, and he also won the Wimbledon men's doubles title in 1890 and 1893, making him the first rugby international to win a senior Wimbledon title. In 1888 his brother Ernest was twice capped for Ireland.

Before Thomas Arnold Harvey became Bishop of Cashel he won eight international caps in the pack between 1900 and 1903 and made two international cricket appearances, scoring 113 runs and taking two wickets. Two of his rugby-playing brothers, George and Frederick (the latter of whom received the Victoria Cross in the First World War), were also capped for Ireland.

Another noteworthy figure was J.C. Parke from Co. Monaghan. In rugby he won 20 caps for Ireland between 1903 and 1909, and he won a silver medal in the 1908 Olympics in men's doubles tennis. Later, he was the Australian Open men's singles and doubles champion in 1912 and the Wimbledon mixed doubles champion in 1914. He also played in the Davis Cup. He was rated the top tennis player in the world in 1914. As if this were not a sufficient CV, he played golf for Ireland in 1906 and was also a noted cricketer, chess player and sprinter. He was wounded at Gallipoli but lived until 1946.

A WAR TO END ALL WARS

The outbreak of the First World War would be a momentous change for the world, and rugby in Ireland would not be sheltered from it. From 1914 until 1918 there were effectively no rugby matches: there were just occasional charity games.

Easter weekend, 1916, is arguably the most iconic few days in Irish history. What is less well known is that on Easter Saturday a special rugby game took place between Leinster and Ulster. In front of a large attendance at Lansdowne

A view of Irish players on packaging for Wills's Cigarettes.

The Ireland team, 1914.

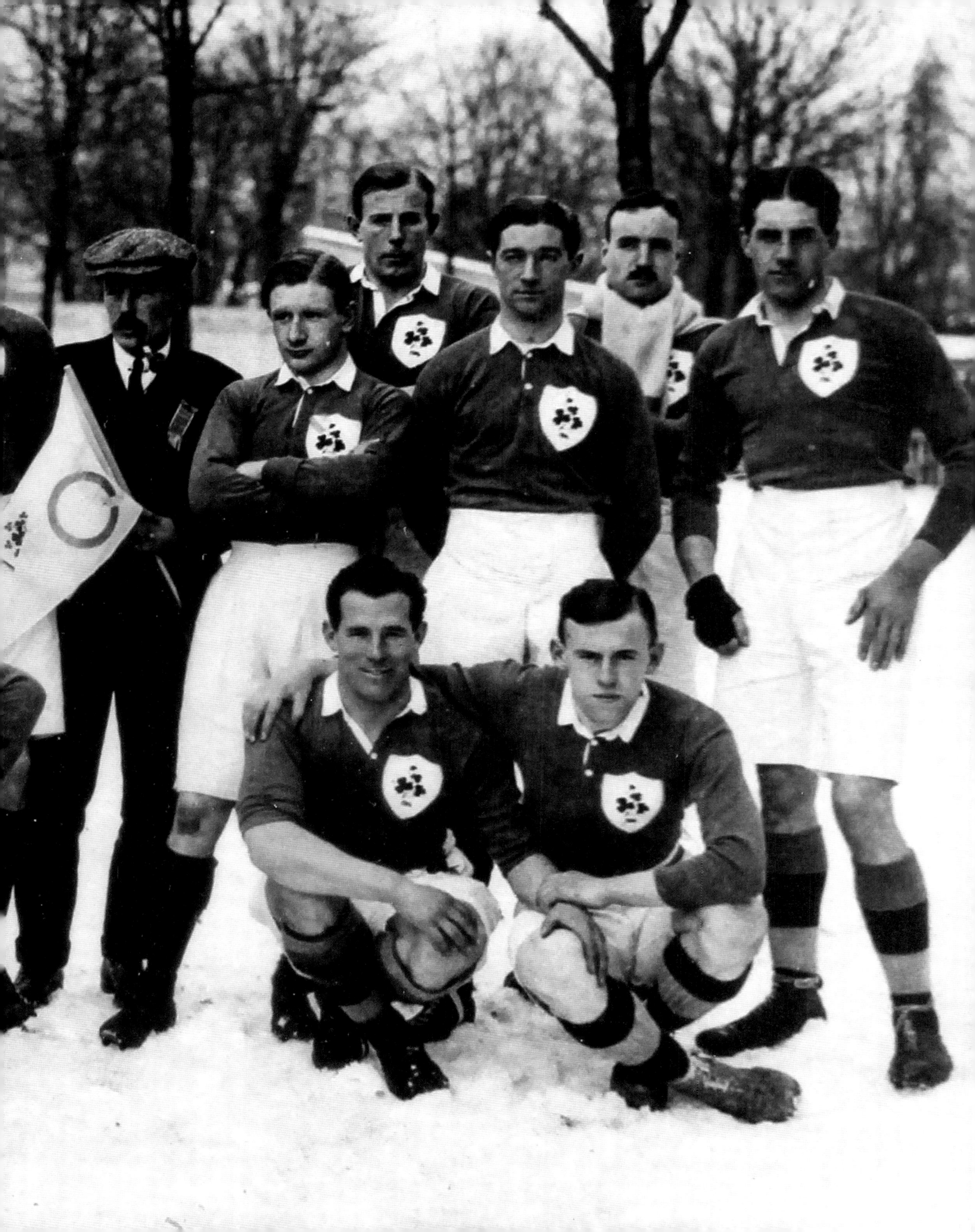

Road and starved by a diet of no meaningful rugby for two years, almost twenty internationals took to the field. They included soldiers, even one major, home on leave for Easter from the British Army.

One of the organisers of the game was Frederick Browning. Two days later he would be shot and killed by the Irish Volunteers just a stone's throw from Lansdowne Road. Browning was imbued with the ideal that there is something in people more powerful than hate as long as they continue placing peace, justice and the common good at the heart of their commitment to life, even as they live through nightmares. This led him to establish the Irish Rugby Football Union Volunteer Corps. Three hundred volunteers answered his call. They were in the main too old to join the frontline battle, and their role was to support the main work of the army. On Easter Monday, Browning was killed when the unit he led was returning to Beggar's Bush Barracks. He was fired on by outposts from Éamon de Valera's garrison in Boland's Mill, in the mistaken belief that they were shooting British soldiers.

In another example from the catalogue of sorrows, 73 members of Lansdowne FC were killed in combat in the First World War. When the first shots were fired in 1914 the club had 300 members, but four years later, after the bloody conflict ended, it was down to just 30. Such were the casualties and injuries that the war sounded the death knell for a number of rugby clubs.

Many Irish rugby players were as heroic on the battlefield as they were on the rugby field. Ernie Crawford was born in Belfast and educated at Methodist College. He was captain of Malone and played for Ulster against the touring South Africa side in December 1912. Wounded in the wrist at the Battle of Arras in 1917, he was discharged from the army with a permanent disability. He had lost manual facility in three of his fingers, but after the war he became one of Ireland's longest-serving full-backs. He won an Irish record-equalling 30 caps, captained Ireland on 15 occasions and served as president of the IRFU in 1957–8. According to legend, he was also the inventor of the word 'alickadoo', a derogatory term in rugby parlance for officials and administrators. His son-in-law Jim Ritchie captained Ireland on his first cap in 1956.

The home of Ulster Rugby, Ravenhill Stadium, opened in 1923. Today it features an ornate arch at the entrance that was erected as a memorial for those players killed in both world wars.

*

After the First World War normal service slowly resumed. In 1926 Ireland went into their final Five Nations match unbeaten and, with the Grand Slam at stake, lost to Wales in Swansea.

Ireland again came close to a Grand Slam in 1927, when their sole loss was an 8–6 defeat to England. New stars were emerging, such as Eugene Davy, who was capped 34 times for Ireland in the 1920s and 30s, captaining the side in the 1932/3 season. In 1930 he scored three tries in the space of 20 minutes against Scotland at Murrayfield.

Then came the 'master of the dummy', Mark Sugden, who became part of Irish rugby legend, particularly after he sold four dummies on the way to his winning try in 1929, the first time Ireland beat England at Twickenham.

The biggest influence, albeit indirectly, on Sugden's career was Harry Thrift, who won 18 caps for Ireland in the opening decade of the century. He captained Ireland once, in 1908, against England because that day Ireland had seven players from Trinity in the side, the largest 20th-century representation in the international team. Thrift was also an international-class sprinter. When Sugden was playing out-half for Trinity, Thrift came up to him and said, 'Sugden, you're the worst fly-half I've ever seen. Why don't you take up snooker?'

Sugden switched to scrum-half, and the rest is history. He formed a lethal combination with the Simon Geoghegan of the 1920s, Denis Cussen. A natural crowd-pleaser, Cussen won 15 caps on the wing for Ireland, scoring five tries. He also represented Ireland in the 100 metres in the 1928 Olympics in Amsterdam and was the first Irishman to break 10 seconds in the distance. Sugden also played cricket for Trinity, for whom he lined out alongside Samuel Beckett.

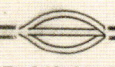

Published with Authority of the
Irish Rugby Football Union

OFFICIAL *Programme*

with Correct Numbers for Players

H. C. Jeffares
Secretary.

IRELAND v NEW ZEALAND

PRICE **3**D

LANSDOWNE RD.
SATURDAY,
7th DECEMBER
1935

PRICE **3**D

GATES OPEN 12.30 o'clock   KICK-OFF 2.15 o'clock

IF IT'S
SPORTS GOODS
GET THEM AT—

Elverys — DUBLIN & CORK

GREAT W

...eers from Leinster Rugby Clubs assembled at Headquarters o...

by Club assembled
...ber 1914.

1914-1918

Rugby Football Union, Lansdowne Road, Dublin

Robert Blair Mayne.

THE MAYNE EVENT

The Second World War would cast a long shadow on Irish rugby and in effect shut down the game for six years.

Second-row forward Lt-Col. Robert Blair Mayne won six caps for Ireland between 1937 and 1939. He had a massive frame, gained from years of lifting weights. His finest hour was the Lions tour of South Africa in 1938, in which he played 20 tour matches, including three Tests – though, curiously, he was the only member of the party not to score on the tour. He also became Irish Universities Boxing Champion.

Mayne was awarded a Légion d'Honneur for his sterling service during the Second World War in North Africa. Craving excitement, he enlisted in the British Army in 1940 and found himself deployed in the desert under Gen. Claude Auchinleck and, later, Lt-Gen. Bernard Montgomery in the Eighth Army. The opposition was formidable because the Germans were masterminded by the 'Desert Fox'. Field Marshal Erwin Rommel and his Afrika Korps wreaked havoc on the British forces before the decisive Second Battle of El Alamein from 23 October 1942. At one point Mayne had come very close to capturing Rommel. The incident was later the basis of a lengthy conversation with his international teammate Con Murphy, who asked him what he would have done if he caught Rommel.

> He told me, without blinking an eyelid, 'I would have slit his throat.' The way he said it, I don't think he was joking.

> After joining the SAS his specialty was in night raids behind enemy lines, where he destroyed 130 enemy aircraft all by himself. No less a person than Field Marshal Montgomery recommended Blair for the Victoria Cross after he saved a squadron of troops pegged down by heavy gunfire. He was some man, because he lifted the wounded one by one and put them in his jeep. At the same time he was mowing down the enemy. It was so sad that he died so young, at just 40, after a traffic accident.

> When we played together for Ireland, because I was so small, the opposition often tried to intimidate me and sometimes tried to take me out of the game. Whenever anyone 'did me damage', Mayne would come and pick me up and say, 'Are you okay, little man? I'll sort him out for you.' The first chance he got, he took revenge for the assault on me, and I was left alone for the rest of the game.

MURPHY'S LAW

When Ireland played France at Lansdowne Road on Saturday 25 January 1947 they had 14 new caps in the side. Lansdowne full-back Con Murphy was the only capped player, having won three caps against England, Scotland and Wales in 1939, and he was also the only Irish international to continue playing in the post-war era. He played for Leinster both before and after the Second World War, as well as in four of Ireland's unofficial internationals in 1946. He also played four times against the British Army in 1943–5.

It was while attending Catholic University School in Dublin that Murphy's rugby passion was born, particularly when he came under the tutelage of Ernie Crawford. Murphy's international debut came against England at Lansdowne Road in 1939. Ireland won 5–0 courtesy of a try from Harry McKibbin, which was converted by Sinclair Irwin.

There followed a 12–3 victory over Scotland. That match featured an unusual event: back-row forward Mike Sayers marked a Scottish drop-out and then dropped a goal from the mark.

The Triple Crown was decided in wet weather at Ravenhill. The match was the nadir of Murphy's international career. As he relived the moment when Ireland lost 7–0 to Wales, a haunted look darkened his face.

> I can still see the ball coming down from the heavens as if it was yesterday. I missed the catch because of the slippy ball. They got a scrum and scored a try. That is the biggest regret of my rugby career because the Triple Crown literally slipped through my fingers. You don't get chances like that too often.

Murphy had great respect for Sam Walker, who was Ireland's second captain of the Lions on their 1938 tour of South

Africa. History was made in the last match of the Test series when all eight Irishmen in the panel played on the winning Lions team. Later, Walker became a BBC commentator.

Murphy had special affection too for Charles Vesey Boyle, who won nine international caps for Ireland between 1935 and 1939, scoring one international try. He would have won more but for the intervention of the Second World War, during which he was awarded the Distinguished Flying Cross. His son Peter would later become the youngest president of the Leinster branch of the IRFU.

Next on Murphy's list was Bob Alexander, an exciting flanker noted for his dribbling who won 11 international caps for Ireland between 1936 and 1939. He also played 14 times, including in all three Test matches on the Lions tour, scoring six tries, more than any other forward on the tour. Alexander also played cricket for Ireland. As a right-hand batsman and bowler he took 29 runs in a test match in 1932. While serving as a captain in the Royal Inniskilling Fusiliers in Myanmar (then Burma) he was killed in action at the age of 33. His international rugby teammate George Morgan won 19 caps for Ireland and toured with the Lions to South Africa in 1938. He, too, represented Ireland at cricket.

Fittingly, Murphy's international swansong was in Ireland's then record 22–0 defeat of England at Lansdowne Road in 1947. Unfortunately for him he just missed out on a golden era for Irish rugby.

Soon, a player would emerge who exemplified the words of Seamus Heaney: 'There was one among us who stood taller than all the rest.'

His name?

Jack Kyle.

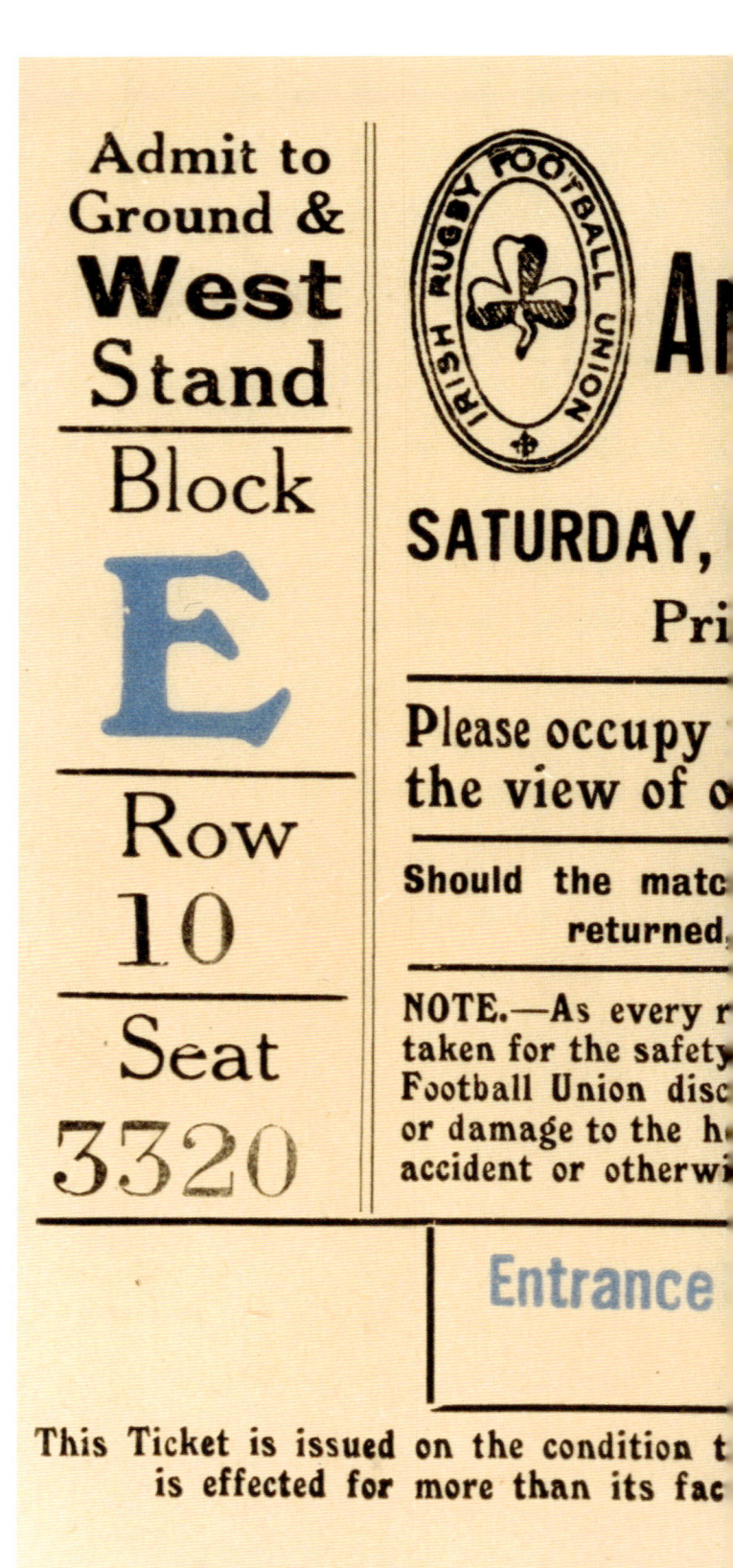

A ticket from the Ireland vs England match, 1946.

...ISH RUGBY FOOTBALL UNION.

...RISH XV v. AN ENGLISH XV

AT LANSDOWNE ROAD,

FEBRUARY, 1946. Kick-off 3 p.m.

10/- (Including Admission).

...Seat by 2.30 p.m. and do not interfere with
...s by leaving before the end of the Game.

...postponed and eventually played, no money will be
...this ticket will be available on the later date.

...ble precaution has been
...ectators, the Irish Rugby
...responsibility for injury
...f this ticket, either from

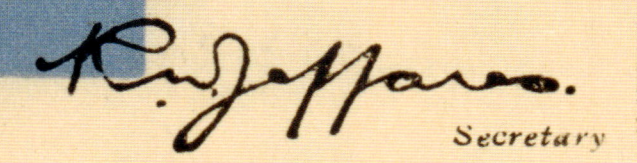

K.W. Jeffares
Secretary

Admit to
Ground &
West Stand

Block
E

Row
10

Seat
3320

Stiles **A & B** Lansdowne Road or
Havelock Square

...o re-sale
...e.

PLEASE RETAIN THIS TICKET

DROUGHT, LTD., PRINTERS, DUBLIN.

The IRFU centenary crest.

2

MAGIC MOMENTS (1948–77)

In an IRFU poll in 2002 Jack Kyle was voted the greatest ever Irish rugby player. Such was his impact during his that his glory days, when Ireland reached its first great rugby peak, in the late 1940s, were known throughout the rugby world as the 'Jackie Kyle era'.

The Irish rugby story is one of peaks and troughs. Grand Slams are no longer rare in Irish rugby, but it was not until 1948 that Ireland claimed its first. Indicative of the fortunes of the national side, it was 2009 before it won its second. Nonetheless, the intervening years saw some memorable triumphs and the emergence of new names, such as Tony O'Reilly, who would become global superstars.

Lions tours have been a showcase in which to achieve legendary status. One such showcase was the most successful Lions tour of them all, to South Africa, captained by Ulster's Willie John McBride. Gareth Edwards, the Welsh scrum-half of the 1970s, has gone on record to say that Willie John was his sort of captain because of his creed of total commitment. Edwards said he would have followed him anywhere – because each match was rugby's high noon for him. He believed in all or nothing: 'Lay down your life or don't come with me.'

Off the field, this era provided some of the greatest characters in the history of the sport, such as Moss Keane and Willie Duggan.

THE JACKIE KYLE ERA

Jack Kyle made his official Ireland debut against France in 1947 and went on to win 46 caps by 1958. This may not seem a lot by today's standards, but they spanned 11 seasons at a time when there were only four regular internationals a year. Kyle also captained Ireland on six occasions and scored 24 points from seven tries and a drop goal. In addition he toured with the Lions in Australia and New Zealand in 1950, starring in 16 of their 23 games, including all six Tests, and scoring six tries. One of these, a startling effort of individual brilliance in the first Test, is still talked about in New Zealand, in the same way that Brian O'Driscoll's wonder try in the first Test in 2001 is still talked about in Australia.

Kyle was the conductor of the orchestra in the first golden era of Irish rugby. He attended Belfast Royal Academy and at 17 was selected for the Ulster Schools XV. He continued with his rugby while a medical student at Queen's University. When Kyle was starting off he

> had the benefit of the advice of Dickie Lloyd, who played for Ireland before and after the First World War. He told me, 'Practise always with the ball in your arms. Walk 25, sprint 25, walk 25 and sprint 25.' To be fast off the mark is as vital for an out-half today as it was then. Things have changed so much in other areas, though. In our day we were trying to avoid the opposition; nowadays, they're deliberately running into people. It's a much tougher game. You need to be able to take the knocks today.

Things really kicked off on New Year's Day, 1948, when Ireland had a shock 13–6 victory over France at Colombes.

> A great character in the team was Barney Mullan. The night before the game in Paris we had a team meeting as per usual. Barney came up with the idea that if we were under pressure

Jack Kyle (centre).

J Norley, Karl Mullen, Tom Clifford and WJ McKay in France, 1952.

during the game and got a line-out he would call a short one and throw it out over the forwards' heads and lift the siege. True to plan, we got a line-out on our own 25. The French players were huge – they looked like mountains to us – so we needed to out-think them. Mullan threw it long and Paddy Reid scored under the posts.

Our strategy back then was 'We're going to run them into the ground.' We had such a fit and fast back-row in particular at the time that we knew we could wear them down, and we did. There's a lot of talk today that 'forward supremacy is the key', but at that time we were always able to win the battle of the packs, which made our job in the backs all that much easier.

Travelling to Paris for us at the time was like going to the edge of the world. We were as green as grass. After our win we were invited to a reception at the Irish embassy. Of course champagne was the order of the day, which was a very novel experience for most of us. Some of the team were knocking it back as if it was stout! To me the incident that best illustrated our innocence was when the Dolphin pair, Jim McCarthy and Bertie O'Hanlon, asked for red lemonade!

On Valentine's Day, 1948, Ireland beat England 11–10 at Twickenham. Then came a 6–0 win over Scotland at Lansdowne Road. The Grand Slam decider against Wales at Ravenhill was the critical game, on 13 March. Ireland fought a tense battle – with nerves as much as with the opposition – before emerging victorious. Kyle believed that the decisive moment came when Ireland lay the Welsh bogey to win 6–3.

We were fortunate to have a wonderful captain in Karl Mullen. He was great for letting everyone have their say.

The night before the Wales game we had a meeting. One of the people who had given us advice was Dave O'Loughlin, who had been a star Irish forward just before the Second

World War. To all of us on the '48 team he was an idol. He had played against the great Welsh scrum-half Haydn Tanner, who was still calling the shots on the Welsh team in 1948. [The previous year his late break had set up a try that robbed Ireland of the Triple Crown.] Dave told us that Tanner was the man to watch and assured us that he would make two breaks during the game. At the team meeting it was suggested that Des O'Brien should be appointed as Tanner's shadow, whose job it would be to ensure that when the Welshman broke he would be quashed. Someone went so far as to suggest that if he didn't do his task properly in this respect he should be dropped. Des was not too happy with this part of the plan at the time, but he was given the assignment nonetheless.

Sure enough, Haydn broke twice. Both times Des tackled him superbly. In fact, so annoyed was Tanner on the second occasion that he slammed the ball on the ground in frustration. These things didn't just turn that match: I'm convinced it was the difference between victory and defeat for us in the Grand Slam.

I especially remember the game against Wales at Ravenhill that day in front of a capacity crowd of thirty thousand. I'd say they could have taken four times as many had there been places for them. We were all understandably a bit apprehensive but deep down felt we could win. Karl [Mullen] made a point of getting the team to discuss tactics and the strengths and weaknesses of our opponents before matches. He made sure that every man had his say, and it was an important part of the pre-match preparations from the point of view of contributing to the great team spirit. We also had a 'council of war' at half-time, and Karl kept us on the straight and narrow.

DALY GRIND

Kyle's clearest memory of the Grand Slam-winning side was of Jack Daly.

At the time we always faced playing the Welsh on their own patch with trepidation. In 1948, though, when we played them, Jack sat in the dressing room punching his fist into his hand, saying, 'I'm mad to get at them. I'm mad to get at them. I'm mad to get at them.' His enthusiasm rubbed off on the rest of us.

Jack was an extraordinary character. Before the war he only played with the thirds for London Irish. As he departed for combat he said, 'When I come back I'll be picked for Ireland.' He was stationed in Italy during the war and had to carry heavy wireless equipment on his back. As a result his upper-body strength was incredible. Before internationals he did double somersaults to confirm his fitness.

He scored the decisive try in Belfast that clinched the Triple Crown in 1948. He turned to Des O'Brien and said, 'If Wales don't score now, I'll be canonised in Cobh tonight.'

In fact, at the end of the game, the fans tore his jersey off his back to keep as a souvenir because Ireland hadn't won the Triple Crown for 49 years. Having scored the winning try to give us the Grand Slam in 1948, he was nearly killed by spectators at the final whistle. His jersey was stripped off his back, and people were wearing pieces of it on their lapels for weeks afterwards. Jack was whisked off from the train station in Dublin the next day by a girl in a sports car whom he had never met but who was sporting a piece of his jersey on her blouse. He stayed with her for a week and lost his job when he went back to London.

The Irish team on that historic day was:

Dudley Higgins	NI Civil Service
Bertie O'Hanlon	Dolphin
William McKee	NIFC
Paddy Reid	Garryowen
Barney Mullan	Clontarf
Jack Kyle	Queen's University
Ernie Strathdee	Queen's University
John Daly	London Irish
Karl Mullen (capt.)	Old Belvedere
Albert McConnell	Collegians
Colm Callan	Lansdowne
Jimmy Nelson	Malone
Bill McKay	Queen's University
Jim McCarthy	Dolphin
Des O'Brien	London Irish

TRAINING WITHOUT STRAINING

Training techniques were very different back then, as Jack Kyle recalled:

> You have to remember that it was such a different set-up from today's. When I started playing, a drop goal was worth four points and a try only three. In fact, in 1946 we lost an unofficial international 4–3 to France when they scored a drop goal and we got a try.
>
> We came down from Belfast on the train in the morning, and in the afternoon we went for a 'training session', using the term loosely, in Trinity College. Johnny O'Meara might throw me a few passes and that would be enough for me. We used an interesting word a lot at the time, 'stale', which I never hear now. Basically, we believed if we trained too hard we would not perform on the Saturday. It was probably an excuse for us not to do any serious work!
>
> I only dropped a goal once for Ireland. It was from a very difficult angle. If I had thought about it I could never have attempted it: it was just instinctive. A lot of times we were working on a subconscious level.
>
> Another time I combined with Jim McCarthy for Jim to score a great try. I got a letter afterwards telling me it was such a textbook score we must have practised it on the training ground. Looking back now, it's amazing how few set moves we had worked out came off.
>
> I was not a great tackler. If I had to play rugby as a forward I would never have played the game. Our back row of Jim McCarthy, Bill McKay and Des O'Brien was so strong that I didn't have to bother too much with the normal defensive duties of a fly-half. McCarthy was like greased lightning and an incredible forager and opportunist. I could virtually leave the out-half to our two flankers. I just stood back and took him if he went on the outside.

Karl Mullen, Michael O'Flanagan, Jim McCarthy and Jack Kyle, 2005.

The 1948 Triple Crown-winning team.

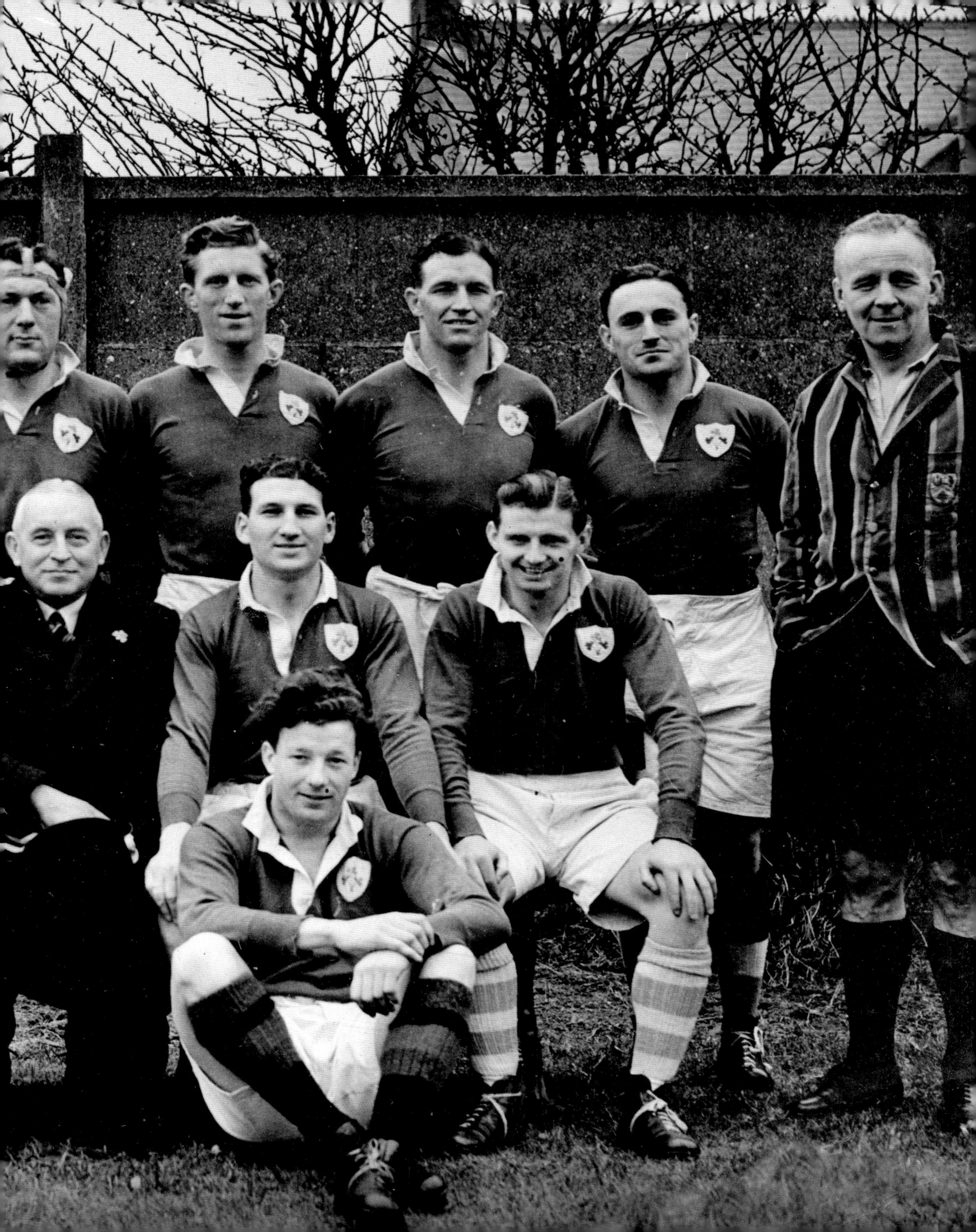

Jim McCarthy was capped twenty-eight times for Ireland between 1948 and 1955, captaining the side four times in 1954 and 1955 and scoring eight international tries. He brought a new dimension to wing-forward play, particularly in relation to helping the out-half breach the opposing half. A flying redhead, he was an invaluable ally to Kyle, combining with him to devastating effect. His back-row combination with Des O'Brien and Bill McKay in those years is among the finest in Irish rugby history.

McCarthy paid homage to Kyle:

> When I was playing for Ireland the best place to be was two feet behind Jackie Kyle. He was a wizard. I'd be struggling to put words on him, he was such a classy player – a man apart. The strange thing about him is that, for all his greatness, he was such a humble man and a real team player.
>
> The classic tale told about Jack concerns John O'Meara's first cap, when he was to partner Jack at half-back. He was naturally a bit apprehensive about partnering the unquestioned best player in the world and was debating how he would address Jack. Should he call him Dr Kyle or Mr Kyle? John travelled up in the *Cork Examiner* van and walked meekly into the team hotel. Immediately he came in the door, the first person to greet him was Jack, who said, 'Congratulations. Johnny. Delighted to see you here. Where would you like me to stand on the pitch?' Who else would have shown such modesty!
>
> It said so much about him that when his rugby career was over he spent decades in Zambia working as a doctor almost single-handedly in a provincial hospital. He never talked about helping the most needy – he lived it.

BIG TOM

Ireland used just 19 players in clinching the 1949 Championship and Triple Crown, only the fourth time the Triple Crown had been retained by a home nation.

Irish rugby players typically came from the white-collar class, but in this period the Irish team literally became white-collared. Ernie Strathdee, who won nine caps for Ireland, was a strong player with an accurate pass and was Jack Kyle's partner (and clubmate) at scrum-half in the 1948 and 1949 season. A Presbyterian minister during his rugby career, he would later become a TV sports journalist.

Fr Tom Gavin played twice in the centre for Ireland in 1949 against France and England. A headmaster and product of Cotton College, Staffordshire, and Cambridge University, he has a unique claim to fame in the annals of Irish rugby: he is the only practising Roman Catholic priest to have played for Ireland.

Although Ireland lost to France in 1949, depriving them of consecutive Grand Slams, the match was notable for the debut of Young Munster's Tom Clifford. He toured with the Lions to New Zealand in 1950 and was one of nine Irish players to make the tour with Karl Mullen (who captained the side), George Norton, Michael Lane, Noel Henderson, Jack Kyle, Jimmy Nelson, Bill McKay and Jim McCarthy.

Kyle had reason to remember Clifford fondly from the Lions tour to New Zealand and Australia in 1950.

> We were given two blazers and our jerseys and two pounds, ten shillings a week for expenses. If you adjusted that figure to allow for inflation, I can't see chaps playing international rugby accepting that today! From our point of view, the trip was a very enriching experience.
>
> We were gone for six months. Although we had journeyed to France to play an international, it was our first real experience of travel. We went out via the Panama Canal and home by the Suez Canal, so it was really a round-the-world trip. We kept fit by running round the ship. Every afternoon we had great discussions about rugby. I learnt more about the game in those conversations than I ever had before or since.
>
> Our champion was Tom Clifford. Apart from the normal luggage, Tom brought a massive trunk onto the ship. We were all puzzled about what he could have in it. As cabins were shared, players were instructed to only store essential items there, but Tom insisted on bringing in his trunk, which immediately caused a lot of grumbles from his roommates, who were complaining about the clutter.

Karl Mullen, 2009.

They changed their tune the first night, though, when some of us said we were feeling peckish. Tom brought us into his cabin and opened his trunk, which was crammed with food which his mother had cooked. So every night we dined royally in Tom's cabin. Someone said that we should all write a letter to Mrs Clifford because she fed us so well on that trip.

Tom had a very healthy appetite. To break the monotony on the journey, we had all kinds of competitions. One night we had an eating competition. Tom won hands down because he got through the thirty courses that were on the menu. On the field Tom had more guts than you could hang on a fence.

The Lions lost the Test series three matches to nil with one game drawn. Despite the disappointment, Kyle easily won the hearts and minds of that most discriminating set of critics – the New Zealand rugby community.

EVITA

There was one big regret from Jim McCarthy's playing days.

> We should have won the Grand Slam in 1951. We had the beating of Wales, but our penalty kicker, George Norton, was injured and we let the game slip through our fingers. We drew 3–3. They sprang a new kicker, Ben Edwards, who kicked a wonderful penalty, and we equalised with a fantastic try from Jack Kyle. We missed the conversion from in front of the posts. We won the Championship that year, but it should have been the Grand Slam.

Uniquely among former Irish rugby internationals, Des O'Brien's biggest sporting regret is that he never tried to qualify for the Wimbledon tennis championships. Then again, O'Brien was not your typical rugby international:

apart from playing 20 times for Ireland, he competed 14 times at the international level for Ireland at squash. He also represented Wales at hockey and was a reserve on the Welsh tennis team.

Like Jack Kyle, O'Brien was a poetry enthusiast. The antitheses of the fabled 'rugger buggers', they shared a love for the poetry of the Belfast native Louis MacNeice in particular. Both players wrote poetry but were consistently disappointed by their literary output, joking that if their rugby were of the same standard, Ireland would never have won the Grand Slam. MacNeice himself was a keen rugby fan.

A renaissance man, O'Brien took a master's degree in architectural history in his 70s and performed in Gilbert and Sullivan productions. He was leader of the pack.

According to O'Brien,

> we were the undisputed kings of wheeling the scrum [the deliberate twisting of the scrum to one side]. In an England game we wheeled the scrum from our own line to their half. Another time we wheeled our opponent's scrum seven times. Every time there was a scrum you could see the fear in the opposition's eyes. Half of our training was spent practising dribbling. When the laws changed shortly after that, the tradition of wheeling the scrums waned dramatically and the art of dribbling died completely. I really feel half of the game died with it.
>
> I found the secret of leading an Irish pack was to keep them under tight control from the start; otherwise, they went off like a cavalry charge and died away in the last fifteen minutes of each half. We had a very tight set scrum that only timed the shove when the ball left the scrum-half's hand. We gave a

The Ireland team, 1949.

stone a man away to the 1951 Springboks, and yet we could shift them back two feet at every scrum. In those days the hooker had to fight for the ball, and two feet was all he needed.

In the five years I played for Ireland nobody had a wife or a motor car. We either walked or cycled. This gave us a natural fitness which players don't have today. I know this might sound like boasting, but I think we were the fittest back row that ever played for Ireland. Jim McCarthy in particular had exceptional fitness. Our other colleague in the back row, Bill McKay, was 400-yards sprinting champion and a boxing champion. The three of us played together 14 times for Ireland and only lost three times.

One of our favourite tactics was to deliberately starve Jack Kyle of the ball for 20 minutes and lull the opposition into a false sense of security. Then we fed him and they were destroyed. He was also in a class of his own when it came to kicking for touch.

George Norton was probably the first Irishman to exhaustively practise place kicks. In his case practice certainly made perfect.

I was lucky enough to play with some great characters like John Smith, the prop from Queen's University. I remember listening to him being interviewed for the radio. He was asked on what side he played in the scrum. In his best Northern accent he replied, 'Sometimes I play on the right side, sometimes I play on the left side – but not right and left at the same time.'

Strangely, O'Brien's most satisfying victory did not come in either of the Triple Crown years.

I think the match that pleased me most was when we beat Scotland 6–5 [O'Brien himself scored the try, with Noel Henderson adding a drop goal] at Murrayfield in 1951. We lost George Norton after 15 minutes, so we had to play with only fourteen players for 65 minutes.

The following year saw O'Brien touring with Ireland to South America.

It was a total success off the field and a disaster on it. We were the first international team to be beaten by Argentina. When we got there we were told we couldn't play any rugby because Eva Perón ['Evita'] had just died. They sent us down to Santiago, Chile, to teach the cadets how to play. After eight days they beat us!

The players didn't take the playing side very seriously. At one stage Paddy Lawler went missing for a few days and nobody had a clue where he was. When he returned, a team meeting was hastily called. The team manager solemnly announced that he had been talking to Dublin, which was a big deal in 1952, and then looked round menacingly and said, 'I'm deciding whether or not to send some players home.' Paddy stood up straight away and replied, 'We've been talking among ourselves, and we're deciding whether or not we should send you home.'

THE LIFE OF O'REILLY

After the heady days of 1948–51, Ireland's form went on a downward trajectory, though there was a new spark in the form of Tony O'Reilly. Having first been capped against France as an 18-year-old in 1955, he was the undisputed star of the Lions tour to South Africa in the same year. The Lions were captained and managed by Irishmen, Robin Thompson and Jack Siggins, respectively. The squad featured five Irish players: Thompson, Tom Reid and Robin Roe in the forwards; and O'Reilly and Cecil Pedlow in the backs. O'Reilly scored no fewer than 16 tries, a record number for a Lions tour, and emerged as top scorer.

In 1959 O'Reilly went even better on the Lions tour to New Zealand and Australia, amassing a staggering 22 tries. It is probably a testimony to his importance to the team that he played in more matches than any other player, 24 in all. However, that time it was another Irish player, David Hewitt, who was top scorer, with 106 points.

O'Reilly was one of ten Irish players to make the Lions tour. The team was captained by Ronnie Dawson. The eight other Irish players were Gordon Wood, Syd Millar, Noel Murphy, Bill Mulcahy, David Hewitt, Niall Brophy and Mick English, with Andy Mulligan making the trip as a replacement to cover for injured players. Under the leadership of Dawson – the fifth Irish player to captain a touring side – the 1959 Lions set a record of 842 points and in the process ran in 165 tries.

The Irish squad takes off on a tour
of Chile and Argentina, 1952.

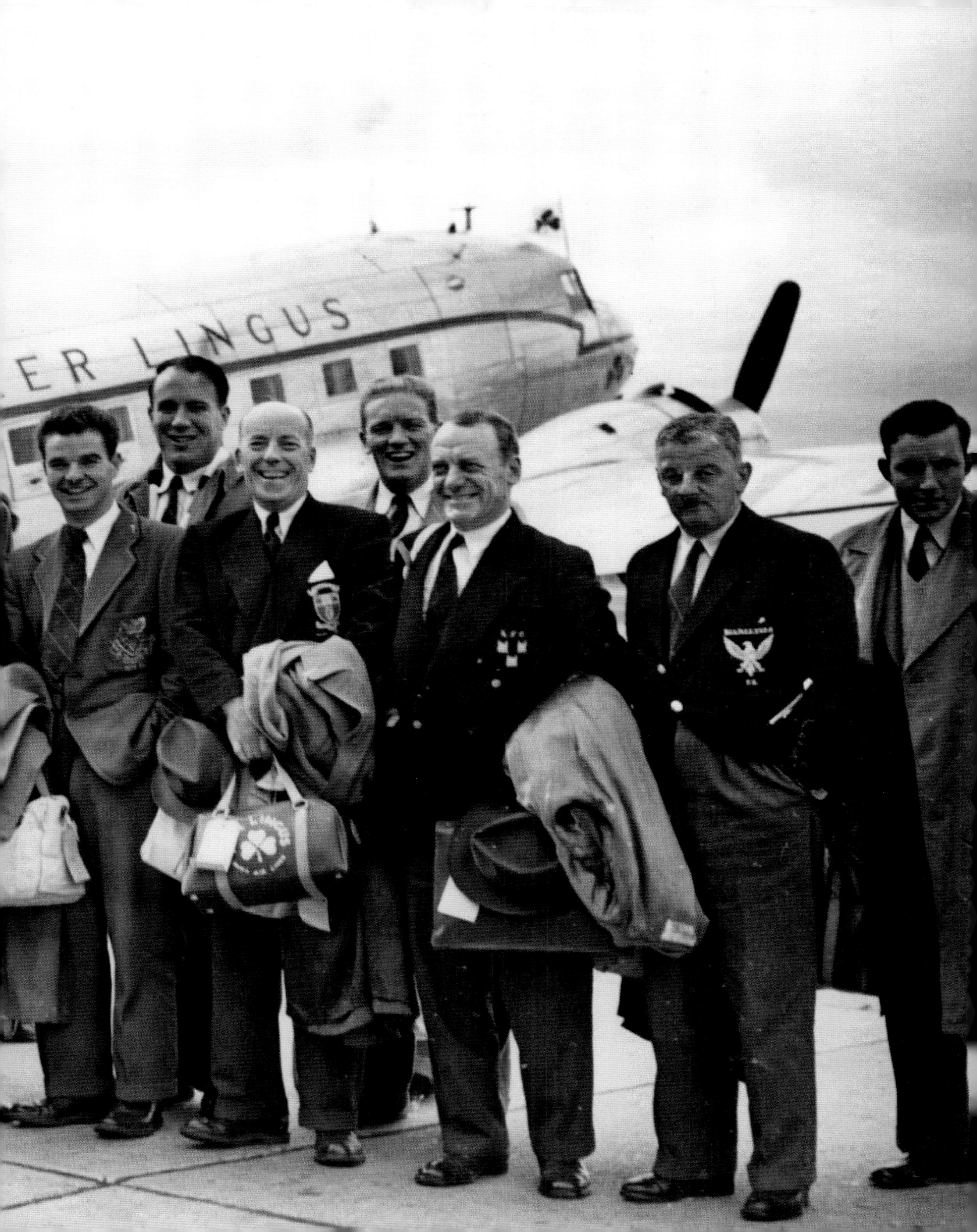
ER LINGUS

Few people were closer to O'Reilly than Jim McCarthy, who knew

> the first time I saw him that he would be a success in anything he turned his hand to. He had it all and more.
>
> Having said that, I don't envy him. I believe he was never fully exploited on the Irish team ... He should have been selected at full-back to get the best out of his attacking abilities. There are two sayings which I think apply to Tony: 'The bigger the reputation, the smaller the gap' and 'To be good, you've got to be twice as good.' Everybody wants to cut the guy with the big reputation down to size.
>
> I was best man at both his weddings. I only played one season with Tony at international level. When he arrived on the scene he was the darling of the media and could do no wrong. After his first match against France the *Irish Independent* said that I had played poorly and had not protected Tony well enough, even though I wasn't playing in the centre. I was dropped for the next match after that report and never played another international. Twenty-five years later Tony put me on the board of the *Irish Independent* just to make up for their injustice to me all those years ago.

Such is O'Reilly's flair with words that it is difficult to imagine that he was once out-quipped. When England beat Ireland 20–0 in 1956, as he walked off the pitch, O'Reilly turned to Tom Reid and said, '20–0? That was dreadful!' Reid responded, 'Sure weren't we lucky to get the nil?'

Gordon Wood was capped 29 times for Ireland between 1954 and 1961 at loose-head prop, scoring one international try. He formed a formidable front row in the late 1950s and early '60s with Syd Millar and Ronnie Dawson. Thirty-five years later Ireland's tour to Australia would see the emergence of a new star: his son Keith, who earned rave reviews for his performances as hooker.

One milestone was secured in 1958 when Ireland beat Australia 9–6 in Lansdowne Road, the first time they beat a touring side. The team in full on that day was:

P.J. Berkery	London Irish
A.J.F. O'Reilly	Old Belvedere
N.J. Henderson (capt.)	NIFC
D. Hewitt	Queen's University
A.C. Pedlow	CIYMS
J.W. Kyle	NIFC
J.A. O'Meara	Dolphin
B.G.M. Wood	Garryowen
A.R. Dawson	Wanderers
P.J. O'Donoghue	Bective Rangers
J.A Donaldson	Collegians
W.A. Mulcahy	UCD
N.A. Murphy	Cork Con
J.R. Kavanagh	Wanderers
J.B. Stevenson	Instonians

Tony O'Reilly.

The Lions and the All Blacks run out onto the pitch, 1959.

THE SWINGING SIXTIES

Bill 'Wiggs' Mulcahy, born in Rathkeale, Co. Limerick, became one the key figures in Irish rugby in the 1960s. He won Leinster Cup medals with Bective Rangers and a Munster Cup medal with Bohemians in 1962. A product of St Munchin's College in Limerick, he learnt there the subtleties of the game, especially those carried on between (broadly speaking) consenting adults in the privacy of the scrum. He was capped on 35 occasions for Ireland between 1958 and 1965. He is also noted for his quick wit. Once, when asked by Tony O'Reilly how he would like the ball thrown into the line-out, he replied, 'Low and crooked.'

He was a typical Irish player. When he went to University College Dublin (UCD) he studied medicine ... whenever rugby permitted. He was one of six Irish players – with Tom Kiernan, Niall Brophy, David Hewitt, Syd Millar and Willie John McBride – selected for the Lions tour to South Africa in 1962. Mulcahy's loss to the Lions after only nine games, after he was severely injured in a match against New South Wales, badly affected the strength of the scrum and was a significant contributor to the Lions' ultimate failure. When fit, he had been the perfect partner for the great Welsh lock Rhys Williams.

Mulcahy was also honoured with the Irish captaincy in 1962. The captain's role was very different then from what it is now because they had no coach or back-up team, so there were many additional responsibilities. They also had no squad sessions. Mulcahy was not an instant success in this role. Ireland went to Twickenham with nine new caps and got hammered 16–0.

Bill 'Wiggs' Mulcahy.

Prince Charles meets the players at Cardiff Arms Park, 1969.

The sweetest moment of Mulcahy's career was going back two years later and getting revenge in the best way possible by defeating England 18–5. It was especially sweet because of Pat Casey's famous try under the posts. Kevin Flynn also got two tries that day. It is probably fair to say that Ireland did not have a great side at the time but that it had some great players. Jerry Walsh's commitment was evident when he came back from an international with two black eyes.

Barry Bresnihan was capped 25 times in the centre for Ireland between 1966 and 1971, scoring five international tries. He went on two Lions tours, to Australia and New Zealand in 1966 and to South Africa in 1968, where he played three Test matches. On the 1966 tour he wrote himself into the history books by becoming the first replacement in representative rugby. His brother-in-law Con Feighery was capped three times in the pack for Ireland in 1972. Con's brother Tom, a prop-forward, was also capped for Ireland.

The year 1969 was almost a great one for Ireland. There was a 17–9 victory over France – their first victory over the French in 11 years. England were dispatched 17–15 in Dublin, and Barry McGann (a former Irish youths international in soccer who once played against the legendary Johan Cruyff) scored his first international try that season when Ireland defeated Scotland 16–0. The Grand Slam was now on.

The Cardiff Arms Park showdown is best remembered for arguably the most controversial punch in the history of international rugby. Noel 'Noisy' Murphy of Ireland was sensationally floored by the Welsh captain, Brian Price. Ten minutes into the match Murphy, in his final international (after winning 41 caps and touring twice with the Lions), was left sprawling on the ground. Ireland lost 24–11.

It was a very physical match. The press made a lot of the fact that Prince Charles was attending his first match as Prince of Wales, and right in front of him Price knocked

Mike Gibson in action at Cardiff Arms Park, 1969.

out Murphy. People today may not appreciate just how sensational the incident was. There was no culture of sending players off, as there is now, so Price continued on his merry way for the rest of the game. The match was really the beginning of the great Welsh team with Gareth Edwards to the fore.

In the autumn of that year the IRFU decided to appoint a coach for the national team for the first time. The role went to Ronnie Dawson.

A low point came in 1970 when 23 players were selected on a depleted Irish squad (deprived of the services of such high-profile players as Ken Kennedy and Roger Young) to tour Argentina. The challenge facing the Irish was compounded by the fact that the tour was in August, which meant that the visitors were ring rusty after a three-month layoff, whereas the home sides had been competing since the previous April. Moreover, Argentina were still bullish in the wake of recent victories over Scotland and Wales. Ireland lost three of their seven matches, including both Tests, 8–3 and 6–3 respectively.

On the plus side, 1970 saw the emergence of a new star. Fergus Slattery's first cap came against the Springboks in 1970 in an 8–8 draw. The terraces behind the goals at Lansdowne Road were empty and the playing surface cordoned off by barbed wire to prevent anti-apartheid protesters from invading the pitch. Slattery recalled the circumstances:

> It was a very controversial match. I was in UCD at the time and there was a forum before the game to debate whether or not Ireland should play South Africa. I spoke in favour and Kader Asmal [founder of the Irish Anti-Apartheid Movement] spoke against.

> The weather was very bad before the match, and they put straw on the pitch. It was like running into a barn. Having said that, the game lost none of its impact for me because of that. Things went pretty well for us that season. We beat Scotland 16–11 and then defeated a Wales side seeking the Triple Crown 14–0.

Slattery would become the nightmare of a generation of fly-halves. A product of Blackrock College, he was capped over sixty times for Ireland as an open-side wing-forward (a world record for a flanker) between 1970 and 1984, scoring three international tries. Perhaps the ultimate compliment came from the 'voice of rugby', the legendary BBC commentator Bill McLaren, who selected Slattery for his rugby 'dream team'.

THE BAN

The year 1971 was a momentous one in Irish sport. The political leanings of the GAA had been clearly manifested in 1905, when Rule 27, commonly known as 'The Ban', was enacted. It prohibited members of the GAA from playing, attending or promoting 'foreign' games such as soccer and rugby.

Ireland's first president, Douglas Hyde, was removed as a patron of the GAA within a few months of his inauguration in 1938 because he had the temerity to attend a soccer game between Ireland and Poland at Dalymount Park, breaching the GAA's ban. In effect the GAA had a vigilance committee whose brief was to attend so-called foreign games and report GAA members in attendance either in a playing or supporting capacity.

Roscommon's most iconic footballer, Dermot Earley, later chief of staff of the Defence Forces, was a victim of this in the 1960s. His army career would afford him many opportunities outside the professional realm. Although he might never have had the career of a Brian O'Driscoll, it nonetheless comes as a shock to discover that Earley turned down the opportunity to play international rugby. While on army duty in the Middle East he played rugby with a side called the Wild Geese, composed of Irish army exiles in the Middle East. In matches against the top club sides, Earley made such an impression that he was invited to become an Israeli international. Politically, this was out of the question.

When Earley played for the army it would have been folly, from a GAA viewpoint, for him to be seen playing rugby. As a result the rugby team could have only 14 players in the team photograph. Sometimes the referee might stand in for him. This became something of a recurring joke in

Fergus Slattery, 1979.

Kevin Flynn in action.

rugby circles. On one occasion a referee walking onto the field said, 'Let's get the photograph over, because I know I have to stand in here for your man.' The press officer of the rugby team came up with an assumed name for Dermot: Lieutenant Earley became 'Lieutenant Late'.

In 1971 the GAA ended the ban – finally legitimising players who played rugby on Saturday and Gaelic games on Sunday.

A SPECIAL WELCOME

The high point of 1972, from an Irish standpoint, came in Twickenham. Ireland were trailing 12–7 when Barry McGann dropped a goal. Then, when everyone thought the final whistle was about to be blown, the evergreen centre Kevin Flynn cut through the English defence like a knife through butter for a superb try. Tom Kiernan added the conversion and Ireland won 16–12.

However, the Five Nations Championship was not completed because Scotland and then Wales refused to play in Ireland after their players received threatening letters from the IRA. The Championship remained unresolved with Wales and Ireland undefeated.

The following year, despite receiving the same threats, England fulfilled their fixture and were given a five-minute standing ovation. Ireland won 18–9 and at the after-match dinner the England captain, John Pullin, came up with one of the great rugby quips: 'We might not be very good, but at least we turn up.'

Mick Quinn, 1983.

In 1973 the scrum-half Johnny Moloney became the first player to score a four-point try for Ireland, helping his country to a 14–9 win over France at Colombes. Earlier that year Moloney's St Mary's clubmate Tom Grace got a try in the last moment in the right corner to tie Ireland's match against the visiting All Blacks at 10–10. Barry McGann missed out on rugby fame when he failed to convert a try that would have won the game for Ireland. The kick was so high that it was difficult to see which side of the post the ball went, but to this day he remains convinced that the ball did not in fact go wide.

Earlier that week the All Blacks had got out of jail against Munster in Musgrave Park with a penalty in injury time in a 3–3 draw.

THE LION KING

In 1974 Ireland won the Five Nations Championship for the first time since 1951, with Mick Quinn replacing Barry McGann at out-half. The side were a good mixture of experienced players like Fergus Slattery, Ray McLoughlin, Mike Gibson, Terry Moore and Ken Kennedy and younger players like Tom Grace, Johnny Moloney, Dick Milliken, Tony Ensor, Stewart McKinney and Moss Keane.

The campaign began on a disappointing note for the boys in green with a defeat to France in Paris. A 9-9 draw against Wales in their first home fixture did not suggest the tide was turning. Despite the best efforts of the thrilling Scottish full-back Andy Irvine, who was destined to shine

Ticket and programme for the Ireland vs
England Five Nations match, 1973.

Willie John McBride, 1974.

on the Lions tour later that summer, Ireland secured a 9-6 victory over Scotland at Lansdowne Road.

Their best game that season was unquestionably against England in Twickenham. Although the final score, 26–21, was deceptively close, Ireland were always in control that day – scoring four tries.

It was a fitting achievement for the Irish captain, Willie John McBride, but greater glory awaited him. To say McBride's rugby CV is impressive is an understatement: 63 caps, 5 Lions tours, 17 Lions Test appearances, captain of the most successful Lions side. In the 1972/3 season he surpassed the record of Scottish prop-forward Hugh McLeod when he made 43 consecutive appearances in international rugby.

McBride also played in 'the game' for the Barbarians against the All Blacks in 1973. Thanks to television the game is immortalised in the famous commentary of the legendary Gareth Edwards try, the most celebrated in rugby history.

> This is great stuff. Phil Bennett covering, chased by Alistair Scown. Brilliant ... John Williams, Bryan Williams ... Pullin ... John Dawes, great dummy ... David, Tom David. The halfway line ... Brilliant by Quinnell ... This is Gareth Edwards ... a dramatic start. *What a score!*

There was no doubt, though, that McBride's finest hour was as an inspirational captain in the Lions tour to South Africa in 1974. That tour provided one of the great hard-luck stories of Irish rugby. The English fly-half, Alan Old, got injured near the end of the tour. Mick Quinn got a call at home from one of the Lions' management team, Albert Ager, who told him to get ready for the trip to South Africa. An hour later Quinn had his bags packed and at the hall door. But then another call came from Ager – a name Quinn will never forget – telling him that in fact he would not be travelling and incongruously asking him if he minded.

On the tour McBride coined the famous rallying cry '99', which meant that all Lions had to support a colleague in trouble. Their record was played 22, won 21, drew 1, lost 0. They won the Test series 3–0. The real strength of that team was its togetherness, loyalty and bravery. When the tour was finished the players presented their captain with an engraved silver water jug that read: *To Willie John. It was great to travel with you.* It remains his most treasured rugby possession.

In his final home international McBride scored his first try for his country as Ireland defeated France 25–6. Such was the emotion generated that the crowd ran onto the pitch to celebrate the try.

To mark the centenary season of Irish rugby, the IRFU arranged a match at Lansdowne Road between Ireland–Scotland and England–Wales in April 1975. It was to be the last time the Ballymena man would lead out a side at the home of Irish rugby.

Events took an unexpected turn after the match when McBride was kidnapped by Eamonn Andrews and whisked away to become the subject of an episode of *This Is Your Life*.

AMAZING GRACE

In 1976 Ireland took on a formidable task with a tour to New Zealand and Fiji under Tom Grace's leadership in the hope of helping the development of the young and inexperienced players. It was only Ireland's sixth overseas tour in its first hundred years. In the circumstances Ireland put up a creditable performance, though they lost the Test against the All Blacks 11–3.

The tour provided a great example of the power of rugby friendships. Tom Grace had marked Grant Batty when Ireland played the All Blacks in Lansdowne Road three years earlier. Batty was not involved with the Blacks in 1976, but he sent 'Gracer' a fistful of New Zealand dollars to buy a round of drinks for the Irish team.

Making his first tour with Ireland was Brendan Foley (father of Anthony 'Axel' Foley), who has two abiding memories of the adventure.

> We began by flying to Heathrow, and there we got onto a jumbo. Back in 1976 none of us had been on a jumbo aeroplane

before. Willie Duggan was famously scared of flying. We all tried to calm him down, and someone said that he should think of it as a ship and remember how safe they were. Willie answered, 'That's what I'm afraid of. How are they going to get this f***ing thing off the ground?'

The tour was going well, but coming up to the Test, people thought we needed to put down a marker for the All Blacks and, in the words of one of the lads, 'show them we weren't pussies'. Nobody was better equipped for this task than our legendary prop-forward Phil O'Callaghan. We were playing Invercargill, and in his loudest, clearest voice Philo shouted to his immediate opponent, 'Hi there, oyster belly.' All hell broke loose, but by the time the dust was settled it's fair to say there was nobody thinking we were pussies!

Phil Orr was one of only three Irish players, with Willie Duggan and Mike Gibson, to be originally selected for the Lions tour to New Zealand in 1977. When Geoff Wheel withdrew from the tour, Moss Keane stepped in for him.

But Irish rugby was about to roar back. A new superstar, and one of the biggest controversies in the Irish sport, would push the game from the back pages to the very front and divide the sporting nation like never before.

Ollie Campbell, Phil Orr and Willie Duggan, 1982.

MAGIC MOMENTS (1948-77) | 49

The Ireland side win a line-out against England, 1968.

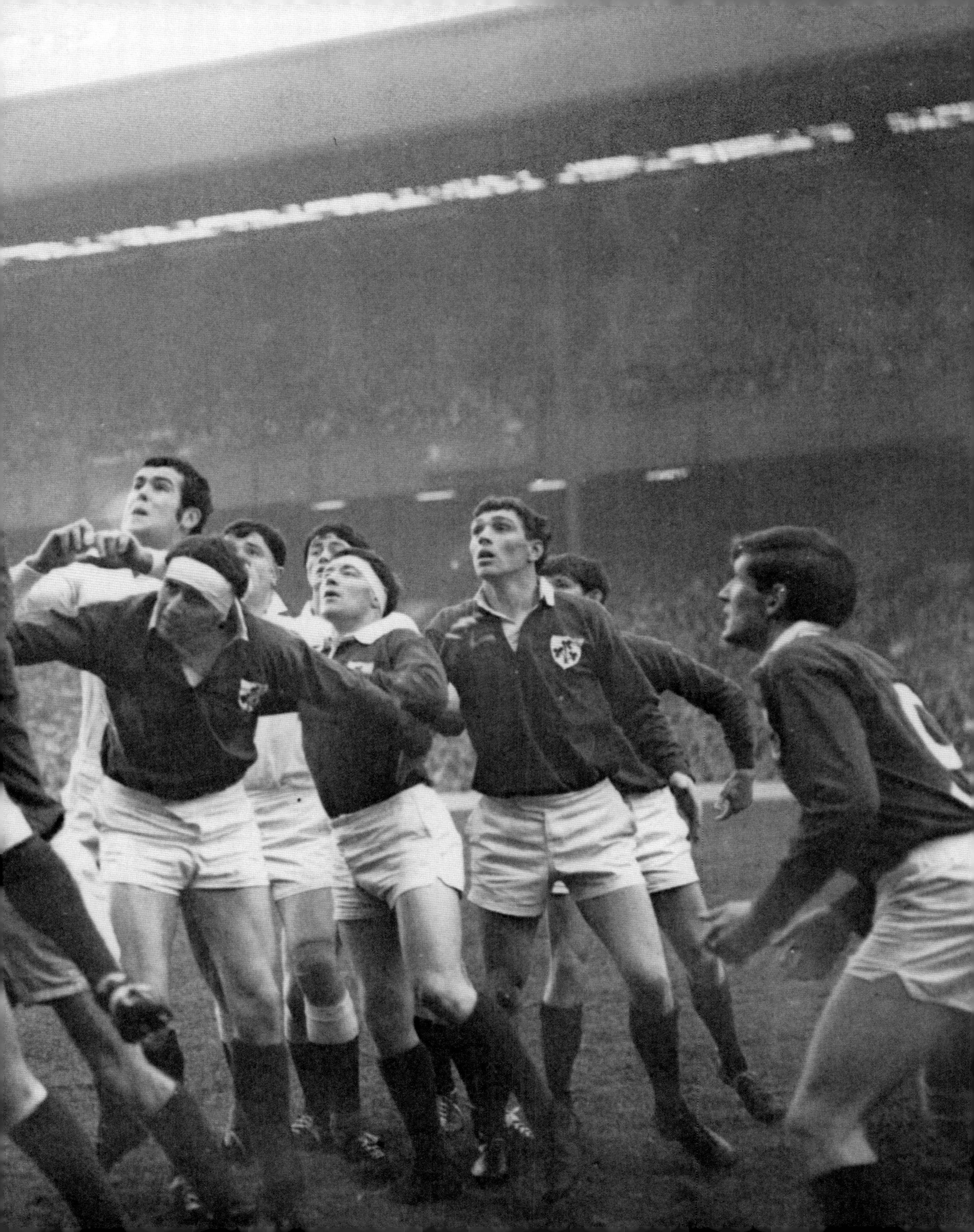

Lansdowne Road Stadium.

3

CROWNING GLORY

(1978–95)

The years 1978–95 would again bring highs and lows for Irish rugby. But above all it would be an era of great drama and some huge controversies.

Rugby tours have a number of striking similarities with religious pilgrimages: uniformity in dress, the chanting of familiar songs and a feeling of community and fellowship throughout. They also have a unique capacity to produce tales of the unexpected. This chapter documents the biggest one in the history of Irish rugby: the reigning European Player of the Year, Tony Ward, being dropped for Ireland's tour of Australia in 1979. Over the next five years the Irish sporting public was split down the middle as to who should be the Irish out-half: Ward or Ollie Campbell.

After 33 years in the wilderness, Ireland would famously reclaim the Triple Crown in 1982 and, under Mick Doyle's 'give it a lash' philosophy, do so again three years later.

The Doyle tenure would come to a disappointing end at the inaugural World Cup in 1987. The second World Cup, in 1991, produced one of the greatest 'nearly' moments in the history of Irish sport.

For better or for worse, the game would be changed forever when rugby went professional in 1995.

THE VIEW FROM NUMBER 10

An interested spectator at Ireland's opening Five Nations victory against Scotland in 1978 was Jack Kyle, watching his country play for the first time since 1965. After Ireland had endured two consecutive poor Five Nations campaigns he saw reason for new optimism.

> It was a great result for Ireland, especially as the win was needed so badly. They played with wonderful spirit. I think Ireland's out-half, Tony Ward, had a splendid match. It was a great debut for him. I would not be despondent about Irish rugby after that performance.

In his first two seasons playing international rugby Tony Ward became one of the first superstars of Irish sport. His status in the game was confirmed when he was chosen as European Player of the Year in both 1978 and 1979. Ireland put in some creditable performances in those years. In 1978 the All Blacks required a try in injury time to claim a 10–6 victory. Ireland were captained that day by flanker Shay Deering – a player revered by his teammates for his lion-hearted bravery on and off the field.

Normally, the effort Ireland put in against Wales in 1979 would have been considered a great achievement: the Irish team scored 21 points in Cardiff Arms Park, thus establishing a new scoring record for an Irish side against Wales on any ground. But this fixture was to be an exception: the Welsh went 3 better and won on a scoreline of 24–21.

The incident that is best remembered from that game is Dick Spring's missed catch, which handed Wales a crucial try. Although his political career later flourished, Spring has never been let forget that incident and has been the butt of jokes about being a 'safe pair of hands'. Everything looked rosy for Tony Ward – but then came Irish rugby's greatest tale of the unexpected.

CAMPBELL'S KINGDOM

Rugby tours are renowned for their ability to surprise. The Irish tour to Australia in 1979 is the example *par excellence*.

The pundits were expecting Australia to hammer Ireland, especially because the previous year they had destroyed the Welsh, who were then enjoying unprecedented success and were laden with immortals of the game, such as J.P.R. Williams.

It was an important tour for emerging Irish players such as Paul McNaughton. He was capped 15 times in the centre in the late 1970s and early '80s and was also a noted soccer player, scoring 21 League of Ireland goals for Shelbourne. He also played senior Gaelic football for Wicklow, earning the distinction of playing at the highest level in Dublin's three main sporting theatres: Gaelic football at Croke Park, rugby at Lansdowne Road and soccer at Dalymount Park.

However, all the headlines were created by the sensational decision to drop Tony Ward in favour of Ollie Campbell. On the same day back home in Ireland, another huge story was breaking: Pope John Paul II would become the first pontiff to visit Ireland. Nonetheless, on its front page the next day the *Irish Press* relegated the news about the Pope to second place. The dropping of Ward was its front-page story.

Both players found themselves unwittingly embroiled in what would become the long-running Ward–Campbell saga. For five years a passionate debate raged about who should be Ireland's number 10. It was Irish sport's first civil war and foreshadowed the fallout from the row between Mick McCarthy and Roy Keane in Saipan during preparations for the 2002 World Cup.

Although he was usually a calming presence when the pressure dial ramped up, Campbell's kicking had let him down in his one previous appearance for Ireland, against Australia in 1976.

> It was one of the biggest disappointments of my life. It was everything you want your first cap *not* to be. I was dropped from the side straight away, which was the only time in my career I was ever dropped off any team.

But in 1979 Campbell produced a kicking masterclass in both Tests, leading Ireland to become the first of the

Ollie Campbell, 1982.

Paul McNaughton in action, 1980.

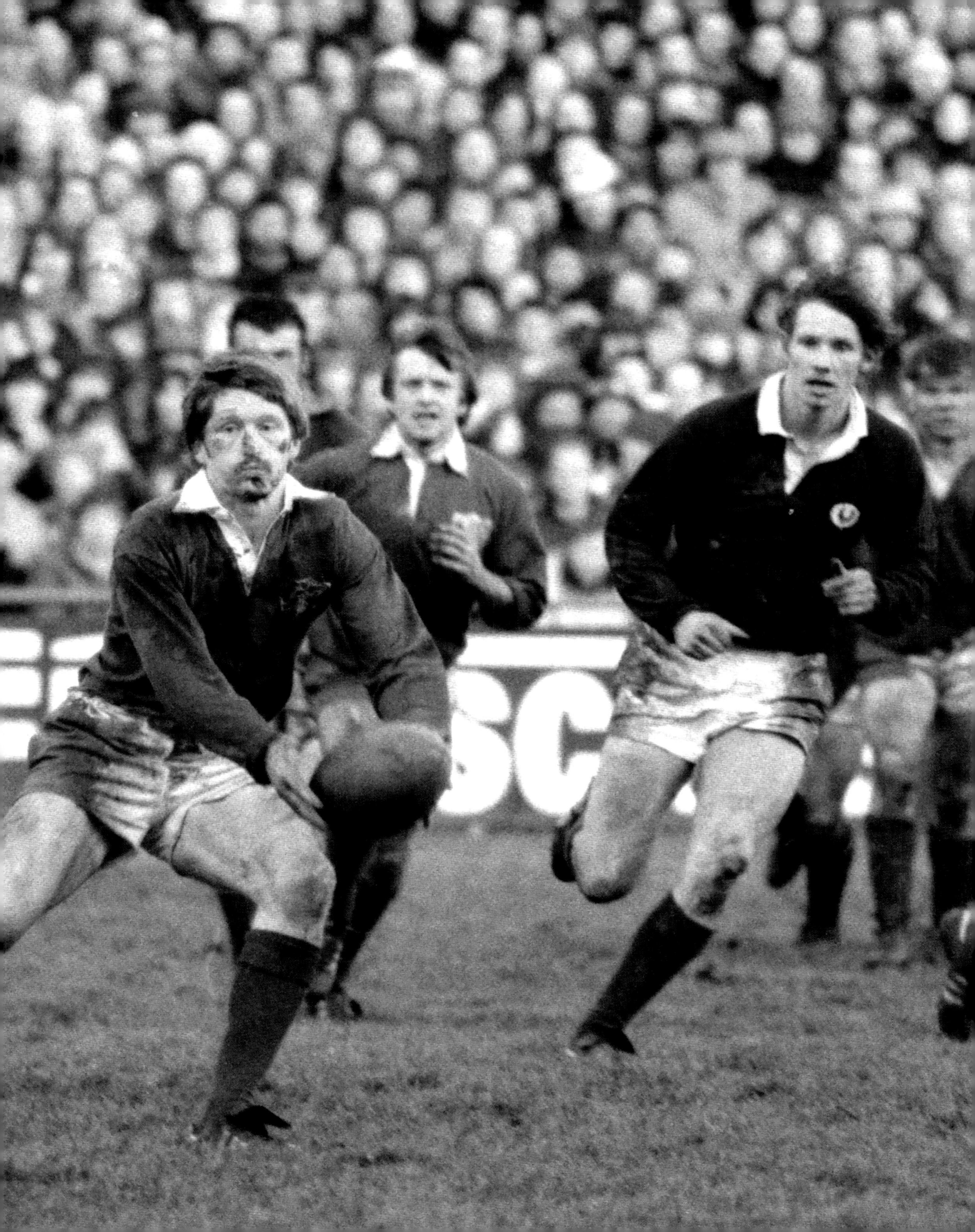

home countries (Ireland, Scotland, England and Wales) to win a Test series in the southern hemisphere. One of his colleagues on that tour, Brendan Foley, offered a window into Campbell's success.

> We were playing Queensland in what was an unofficial third Test. The teams were level, 15–15, and Ollie had kicked all our points when we got a penalty that would win the match. The hooter had just gone. The home fans went crazy. Not alone did they start booing and hissing and making an unbelievable racket as Ollie lined up what was an incredibly difficult kick in the circumstances, but they started throwing bottles of beer onto the pitch. Ollie showed nerves of steel to land the kick.
>
> When the final whistle blew I ran up to him and asked him how he managed to score despite all the noise and all the bottles. He looked at me in bemusement and said, 'I never heard any noise or saw any bottles.' That just shows how focused he was. Afterwards, Ollie was picked for the first Test, and the rest is history.

The Ward fans did not go quietly into the night. Dermot Morgan, to become better known as Father Ted, appeared on a prime-time television programme, *The Live Mike*, singing his song about the saga, 'Don't Pick Wardie.' It was a sign that Irish rugby had moved from the back pages into mainstream popular culture.

CLOSE ENCOUNTERS OF THE WARD KIND

In 1980 Ollie Campbell set a new points record (46) for the Five Nations Championship, with Ireland claiming victory at home over Scotland and a then record 21–7 victory over Wales. Along with Rodney O'Donnell, Colin Patterson, John O'Driscoll and Colm Tucker, Campbell was chosen for the Lions tour to South Africa in 1980 with an Irish manager in Syd Millar and an Irish coach in Noel Murphy. Tucker was an interesting selection because he was unable to command a regular place on the Irish team. Sadly, serious injuries sustained on the tour would prematurely end the promising careers of both Colin Patterson and Rodney O'Donnell. John Robbie, Phil Orr and Tony Ward subsequently joined the squad as replacements, to Campbell's amusement.

With the first Test looming, and with both out-halves – Gareth Davies and me – injured, a fit one was needed. Who was flown out? Tony Ward. Not only did he play in the first Test, but he scored 18 points, which was then a Lions individual points scoring record in a Test match. Was there to be no escape from this guy?

Ward was a sub to Campbell in the third Test in Port Elizabeth. To his horror, Ward discovered in the dressing room that he had forgotten his boots. It was too late to retrieve them from the team hotel. Even worse, nobody had a spare pair to lend him. He consoled himself with the thought that he probably wouldn't need them. The seating arrangements for the subs that day were bizarre, to say the least: they were to sit at the very top row of the stadium. As the match began, Ward was making the long journey up countless flights of stairs with John Robbie when he heard somebody shouting for him.

Campbell jokes about a lost opportunity to scupper his rival's career.

> I was injured in the very first moments of the match and was pumping blood. [Campbell still has a small scar on his face as a 'souvenir'.] It was panic stations all round. John Robbie got a pair of boots from a ball boy for Wardie to wear. At size nine they were too big for him, but an even more serious problem was that the studs were moulded. The pitch was waterlogged that day, and even if they had been the right size, they would have been a disaster in the conditions, but they were all he had at the time. If only I had known, I was straight off, and he was not getting my boots! It would have been Wardie's ultimate nightmare, and his reputation would have been destroyed at a stroke!

Luckily for Ward, he didn't have to resort to Campbell's oversized boots.

APARTHEID SOUTH AFRICA

In these years the spectre of apartheid hovered ominously on the horizon, as it did for a generation of Irish rugby players travelling to South Africa. It was a disturbing time for Tony Ward.

I first recall my own experiences of life in South Africa on the Lions tour in 1980. I candidly confess that I had no hesitation about going to South Africa, despite the apartheid regime at the time, once the call came. I wanted to be a Lion and it was really as simple and as selfish as that. I don't deny it. Donning that red jersey of Wales, those white shorts of England and the Irish and Scottish green and navy socks represented the be all and end all of my very existence at that time. I offer no justification. I didn't even think: I simply went. However, was I in for a rude awakening! I have never forgotten my first few minutes in South Africa. As I walked through customs I spotted those toilet signs, *Black only toilets* and *White only toilets*.

The agonising plight of the majority of the population struck Ward most forcefully on a visit to the paradisal world of a golf course in Bloemfontein on an excursion with John Robbie, Paul Dodge and Clive Woodward.

On the course we were surrounded by about thirty black youngsters – about late teens and all literally dressed in rags. They wanted to caddy for us. 'Master, Master,' they called me. This was the bit I could never take: people calling me 'master'. We selected two kids, and I took them aside and I said, 'This is John and Paul, and I am Tony', but after that they didn't call us anything at all. It really confused them.

I was one of a number of players brought to visit a children's hospital by former Irish scrum-half Dr Roger Young in Cape Town. It was a harrowing experience to see so many seriously disabled children, but for me what compounded their tragedy was that, even in the wards, there was segregation between whites, blacks and those of mixed race. It was a hospital similar to Crumlin, full of sick children – some very serious, some not so serious – yet within that children's hospital there was the black children's wing and one for the whites. It was unbelievable. I found it the saddest sight I had ever seen. For me that was as much as I could take, and the sad feeling of that moment will stay with me forever.

Then Ward had an encounter with a remarkable man.

The most formative influence on my subsequent attitude to tours in South Africa occurred when I, Bill Beaumont, Colin Patterson and some other players went to visit the Watson brothers. Both Cheeky Watson and his brother Valence, who lived in Port Elizabeth, had decided some years previously to play rugby with a non-racial team in the New Brighton township Kwaru rather than to continue to play with a whites-only club. Cheeky was a top-class rugby player and had even won a Springboks trial. I have never forgotten Cheeky telling me his story: 'By 1979 we had developed into a brilliant side, playing superb rugby. However, we went into it unaware of what we were up against. You could not go and play against the blacks just like that. We were arrested and fined countless times. Military intelligence was actively trying to destabilise non-racial sport in South Africa, and we had been singled out as enemies.'

Back in 1976 Cheeky was approached by then South African coach and selector Ian Kirkpatrick, who informed the very promising winger that he was prepared to give him written guarantees that he was going to be on the following year's Springbok team to France – on condition he stopped playing for Kwaru. The then 20-year-old refused to compromise and became perhaps the only player in rugby history to have spurned the hallowed Springbok jersey on ethical grounds.

Cheeky was renounced by his white friends because he was playing with a black club. Naturally enough, the authorities did not rejoice in the Watsons' principled stand. The clandestine repressive regime went into action, with the family house being burnt down by 'unknown assailants'. To rub salt into their wounds, the Watson brothers were accused of deliberately burning down the house in order to cash in on the insurance and were arrested. The evidence against the government case was overwhelming and the court action collapsed.

The trial, though, left the Watsons nearly destitute. The harassment continued and even intensified, with the disinformation department of military intelligence spreading rumours about them. The brothers received phone calls threatening them and their children. Cheeky could not find work. One of his brothers, Gavin, was stabbed in the family shop, and there were two attempts on the life of another brother, Ronnie.

Cheeky joined an action group, Concerned Citizens, whose aim was to explain to the white community the profound injustice of the system and to expose the whites to the real situation in the townships. In a bid to combat that threat, Colonel Kaletski of the military intelligence offered Cheeky the opportunity

Tony Ward.

[to become] an informer, with all the advantages that would have brought him. Cheeky typically acted against his own self-interest and declined the offer. As a result there were endless intimidating calls to his home, police were constantly breaking the door down to enter the house, and Cheeky was arrested numerous times for breaking the law by entering the black township without a permit.

A year later, in 1981, Ward would make a very different decision about travelling to South Africa from the one he had made in 1980.

With an Irish tour to South Africa in the offing for the following summer [1981], I decided I would not travel on the day I returned from the Lions tour. When I left South Africa in June of 1980 I did so certainly enriched for my rugby experiences, certainly content to have achieved the personal honour of Lions status. But, overall, I was deflated and deeply hurt by what I had seen, heard and experienced. So when, twelve months later, Ireland were to tour South Africa, I had no decision to make. My mind – no, my conscience – said, 'No – never again.'

I had no doubt whatsoever that politics and sport were one and the same in South Africa. To my mind, rugby was used as a political weapon, and that is why I refused to go on the tour. My view was that rugby was so important to the Afrikaners that if we refused to tour they would be forced to confront the question 'Why is this happening?' Of course, the opposite view was the 'building bridges' argument, which was widely proffered by rugby people in both Ireland and the UK at the time.

Several other players – including Moss Keane, Hugo MacNeill and Donal Spring – also refused to participate in the tour for reasons of principle.

There was to be an unexpected postscript for Ward.

Because of my decision to boycott Ireland's tour of South Africa in 1981, in 1990 I was invited, with fellow former international Donal Spring, to a special meeting with Nelson Mandela during his visit to receive the Freedom of the City of Dublin. We had all heard about this man who had been locked away for 26 years, and then suddenly he appears. I met him and his then wife, Winnie, with Donal Spring and the Dunnes Stores workers [who conducted a nearly three-year strike over handling South African goods] when he received the Freedom of Dublin [...] He just shook our hands and thanked us. It is a memory I will always treasure.

CENTRE OF EXCELLENCE?

In 1981, after a disappointing loss at home to France in the opening Five Nations game, Ollie Campbell was moved to the centre to allow for Tony Ward's return as out-half. How did Campbell react to the change?

I never minded the idea of playing in the same team as Tony – provided I was at out-half. Playing in the centre is a very different position, and to be honest I was never really comfortable there. After Tony was brought back onto the Irish team, and I was at the centre, John O'Driscoll went out with me for a walk through Stephen's Green just before the game. Suddenly John told me that he was delighted I was playing there. My morale lifted straight away, and I inquired why. He said, 'Now at least we will have somebody at out-half who can make a tackle!'

In 1981 we lost all four matches by a single score after leading in all four at half-time. It was Ireland's best ever whitewash! Our coach, Tom Kiernan, repeatedly told us that, whatever about the results, if there was to be a Lions tour that year, the country that would have the most representatives would be Ireland. I'm not sure if that was true, but it certainly kept our morale and self-belief up.

Given the ferocity of the debate about them, Campbell and Ward might have been expected to be bitter enemies, but, as now, they remained close friends.

GLORY DAYS

The following season, things came together for the Irish side. A record score from Ollie Campbell, kicking all of Ireland's points (with six penalties and a drop goal) in their 21–12 victory over Scotland, allowed the Irish to clinch the Triple Crown in 1982, ending a 33-year famine since their previous win in 1949. One of Campbell's enduring recollections of the game was of the fans.

> There were a lot of great moments that season – I suppose most famously [Gerry] 'Ginger' McLoughlin's celebrated try against England. On a personal level I remember a break I made which set up Moss Finn's first try against Wales, the virtual touchline conversion of Ginger's try in Twickenham and the drop goal against Scotland. That score came from a special loop movement we had devised in January with David Irwin but kept under wraps. It should have led to a try, but I gave a bad pass to Keith Crossan and the move broke down, so we had to settle for three points.
>
> Life for that team was never really the same afterwards. Most of the team had grown up with no international success. There was a huge sense of achievement and a bonding that has lasted since.
>
> When we won our first match, all we were trying to do was to bring a sequence of seven consecutive defeats to an end. Two weeks later we won at Twickenham, and suddenly we were in a Triple Crown situation. It was something as a team we had never thought about. But we knew we were onto something big when we saw the big crowds watching us in training. That was something we had never experienced before.
>
> It was a very exciting week, as we had a general election at the time following the fall of Garret FitzGerald's first coalition government, but nobody seemed to care about it. Everybody was more excited about the possibility of a Triple Crown. Ireland had never won one before at Lansdowne Road.
>
> The tension mounted, but then Tom Kiernan, the Irish coach, decided to have a closed practice session on the Thursday before the game. Suddenly the Triple Crown match became just another game, and I have never felt so at ease and comfortable going into a game. It was a masterstroke.
>
> Two weeks previously I had missed a penalty against England that would have sewn the game up. On the Sunday afterwards I went to Anglesea Road with my five balls and kicked for two hours from the same spot I had missed the previous day. Ninety per cent of all the kicks I took in practice over the next two weeks were from this spot.

> After just three minutes of the Scotland game, when the first penalty arrived, I relaxed. Amazingly, it was from exactly the same spot. I felt I would have kicked it with my eyes closed, but I didn't take the chance. We were on our way and, for me at least, never before had the value of practice been more clearly demonstrated.

The team that defeated Scotland in the deciding match was:

H. MacNeill
M. Finn
M. Kiernan
P. Dean
K. Crossan
O. Campbell
R. McGrath
P. Orr
C. Fitzgerald (capt.)
G. McLoughlin
D. Lenihan
M. Keane
F. Slattery
W. Duggan
J. O'Driscoll

THE KEANE EDGE

Many of Donal Lenihan's memories of that time revolve around his second-row partner, Moss Keane.

> I usually roomed with Moss. He was coming to the end of his career at that stage. Our room was like an alternative medical centre, with pollen, garlic tablets and a half-dozen eggs. The mornings of internationals I woke up to see Moss eating three raw eggs. It's not the sort of sight that you want to wake up to! Having said that, Moss was an enormous help to me in the early days. I especially appreciated that he let me make the decisions about the line-out.

Stories abound about Moss. It is probable that some are even true. One goes back before the Triple Crown decider against Scotland. Bill Beaumont rang him to wish him well: 'Moss, if you win they will build a statue of you in Cork.'

Moss Keane, 1984

Keane replied, 'Billy, you boll*x. I'm a Kerryman.'

After the Triple Crown was won, Moss approached the team captain, Ciaran Fitzgerald, and said, 'I'm taking the cup to Currow next weekend. No more about it – my mind is made up.'

'But, Moss, there is no trophy. The Triple Crown is a mythical trophy.'

'Is there a medal?' Keane asked.

'No, Moss.'

'You mean to say we went to all that f***ing trouble and they won't even give us a f***ing medal!'

Ireland's captain, Ciaran Fitzgerald, gives much of the credit for the triumph to a true legend of Irish rugby.

> Tom Kiernan was always two moves ahead of you. I often heard myself saying things about which I would later get a flashback and see that Tom had discreetly planted the thought in my mind either the previous day or a week earlier. He was a great man-manager. He was always prompting you because he wanted the ideas to come from the players themselves, because they took more responsibility for their own decisions.
>
> I wanted the players to do more physical work, but Tom always subjected everything to a cost-benefit analysis and asked, 'Was it worth it?' He always said that what exhausted players was not training sessions but constantly travelling up and down to Dublin. P.J. Dwyer, as chairman of selectors, was also a great prompter of ideas.
>
> My clearest memory of 1982 was when Gareth Davies limped off in the Welsh game. We could see it in their eyes that they knew we were going to beat them.
>
> The England game really established that we were a side to be reckoned with. I remember travelling on the bus back to the hotel. When everybody else was ecstatic, Willie Duggan was sitting at the back of the bus working out the practicalities of what was needed for a Triple Crown decider in terms of extra tickets for players and so on.

Fitzgerald's own role as captain was also crucial. What was the secret of his success?

> I think I'm very sensitive to people and curious about them. I was still a relatively inexperienced player, in comparison with most of my pack. I knew there was no way I could use my army style to deal with these guys. You have to remember there were a lot of world-class players in the forwards like Orr, Keane, Slattery, O'Driscoll and Duggan. The previous year Ireland had won no match, and those guys were fed up hearing from people who knew virtually nothing about rugby: 'You're only a shower of ...' That really annoyed them and they were fired up to prove just how good they were.
>
> Whatever you say to players of that calibre has to be effective. Every player is different. The most important thing is to find out how to bring out the best of each player and find a strategy appropriate to his personality. In 1982, before the decisive Triple Crown match against Scotland, the *Irish Press* wrote a very critical article about John O'Driscoll, who was a superb player and central to our success that season. The day before the match I quietly went to him in the Shelbourne Hotel and expressed my sympathy about the article. He knew nothing about it and asked to see it. He read it but said nothing. The next day he played like a man possessed.
>
> As captain, no matter what position you play in, you can't see everything that is happening on the pitch. You need guys you can quickly turn to in the heat of battle and who can read the game and tell what is needed in their area. Fergus Slattery was a great player in those situations. Ollie Campbell, apart from being an outstanding player, had a great rugby brain, and I relied on him to control the game for us. His partner at scrum-half, Robbie McGrath, also played a crucial role. He was a very underrated player who never got the acclaim he deserved.

After Ireland won the Championship again in 1983, John O'Driscoll was selected to tour New Zealand with the Lions in the company of his Irish colleagues Trevor Ringland, Michael Kiernan, David Irwin, Ollie Campbell (who scored 124 points on the tour) and Donal Lenihan, under the captaincy of Ciaran Fitzgerald. Although O'Driscoll played in two Tests, it was not the experience he hoped for.

Ciaran Fitzgerald.

The Ireland Team, 1982.

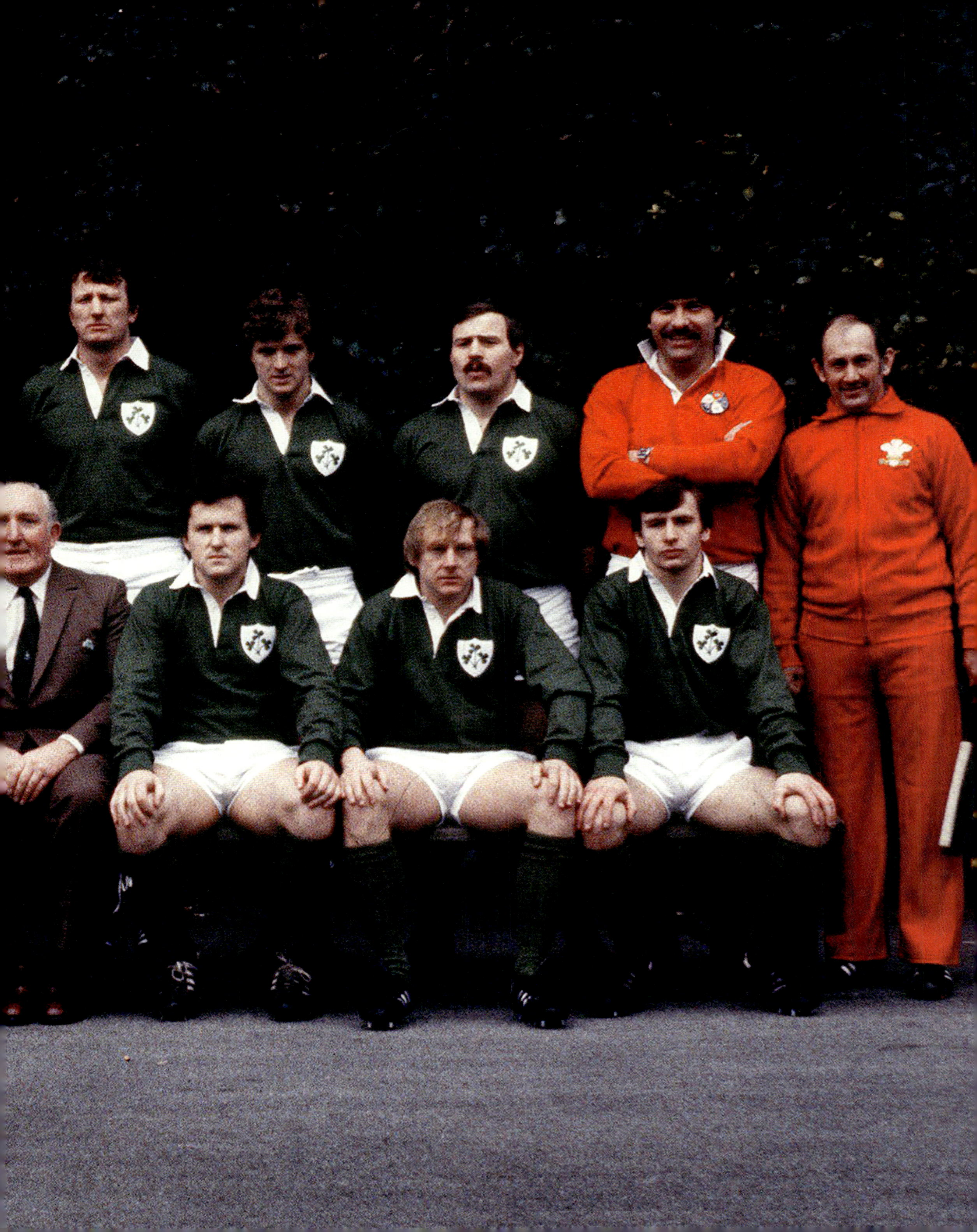

I was injured in the first match and didn't play for three weeks. You need to be playing on a tour like that. We were not as evenly balanced as we had been in 1980. The press were very unfair to Ciaran Fitzgerald, which didn't help. By the standards of the time the criticism of him was way over the top. Nowadays, that kind of sustained media assault has become commonplace.

After the highs of '82 and '83 the following season was a disaster, as we were whitewashed. The balance between success and failure is relatively fine. Ollie Campbell got injured, which disturbed our rhythm a lot. We lost confidence when we started losing. I was ill for the 84/5 international season and never regained my place. Even though I was a few years younger than them, I was regarded as being the same vintage as Willie Duggan and Fergus Slattery and as part of 'Dad's army'. In fact, I continued to play for Connacht for a number of years and hoped to make it back onto the Irish side, but it was not to be. I never actually retired.

Donal Lenihan, however, recalls the whitewash of 1984 with some affection, especially regarding Ireland's captain that season, Willie Duggan.

The best Irish forward I ever played with was Willie Duggan. He was the Scarlet Pimpernel of Irish rugby because he was so hard to find for training! Having said that, he wouldn't have survived in international rugby so long without training. Willie took his captaincy manual from a different world. His speeches were not comparable with anything I'd ever heard before or since.

One of my clearest memories of Willie's captaincy is of the morning after the Scotland game in 1984. The papers all had a picture of Duggan with his arm round Tony Ward and speaking to him. It was just before Wardie was taking a penalty. It appeared that Willie was acting the real father figure but, knowing him as I do, my guess was he was saying, 'If you miss this penalty, I'll kick you all the way to Kilkenny!'

The 1980s saw a curious combination of Irish results: whitewashed in 1981, Triple Crown and International champions the following year, joint champions in 1983, whitewashed in 1984, Triple Crown and international champions in 1985 and whitewashed in 1986.

The year 1984 saw a premature end to Ollie Campbell's career because of injury. But he would continue to play a meaningful role in Irish rugby, notably through his long association with the Charitable Trust. Established in 1978, the Trust helps seriously injured rugby players and their families with everyday needs such as medical care, wheelchairs, physical therapy and education, transport (including vehicle alterations), home alterations and just being there for players and their families when they need someone.

DOYLER

After the disappointments of 1984 things took a dramatic turn for the better with the appointment of a new coach, Mick Doyle, and his bold philosophy of 'giving it a lash'. As Leinster coach he had taken the team to five interprovincial titles between 1979 and '83 (1982 shared). After Ireland lost to Scotland in 1984 Moss Keane and Willie Duggan persuaded Doyle to run for the job of Ireland coach.

Doyle knew how to tilt the odds in the team's favour, as Ollie Campbell recalls:

Mick was very shrewd. My only experience of him was as coach of Leinster. We played Romania when they toured Ireland in 1980. We arrived at the ground well over an hour before the game. I thought then we had mistimed the arrival. The previous week Romania had hammered Munster, and Doyler had noticed in the lead-up to the match that the Romanian players were constantly in and out of the toilet. Being the cute Kerryman that he was, Doyler gave a newspaper and a match programme to each of our substitutes and told them to lock themselves in the toilets until the game began. We demolished the Romanians in the match. The next day the phrase that was used in the newspapers was 'The Romanians were strangely heavy and leaden-footed.' Was it any surprise?

Doyle saw the opportunity to forge a new shape for the team almost by accident. With the retirement of Ollie Campbell in 1984 the popular opinion among rugby fans was that the stage was set for Tony Ward to return to the Irish team. However, an injury to Ward sustained while playing for St Mary's against Monkstown in Sydney Parade on a dark autumn afternoon opened the way for Paul Dean to become Ireland's out-half. Ward had been due to travel to Cork to play for an Irish selection against Highfield in an exhibition the following day. But Ward's difficulty was Dean's opportunity, and Dean played out-half to Michael Bradley. The rest of the back line comprised Brendan Mullin and Michael Kiernan in the centre, Trevor Ringland and Keith Crossan on the wings and Hugo MacNeill at full-back. They went on a scoring spree against Highfield – a back line that was to drive Ireland to win the Triple Crown and win it in style.

Having been a virtual novice in 1982, Hugo MacNeill was one of the more senior players when Ireland regained the Triple Crown in 1985.

> That year there was a great uncertainty and apprehension before the Scotland game. The Scots had beaten us 32–9 at Lansdowne Road the previous March, and we were going into their back yard with a young team. So many experienced players retired that year: Ollie Campbell, Moss Keane, Fergus, Willie Duggan and John O'Driscoll had all moved on. Mick Doyle asked us, 'What are we afraid of?' The answer most people would have given him was 'the wooden spoon'. But literally from the first minute I sensed that something special was about to happen to us all. Deano [Paul Dean] moved it wide, Keith Crossan split the line, Brenny [Brendan Mullin] passed to me, and the ball squirted forward as I was tackled over the line. If I'd had the ball in my other hand, we'd have scored a breathtaking try with our first attack. Our confidence was instantly lifted. We thought, 'Wow, did we really do that?'
>
> The Scots got on top of us slowly and it looked like it was going to end badly, but then we produced a little piece of magic. The back row created a position on the far side; the ball went wide and through the hands of nearly every back on the team before Trevor Ringland scored in the corner. We won 18–15.
>
> It was an extraordinary day, made all the more special by the scenes in the dressing room afterwards. I played 37 times for Ireland as well as for the Lions, and if you ask me to single out one moment from all those years that will live with me forever, then it is the Murrayfield dressing room on the late afternoon of 2 February 1985. There was an ecstatic air about the place … It was almost childlike. We had all played hundreds of championship matches as children in our back gardens, but

Mick Doyle, 1983.

Michael Kiernan celebrates his drop goal against England, 1985.

this was the real thing. It was the most amazing feeling I ever had in my career.

We had no recognised place-kicker and had such a young side. After our win there was so much excitement and freshness that no one could sit down. I had come through the schools and universities with these guys, and I really enjoyed the buzz.

MacNeill feels that Mick Doyle was pivotal to the glory days of 1985.

In 1985 grey clouds hung over the entire country. To those back home in Dublin in the 1980s, I was one of the rats that deserted the sinking ship. I was studying at Oxford ... a world away from the recession and depression at home. I was working on a thesis, 'How Do You Reduce the Irish Unemployment Problem?' It wasn't easy. There was almost 20 per cent unemployment, and I always think that's why our triumph in

'85 was so important ... It lifted a nation at a time when it desperately needed lifting. It wasn't just that we won the Triple Crown: it was the style we played when winning.

Doyler best summed up his philosophy when he said, 'I want you to run, and if it doesn't work out I want you to run again.' On a personal level I had reason to be grateful to him that season. One game didn't go well for me. After the game a number of journalists were calling for a change at full-back. Mick said to me in training, 'Hugo, I want you in this side, okay?' We had a good chat and he made me feel confident again. He had a great gift for man-management.

We hadn't won in Cardiff Arms Park since 1967 going into that match, but we beat them 21 points to 9 with great tries from Keith Crossan and Trevor Ringland. There was some discussion before the match about what we would do when the crowd started singing at us to intimidate us. Brian Spillane said, 'We'll sing back at them!.' In some of the pictures showing the arm-linked scene, you can see Brian singing at the crowd. Don't ask me what, though!

Ciaran Fitzgerald was described by Mick Doyle as 'one of the best leaders I've ever had in a team'. One of the enduring images of the year is Fitzgerald's efforts to rally the team as they appeared to be letting the Triple Crown slip through their fingers in 1985 against England – in the wake of their dazzling and stylish victories away to Scotland and Wales. Even those who had no experience of lip-reading could clearly make out his plea from the heart: 'Where's your pride? Where's your f***ing pride?'

It was a revealing window onto Fitzgerald's exceptional gifts as a captain – his ability to work so well with the different personalities in the team, to handle their idiosyncrasies as individuals and to collectively fire them with a burning will to win when they stepped on the field of play. Never was the motto 'All for one and one for all' better displayed, as far as the Irish team were concerned, than when Fitzgerald was captain.

That game against England was a torrid affair, but Ireland came out on top, 13–10, courtesy of Michael Kiernan's late drop goal.

After the high of his second Triple Crown triumph, Hugo MacNeill was soon brought down to earth with a bang.

> I was at Malahide at a festival or something. It was not long after the Triple Crown and we had a very high profile then. At one point I was conscious of a group of girls looking at me. I heard murmurs of 'Yes, it is,' 'No, it isn't.' Shortly afterwards I felt someone tap on me on the shoulder. It was a young lady who asked me if I was Hugo MacNeill, the Irish rugby player. When I said I was she turned round and went back to her friends. I heard her whisper, 'Jaysus, I've never been so disappointed in all my life. He's nowhere near as good looking in real life as he is on television!'

The season finished on a high note for the team with a successful and enjoyable tour to Japan, Ireland winning all five games. But Ireland's star waned dramatically the following season. Hugo MacNeill offers an explanation:

> We won the Triple Crown playing good rugby, but I think we got complacent the following season. If you look back at our matches in 1985, we could have lost all of those matches. We had a lot of good fortune. In 1986 we were not going to surprise people playing more of the same. We needed to advance our game, but we didn't.

A WHOLE NEW WORLD

The year 1987 was also one of missed opportunities and some rumours of discontent within the Irish camp. Ireland probably should have won the Triple Crown in 1987 but let the game against Scotland slip away from them. The mood was brilliant after Ireland beat Wales in Cardiff, and the Irish players, in a show of affection, threw Mick Doyle in the bath!

Hopes were high as Ireland set off for the inaugural World Cup. But within 24 hours of their getting to New Zealand, things started to unravel when Doyler had a 'coronary incident'. He was rushed to hospital but returned to the squad within days. By his own admission, he should have been sent home after that.

As Doyle later conceded, Ireland made a blunder in the build-up to the tournament by trying to wrap their players in cotton wool and not allowing them to play any club matches after March, whereas the Welsh players were involved in club rugby right up to the first half of May. Ireland looked rusty in that opening match in Wellington, while Wales were sharp and incisive and ran out comfortable winners, 13–6.

The game is as much remembered for an incident before it as for the action on the field. The band played a horrendous version of 'The Rose of Tralee' instead of the national anthem. It was excruciatingly painful and embarrassing for the Irish players.

After the defeat to Wales, changes were inevitable for the second game – a somewhat flattering 46–19 victory over Canada. There followed a more comfortable 32–9 over Tonga before a crushing 33–15 defeat to Australia in the quarter-final. The Aussies led 24–0 after 25 minutes. Late tries from Hugo MacNeill and Michael Kiernan gave a

Trevor Ringland in action against Wales, 1987.

Donal Lenihan leads the Irish team out at the 1987 World Cup.

Donal Lenihan and coach Mick Doyle at a press conference.

slightly misleading gloss to the score. Mick Doyle struck the wrong tone in interviews after the match when he stated that Ireland 'won the second half'.

Surprisingly, Brian Smith, one of the Australian players to score a try that day, would go on to win the first of his nine caps for Ireland at out-half two years later. He returned to Australia after defecting to rugby league just before the 1991 World Cup. That he played for Australia against Ireland in the 1987 World Cup and could also have ended up playing for Ireland against Australia in the 1991 World Cup was not to everybody's taste. The tournament was the end of the Mick Doyle era, and he was replaced as Ireland coach by Ulster's Jimmy Davidson.

FACE-OFF

The Davidson reign did not bring huge success, a particular low point being a 35–3 defeat to England at Twickenham in 1988. However, it produced two unforgettable moments in Irish rugby. In 1989 Corinthians' Noel Mannion scored one of the greatest tries in the history of Irish rugby during Ireland's 19–13 win against the Welsh in Cardiff. Wales were attacking on the Irish 22-metre line when Bleddyn Bowen's fly kick was smothered by the Ballinasloe man, who raced a gut-busting seventy yards by the right touchline before grounding the ball just before he ran out of breath.

One of the most famous pieces of sporting theatre came the same year before Ireland played the All Blacks. Team captain Willie Anderson led the Irish team literally up to the noses of the All Blacks during their haka in an effort to intimidate them at Lansdowne Road. Ireland may have won the dance, but they lost the match 23–6.

Ireland's status in the game in this year was reflected in the fact that only four of the side were selected to tour with the Lions to Australia in 1989: Steve Smith, Donal Lenihan, Brendan Mullins and Paul Dean. Unfortunately,

Dean's career was ended when he sustained an injury in the opening game of the tour.

Although 1990 brought another bruising Irish defeat to England, the Twickenham game was notable for the selection of Ken Murphy at full-back. This created history when – like his grandfather Noel F. and father, Noel A. – he played for Ireland at senior level: the first grandfather-father-son combination to do so.

After just one Championship win in each of his three years, Jimmy Davidson was replaced as coach by Ciaran Fitzgerald, who had another former Irish captain and fellow St Mary's College alumnus, Johnny Moloney, as his assistant. Their first fixture in charge was a victory over a touring Argentina. The sense of a new broom was accentuated when London Irish scrum-half Rob Saunders was chosen as captain, the first debutant to get this high honour on his first cap since Jim Ritchie in 1956. If results were disappointing, apart from a 21–21 draw with Wales, Irish fans were not downbeat. The side played some thrilling rugby – and there was an electrifying new winger, Simon Geoghegan, who lit up the season and scored tries in three consecutive games against Wales, England and Scotland. Some supporters, though, heard alarm bells as Ireland's warm-up tour to Namibia saw defeats in both Tests.

Ireland's build-up to the 1991 World Cup tournament was not ideal in various ways. The team's preparations were impeded especially when they lost warm-up matches to club sides, which eroded confidence and morale. And, as in many other spheres of life, money was also an issue. Phillip Matthews, Des Fitzgerald and Brendan Mullin were the players' representatives who negotiated with the IRFU over the way the squad were to be remunerated. A deal was scrambled together only at the eleventh hour after some frenetic contacts with Ronnie Dawson.

On the field the tournament was a story of what might have been for Ireland. Their campaign kicked off with a historic occasion on the double: their first international against Zimbabwe and the first time an international was played at Lansdowne Road on a Sunday, with Ireland emerging victorious, 55–11.

The key game came against Scotland: a win would bring a quarter-final against Western Samoa, but a defeat would mean another quarter-final against Australia. Scotland won 25–14.

A bust-up among the forwards set the tone for a game in which the Aussies – despite two scores from David Campese, the undisputed player of the tournament – never managed to kill off the fighting Irish. Twelve points from Ralph Keyes kept Ireland within striking distance but never in front – until a moment that sent the Irish fans into a frenzy. With Ireland trailing 15–12, full-back Jim Staples launched a kick in the dying moments, and winger Jack Clarke set off in pursuit before feeding the charging Gordon Hamilton. The flanker stormed past Campese and sprinted forty yards to score in the corner. Hamilton was mobbed by his teammates and also by a swarm of supporters in some of the most exuberant scenes Irish rugby had ever witnessed. Then Keyes added the conversion from the far left to give Ireland a three-point lead.

But before the crowd could catch their breath, the game turned decisively once more. Ireland conceded a penalty and Michael Lynagh seemed set to take it to level the scores. Instead, he opted to take a quick tap penalty. The shocked Irish defence rushed to cover but in the process allowed too much space for Tim Horan and Jason Little – and Little whipped the ball out to Campese, who lofted the ball to Lynagh, and he crashed over for a try. The Wallabies got out of jail and would go on to win the World Cup.

Had Ireland won that game it would have created a whole new level of interest in rugby throughout the country. It could have been akin to the hysteria that the Irish soccer team generated a year earlier during Italia '90.

After the high hopes induced by the Australia game Ireland were quickly brought crashing back to earth in the following Five Nations – experiencing the ignominy of the wooden spoon.

The mournful mood continued that summer when Ireland toured New Zealand. Despite some gutsy

Mick Galwey, 1992.

performances – notably in the first Test, when they lost narrowly, 24–21 – the series ended with a record defeat of 59–6 in the second Test.

That November, Ireland lost 42–17 to Australia in Lansdowne Road. The demands of juggling a business career and coaching Ireland finally became too much for Ciaran Fitzgerald. In an age when the word 'duty' sounded increasingly old-fashioned, Fitzgerald had made huge personal and professional sacrifices for Irish rugby. He was succeeded as Irish coach by Gerry Murphy.

The new coach had a memorable start to his career. He was visited in his home for an interview for RTÉ by Des Cahill. Murphy was on the phone to Michael Bradley when Cahill arrived, and he ushered his guest into the sitting room before resuming the telephone conversation. Cahill was waiting fifteen minutes for the conversation to end and amused himself by looking at pictures on the wall and looking out the window. He then sat down and, for the first time, noticed that Murphy had what had once been a beautiful white carpet. It was now covered in mud. Cahill was thinking that Murphy must be a confirmation of all the stereotypes about rugby players being untidy.

Then Murphy joined him. Cahill was unnerved when he saw Murphy constantly looking down at his guest's shoes. Eventually, Cahill looked down himself and was horrified to discover that his own shoes were caked in mud. He remembered walking into a puddle after he had parked his car, but he hadn't realised that he had accumulated so much muck. Destroying his host's exquisite carpet was not the most auspicious start to the interview.

GEOGHEGAN AND GALWEY

The 1990s were a disappointing decade for Ireland. It was no coincidence that their best performances early in the decade coincided with the best of the flying winger, Simon Geoghegan. Great tries in 1991 against Wales and England established the then-Baker Street resident as the rising star of Irish rugby. However, in 1992, Ireland lost every game,

Willie Anderson faces up to the Haka, 1988.

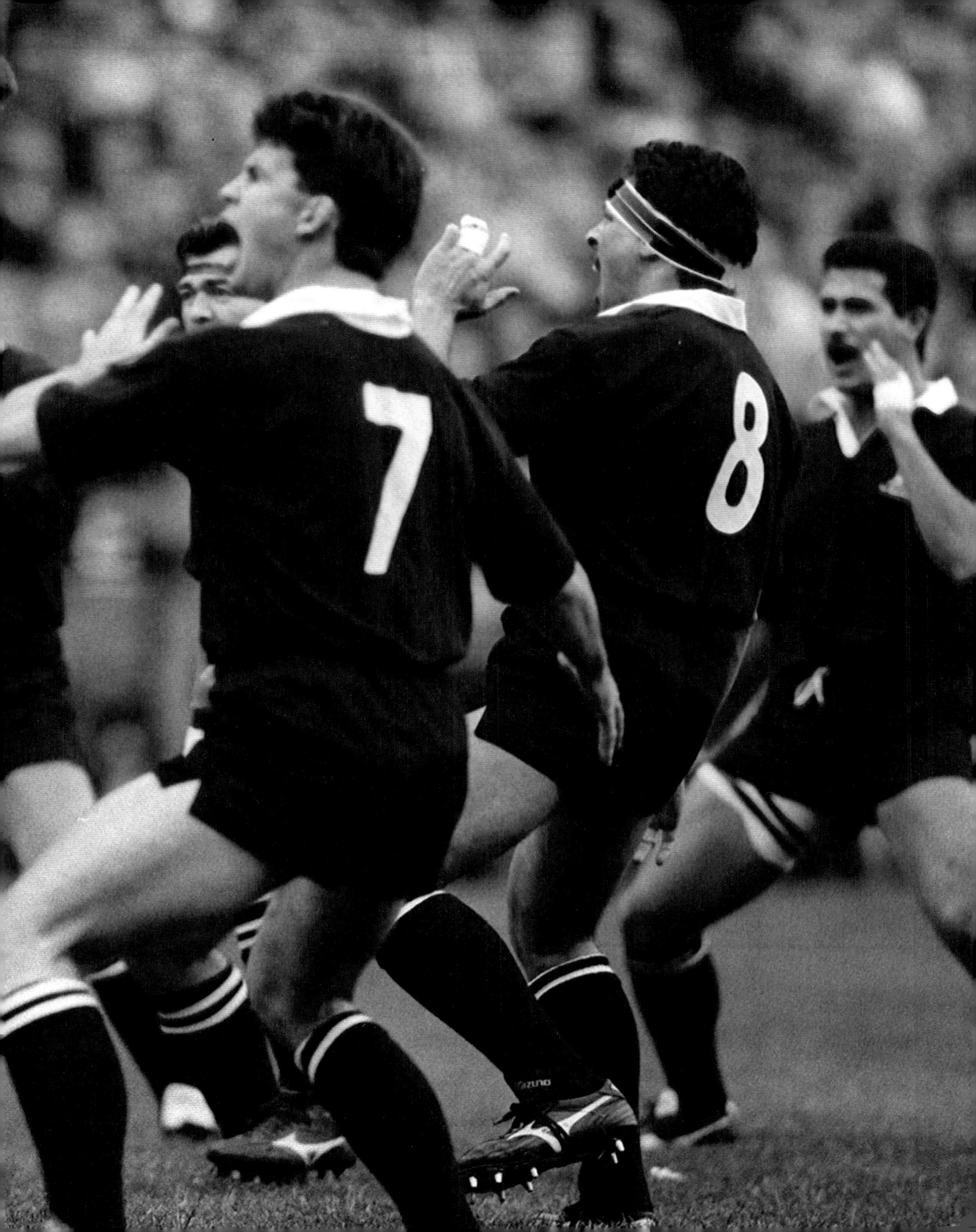
7
8

Gordon Hamilton celebrates his try against Australia, 1991.

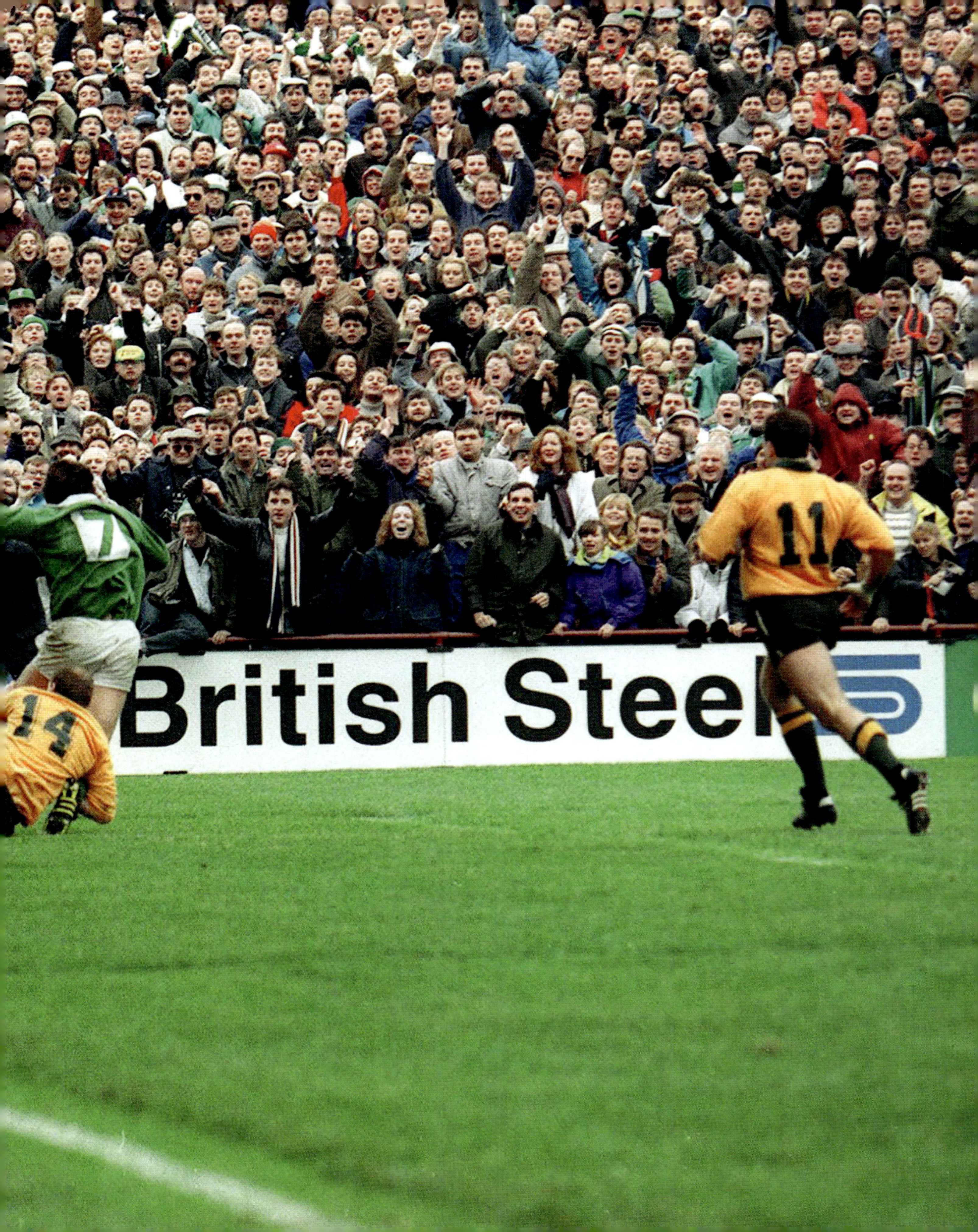
British Steel

Gary Halpin gives the finger to the All Blacks, 1995.

Eric Elwood in action for Connacht, 2003.

so he got little chance to impress. Things went from bad to worse for him the following season when he had hoped to make the Lions tour to New Zealand.

Ireland would defeat England 17–3 in March 1993 and, in a team performance in which all the boys in green were heroes, it is difficult to single out one player for special attention. But Mick Galwey would have to be in the running. Six weeks before the England match he lay in a Dublin hospital with his neck in a brace and his rugby future shrouded in uncertainty. At one point he was even told that his playing career was history. A shadow on his X-ray imperilled his prospects. For four terror-filled days he waited for the all-clear. Then it was out of hospital and onto the training field. A week later he played for Ireland against France.

The next game saw Ireland overcome the Welsh in Cardiff, with Connacht out-half Eric Elwood making a hugely impressive debut.

The win against England had been sealed with Galwey scoring a fine try – helping him to become one of only two Irishmen to secure a place on the Lions tour to New Zealand, with Nick Popplewell.

When injury ruled Geoghegan out of Lions contention, it was his partner on the wing, Richard Wallace, who got the call to go south as a replacement for the Lions, not Geoghehan, the golden boy of Irish rugby.

Still basking in the glory of a win over the All Blacks, the English expected retribution against Ireland in 1994 in Twickenham, but a splendid try from Geoghegan helped Ireland to secure another shock win – this time on a score of 13–12. Geoghegan also toured with Ireland to Australia that summer. He scored 11 tries in his 37 caps for Ireland. Sadly, injury brought his career to a premature end, and Irish and world rugby were deprived of one of their most thrilling wingers.

New players were emerging, such as the number 8, Victor Costello, who played for Ireland 39 times before retiring in 2007. He previously represented Ireland in the shotput event at the Barcelona Olympics in 1992. His father, Richard, had also been capped for Ireland at rugby, and his sister Suzanne represented Ireland in athletics.

THE 1995 WORLD CUP

A lovely moment, from an Irish perspective, occurred during the 1995 World Cup. Scrum-half Niall Hogan was conferred with his degree in medicine by a delegation from the College of Surgeons in a special ceremony in Johannesburg the day before Ireland played Wales.

It was at this World Cup that New Zealand's Jonah Lomu would become a global superstar. The tournament also produced a high point – if a notorious one – in the career of the late, great Gary Halpin, who scored a try against the All Blacks and infamously gave them the finger afterwards. As a sport, rugby must harness and celebrate the power of personality, and few matched Halpin in that department. About his gesture, Halpin believes that there are

> worse things you can do in life. But it was a really stupid thing to do. It wasn't a conscious thing. There was a frustration there. [Sean] Fitzpatrick [of New Zealand] is a bit of a wind-up merchant, and you don't get too many chances to stab the dragon.
>
> He had said a few things about us which were disrespectful, about how the Irish are always full of fire and passion to begin with and then they run out of gas. Thing is, he was probably right!
>
> It was really funny in the aftermath of that game. I got my fifteen minutes of fame. I spent the rest of that summer in Africa – my wife, Carol, and I, we went touring. I literally got a Daktari jeep and toured as far as Lusaka in Zambia, and we were all over Zimbabwe as well, staying on a tobacco farm at one point. The great thing was that, while I was there, I was thinking we [in Ireland] have a rivalry with England, but, man, these South Africans have a rivalry with New Zealand like you wouldn't believe! So everywhere I went that summer it was 'This is the guy who gave the finger to the All Blacks.' I couldn't get out of bars – everyone wanted to meet me and buy me a drink. It was pretty good chaos!

Halpin was almost as famous for his quip about the game:

> People forget that I sidestepped Jonah Lomu three times in that game. The only problem was that I didn't have the ball at the time: he did!

Ireland eventually lost the match 43–19 before going down 36–12 to France in the quarter-finals.

The tournament produced one of sport's fairytale endings: on their World Cup debut, Nelson Mandela's rainbow nation upset the favourites, leaving the All Blacks to blame food poisoning.

A GAME CHANGER

Shortly after the World Cup, on 27 August 1995, rugby turned professional. Tony Ward recalls that professionalism

> has dramatically changed the face of rugby on so many levels. Officially, the game turned professional in 1995, but towards the end of my career the cracks in the old amateur ethos so beloved by the authorities were appearing. My only brush with the clandestine world of illegal payments came when a Welsh rugby legend invited me to play a match in Aberavon. I had got to know him very well on the Lions tour in 1980. After the game he slipped me a brown paper bag with my 'expenses'. The subterfuge about 'under the table' payments was at James Bond levels for years, but finally, in 1995, the genie was let out of the bottle, and the professional era was formally ushered in.

Rugby in Ireland and beyond was no longer what it used to be.

Simon Geoghegan celebrates his try against England, 1994.

CROWNING GLORY (1978–95) | 83

Justin Bishop wins the ball ahead of Australia's Matthew Burke, 1999.

4

TRUE PROFESSIONALS (1995–2008)

At the end of 1995 the rugby world was frantically seeking a safe landing in a turbulent wind tossing it around. It was living through the breakdown – and breaking open – of much that had defined its first 120 years. Irish rugby administrators faced a disconcerting reorientation. The situation could either help people find new meaning or cause rugby people to close down and slowly turn bitter. Change happens, but transformation is always a process of letting go and of living in a transitional space for a while.

Eventually, Irish rugby would require an imaginative new structure to which rugby folk could commit themselves with conviction – one that would bring not just short-term but long-term life benefits. The edifice of that new structure will be the focus of part two of this book. Until then, our focus will primarily be on events on the pitch – though the first decade of the new era would be overshadowed by controversies about coaches and a series of bruising defeats.

NEW KIDD ON THE BLOCK

Ireland's first coach in the professional era was the New Zealander Murray Kidd. He had made his name with Garryowen, who had won the All-Ireland League in 1992.

Ireland won their first game in the professional era against Fiji on 18 November 1995 at Lansdowne Road on a score of 44–8. Another victory came two months later over the USA.

The 1996 Five Nations brought one win against Wales, the low point being a 45–10 mauling by France. However, the wheels really came off the wagon the following autumn. A loss at Lansdowne Road to Australia was acceptable, but defeats at home to Western Samoa and Italy were not, and the Kidd era was brought to a conclusion. Subsequently, he returned to work with the Cork club Sundays Well. There, the future Irish star Donnacha Ryan would credit Kidd with playing a formative role in his development.

Irish rugby fans looking for a messiah hoped they might have found one in Kidd's replacement, Brian Ashton. He had a much more substantial CV than his predecessor. Ashton's reputation was based on his triumphs as an innovative coach in Bath, playing both winning and thrilling rugby and unleashing the talents of such household names as Stuart Barnes, Jeremy Guscott and Mike Catt, the future Irish backs coach. At the time, Bath had 23 internationals in their squad, and their standards were very high. Such was the faith in Ashton's abilities that he was given a contract for six years.

The problem was that, while his Bath side were laden with gifted playmakers ideally equipped for playing his expansive game, the Irish side he inherited were not. A 'development tour' to New Zealand in 1997, to put it at its kindest, did not show much evidence of progress. The former Irish centre Rob Henderson looks back on the tour with horror.

> Oh, my God, was that a low point! Terrible. We played eight games on that tour – lost seven and won one. I played in seven games, and each of those we lost. The side we beat, when I wasn't playing, was New Zealand's equivalent of Ballybunion rugby.

Ashton achieved two wins at international level with Ireland, over Wales and Canada, but a crushing home defeat to the All Blacks, 63–15, and a 37–22 defeat to Italy (the third time they had been defeated by Italy in two years) were particular low points. Ashton did not endear himself to the Irish public in the way Joe Schmidt and Andy Farrell subsequently would, and his decision not to attend All-Ireland League games – preferring to stick to the English league, where many of the Irish players were playing – was not helpful to his cause. Likewise, his infamous comment after the defeat to Scotland – 'I'm not quite sure whose game plan that is, but it's nothing to do with me' – was detrimental in the court of popular opinion, not to mention to his relationship with his players and, ultimately, to his employers. There could be only one outcome, and Ashton's tenure as Irish coach came to an end.

TOUCH WOOD

The 1997 Lions tour began on a strange note for two Irish players. Paul Wallace was selected to replace the injured Peter 'The Claw' Clohessy before the tour even began. Wallace was at the airport when he saw The Claw coming towards him on the way home. It was awkward for Wallace, but he made it onto to the Test team and would come to be considered one of the stars of the tour. Other Irish players to impress were Jeremy Davidson and Eric Miller.

One of the massive hits on the tour was Keith Wood. He won 58 caps and became Ireland's most-capped hooker, having surpassed the great Ken Kennedy. Wood was not a typical hooker: kicking like a fly-half, linking like a centre and jinking like a winger, he was always inspired by his father's words: 'Never be ashamed at being proud of what you are good at.'

Wood first made his name with Garryowen, but in 1996 he crossed the channel and joined Harlequins. A year later he became the club's captain, remaining with Harlequins until his retirement, except for the 1999/2000 season, when he returned to play with Munster, leading them to the narrowest of defeats in the European Cup final. He first

Brian Ashton and Keith Wood.

Jeremy Davidson, Keith Wood and Paul Wallace during the Lions tour, 1997.

captained Ireland against Australia in November 1996 and immediately established himself as an inspirational leader.

Wood's motivational qualities are evident in one of the most famous legacies of the 1997 Lions tour. England's John 'Bentos' Bentley made as big a name for himself off the pitch as on it in the acclaimed documentary about the trip, *Living with Lions* (1997), and Woodie's fiery outbursts before games are among the most striking features of the film.

IN FROM THE WEST

Warren Gatland had brought success to Connacht, leading them to a quarter-final of the European Challenge Cup in 1998. When Brian Ashton 'moved on' in the middle of the Five Nations tournament that year, the IRFU came knocking on Gatland's door.

His first match was a daunting trip to Paris. The French were 33–1 on. From the outset, Gatland did things differently. He made an appeal to the Irish public for support, and the team received two thousand fax messages. Against all the odds, Ireland played well and were unlucky to lose 18–16. But there would be no wins that season and, from a results standpoint at least, a tour to South Africa that summer failed to turn the tide. Still, there were some encouraging performances.

In 1999 things did not go much better, and Ireland won only one match in the final Five Nations, against Wales. A tour to Australia brought more defeats but was notable for the debut of a young centre who would alter the Irish rugby landscape: Brian O'Driscoll. He looks back on this period with mixed feelings.

> My debut for Ireland came in June 1999. I had been brought on the tour of Australia, having sat on the bench for one of the Six Nations games. I played a few games on the tour before the first Test, when I was selected to play in the centre with Kevin Maggs ... in Brisbane. I was lucky to play for Ireland when I was so young [20 years of age]. It was a huge honour for me and something that I had always hoped to rise to at some stage of my career, but for it to have come at such an early age was incredible for me and something I really cherished. I had mixed

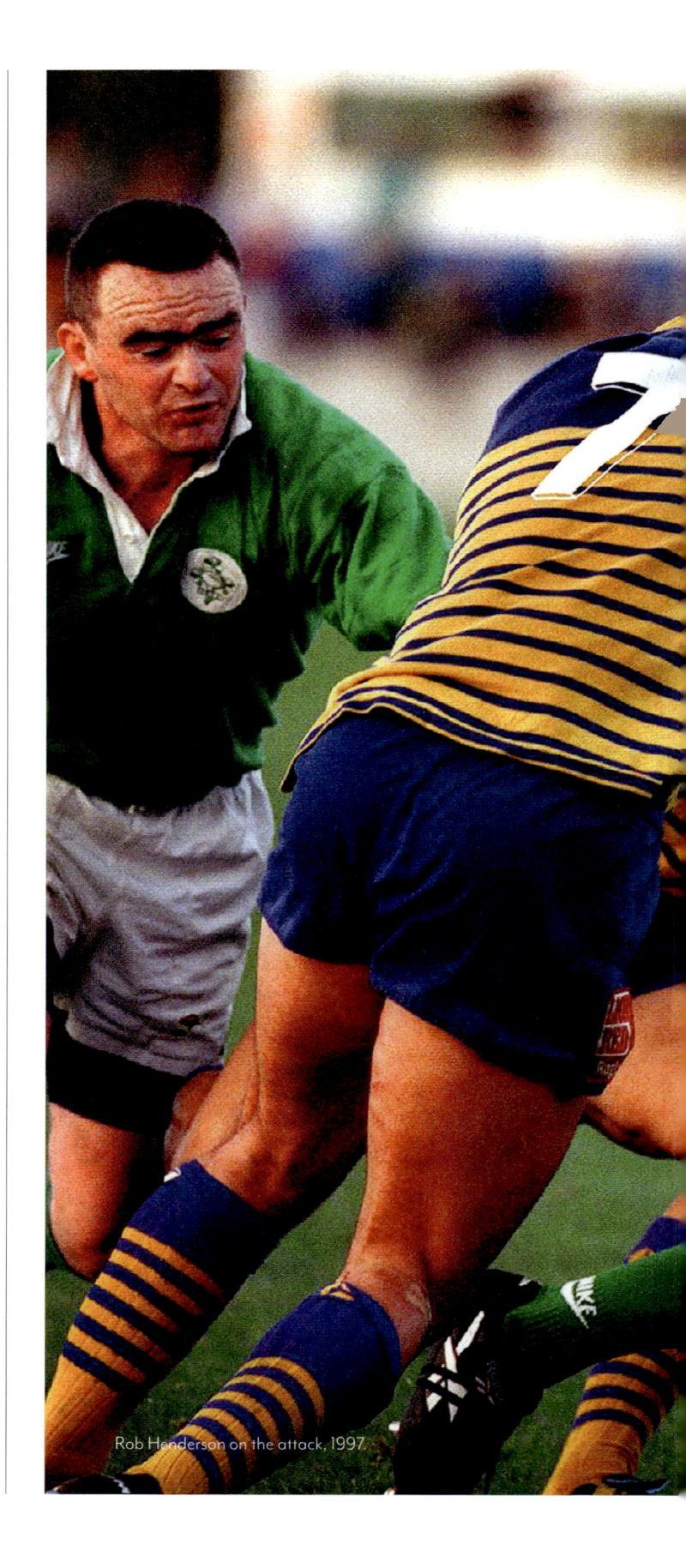

Rob Henderson on the attack, 1997.

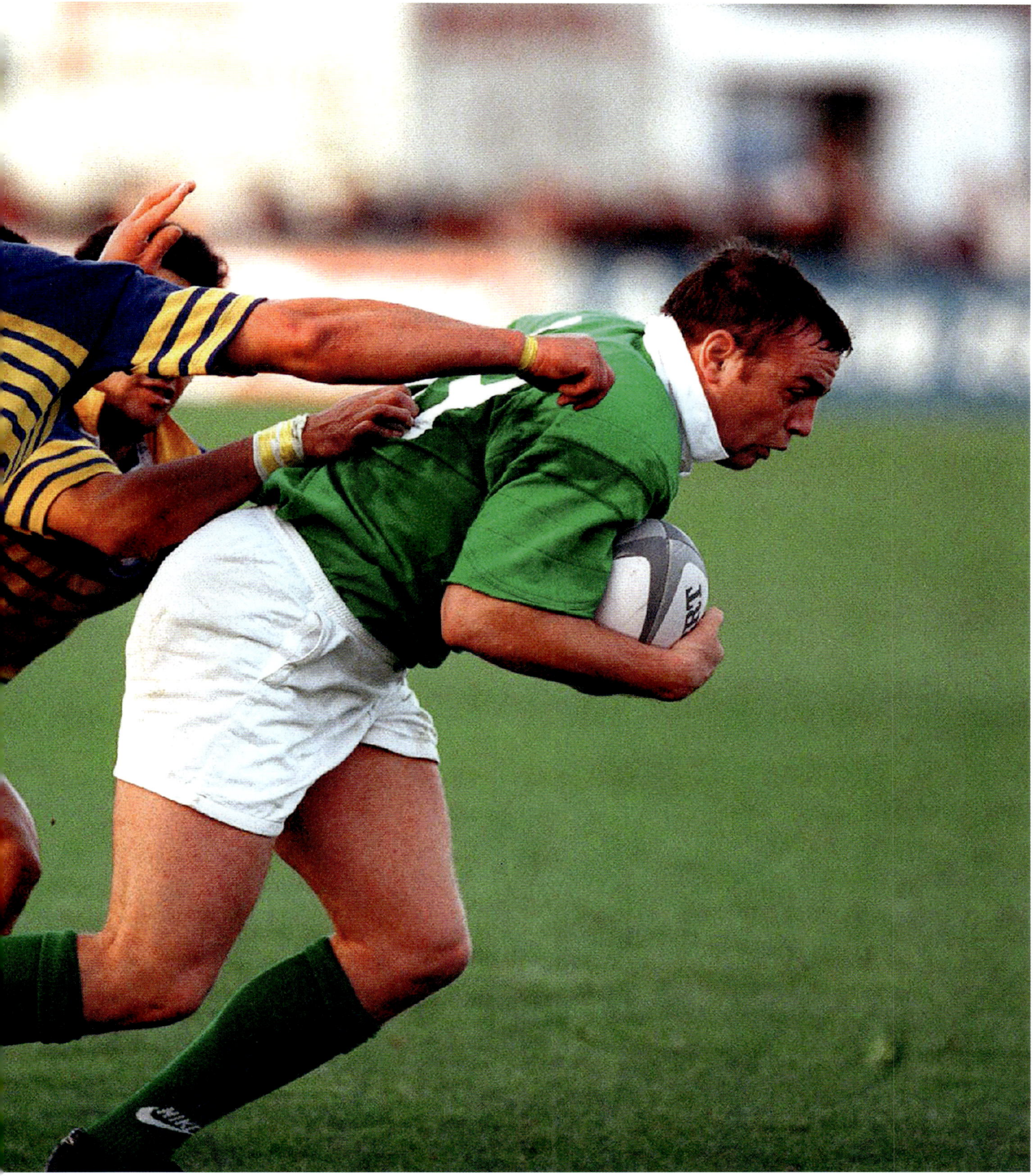

emotions because we got a bad beating, but at the same time I'd won my first cap.

I probably got to enjoy my second Test more because we really pushed the Aussies all the way. I had heard people say that your first cap always goes by so quickly that you can't really take it all in and enjoy it. That was my experience too.

At the start, things weren't going so well for Ireland. The low point was probably losing to Argentina in the World Cup back in Lens in 1999. That defeat was crushing. I think we panicked as a team towards the end, and probably our 13-man line-out showed we were a bit scarce of ideas.

I think we probably reached an equal low when we lost so heavily to England the following year. After that a lot of changes were made and the team started to improve, and we started to win again ... When you have bad losses, as well as great victories, you become very philosophical and realise that, when you are down, the team is probably not as bad as people say you are – or, when you win, you are not the world-beaters that everybody says you are.

After the team failed to qualify for the World Cup quarter-finals in 1999, Warren Gatland's job was in jeopardy. The heavy defeat to England the following year put him in further peril.

But happier times were round the corner, and O'Driscoll dramatically announced his arrival on the world stage with a stunning performance in Paris in 2000, culminating in three tries and Ireland's first win in Paris since 1972. O'Driscoll became one of the biggest names in international rugby overnight.

When we went to play France nobody expected us to even challenge the French, which probably took a lot of weight off our shoulders. I look back at the pictures and see the joy on our faces for having achieved something that Irish teams had failed to do for 28 years. We were overwhelmed at the end,

Dejected Irish players after the World Cup loss to Argentina, 1999.

Brian O'Driscoll breaks through in Paris, 2000.

and it was really a fantastic feeling. For me to have scored three tries was a nice bonus!

The third try sticks out most of all. What most people probably don't realise is that I shouldn't have been where I was when I got the ball. I was just trying to catch a breather before I got back into position, but the ball squirted out in front of me, and I went for the gap. That try took us to within two points of them and convinced us that we could win the game. A lot of people have remarked that Émile Ntamack didn't make a great effort to tackle me, and I'm only glad he didn't come crashing into me.

In many ways, though, the most important win in that campaign was the Scotland match, which marked a turning point in modern Irish rugby. It followed a 50–18 hammering by England and was Ireland's first win over Scotland since 1988. In that emphatic and thrilling 44–22 victory over Scotland, which showed that Ireland had found a winning formula at last, Gatland introduced five new caps: Simon Easterby, John Hayes, Shane Horgan, Ronan O'Gara and Peter Stringer.

The most famous 'golden generation' in sport in recent decades has probably been the Class of '92, the Manchester United youth team that brought unprecedented success to the club. That team included Phil and Gary Neville, Nicky Butt, Paul Scholes, David Beckham and Ryan Giggs. But Gary Neville claims that the Class of '92 would have won nothing had they not been 'backboned' by senior players such as Roy Keane and Eric Cantona. In like manner, Gatland knitted the exciting new talent with senior players.

The thing Moss Keane hated most about Irish rugby was people who kept talking about 'passion'. What he loved

Peter Stringer, Mick Galwey and Ronan O'Gara during the national anthem, Six Nations 2000.

Warren Gatland looks on as the Irish team prepare to go out for the second half, 2001.

most about it was people who played with the passion of a medieval martyr. Four players from this era who Moss adored for that reason were Keith Wood, Mick Galwey, Peter Clohessy and Anthony Foley. The famous photos of Galwey with his arm round Ronan O'Gara on one side and Peter Stringer on the other as Ireland lined up for the national anthems speak volumes.

Ireland had gone from a wooden spoon in 1998 to missing out on a Six Nations on scoring difference in 2001. One potent symbol of the upturn in Ireland's fortunes came that year when Keith Wood was voted World Rugby Player of the Year.

On the Lions tour that year, O'Driscoll's reputation rose even further on foot of a stunning try in the first Test. He has looked back on that time:

I know some people will probably feel this is strange, but I was far more nervous watching the 1997 Lions tour of South Africa, when I was back home in Dublin staring at the television set, than I was on the field in Brisbane for the first Test in 2001. When you're playing you have no time to dwell on things. Mind you, I was aware of the crowd at the Gabba. Just looking up into that sea of red as we ran out was enough to put us on our toes, but when the Wallabies appeared and the boos drowned out the cheers it was just unbelievable.

If we had gone on to win the series, that first Test would probably have been a major highlight of my career, but because we lost the series it doesn't have the same glow in my memory. We were fairly surprised at what we achieved in the opening fifty minutes of the first Test in particular, but all the gaps were closed up for the next two Tests. When you are a part of a tour like that, every result counts in terms of morale and encouragement. The first Test gave us a big lift, but the other two losses were crushing blows.

The tour left an enduring impression on O'Driscoll's mother, Geraldine.

> Probably the most interesting experience of all came in Australia during the Lions tour. After the first Test, when Brian scored the famous try, Brian's father Frank and I got on the bus with a gang of Lions supporters. We sat at the back of the bus and nobody knew who we were. Then the crowd burst into song. They started singing 'Waltzing O'Driscoll'. Frank and I said nothing. We just nodded at each other, but it was actually very emotional.

Another noteworthy moment of that tour came when David Wallace played for the Lions – making history by becoming the third member of one generation of a single family to play for the Lions, after his brothers Paul and Richard.

STEADY EDDIE

Warren Gatland's assistant coach was Eddie O'Sullivan. Although many marriages are made in heaven, the Gatland–O'Sullivan one most definitely was not. The saga of their 'feud' has already been widely ventilated in public by both men and by many others. Given the improvement in Ireland's fortunes, Gatland did not foresee that his 29–40 loss against the touring All Blacks in autumn 2001 – after a Six Nations campaign that year that was severely disrupted by foot-and-mouth disease – would be his last game in charge of Ireland. He was replaced as coach by his erstwhile assistant.

The abiding image of O'Sullivan's second year in charge is of the English captain, Martin Johnson, infamously snubbing President Mary McAleese on the red carpet at Lansdowne Road during Ireland's 2003 Grand Slam decider. England swept Ireland aside that day 42–6 and went on to win the World Cup that autumn.

Eddie O'Sullivan.

Alan Quinlan, Paul O'Connell and Malcolm O'Kelly, Rugby World Cup 2003.

O'Sullivan used imaginative ways to motivate the team. A speech made just before, during or straight after a game rarely means anything. It is what is said in the weeks leading up to it that helps win a match. In the run-up to the World Cup in 2003, O'Sullivan brought in two very different guest speakers to talk to the squad in the Citywest hotel: the explorer Sir Ranulph Fiennes and the former champion boxer Marvin Hagler. They both struck a chord with several players in the squad. Hagler said, 'Feed the positive and starve the negative in everything you think and say and do.' Fiennes talked about the preparation that was needed for a major expedition and the steps needed to achieve what you wanted to achieve.

In the build-up to the 2003 World Cup, rugby pundits throughout the world believed that Geordan Murphy was destined to become one of the stars of the tournament and even one of the giants of world rugby. But in one of the warm-up games against Scotland, Murphy broke his leg, and the 'George Best of rugby' missed out, having emerged as the star of the previous Six Nations. It was a huge setback for the team. With Murphy in the side, O'Driscoll would have got extra space, because opposition defences would have to figure out which one of Ireland's two big threats would make the break.

Although Ireland were in the 'group of death' with Australia and Argentina, they did atone for the defeat in Lens four years earlier and qualified for the quarter-final, only to lose to Australia. Paul O'Connell has looked back on the tournament:

> Overall, the World Cup went well for me personally. It was horribly disappointing to lose to Australia. Although sometimes

the media didn't believe us, we felt we had a good team. The days of moral victories mattering for us were over. We knew that if we won that game a lot of things could happen for us. We didn't play fabulously well against France, and a couple of defensive mistakes cost us dear.

I have been on tours like that before, when I was homesick, but not on that one because it was such a carnival of rugby. For two weeks we were staying in a hotel outside Sydney by the beach going surfing every day and swimming in the sea after training as part of our recovery. We were in Melbourne at the time of the Melbourne Cup, and there was massive hysteria about it. The whole experience was the kind of stuff you dream of.

And happier days for the Irish team were round the corner.

DEMPSEY'S DEN

Girvan Dempsey guaranteed himself a place in Irish rugby immortality when he scored the try that beat England in 2004.

Against all the odds, Ireland ended England's 22-match winning streak at 'Fortress Twickenham', which stretched back to the 1999 World Cup, when England were beaten by New Zealand. It was England's first Championship home defeat under Sir Clive Woodward, whose coaching regime began in November 1997. The icing on the cake was that the English were parading the Webb Ellis Cup at Twickers for the first time since their World Cup victory in Australia. For Dempsey, the only people who were not shocked by the turn of events were the Irish team.

Although nobody gave us a chance, we went into the game with a lot of self-confidence and felt we could take the scalp of the world champions. All week Eddie O'Sullivan had been asking, 'Why can't we beat England?' Training had gone well beforehand. Going onto the pitch, the noise from the English fans was incredible. They got a try from Matt Dawson early on. Brian O'Driscoll called us together and said, 'Right, lads. This is a big game. Let's buckle down.' I know it is a cliché, but the try was straight off the training ground. We had worked that move again and again in Naas, and everyone played their part perfectly.

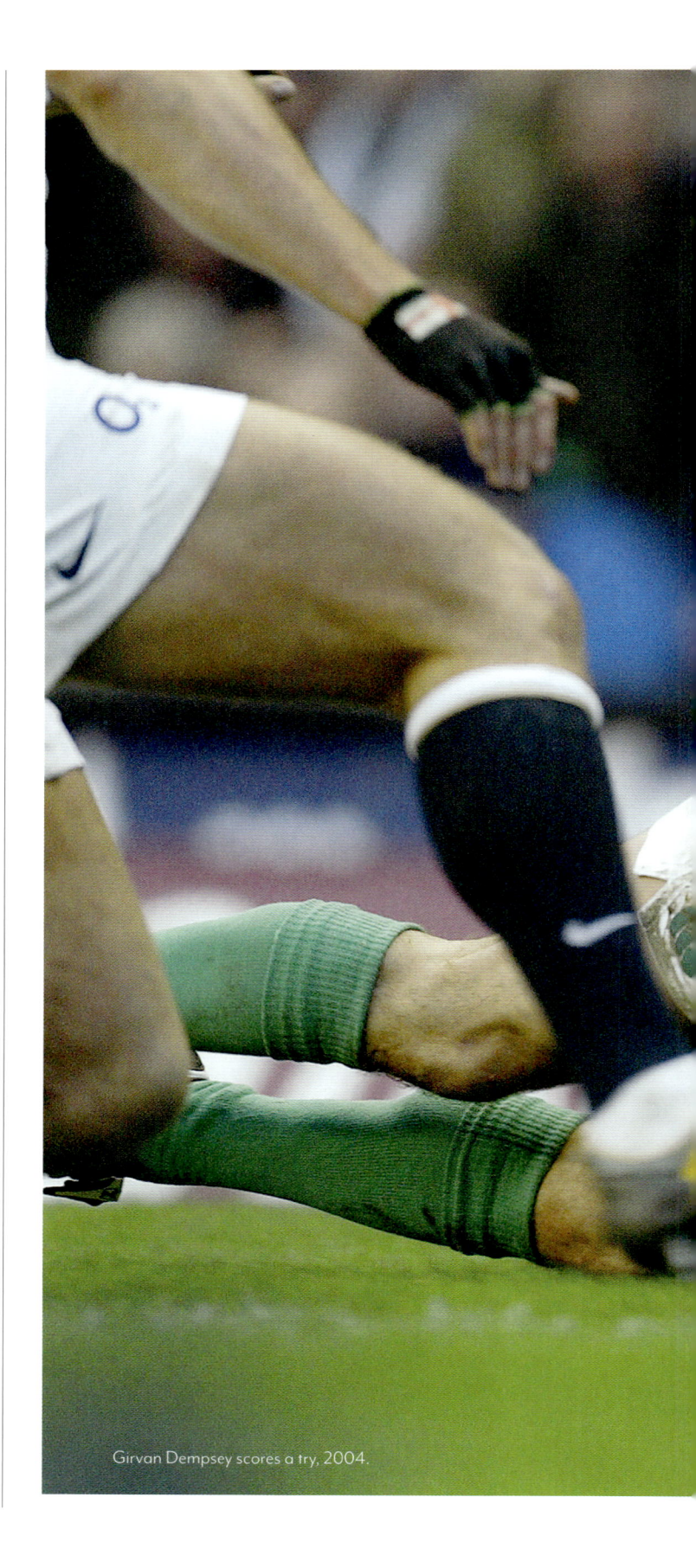

Girvan Dempsey scores a try, 2004.

TRUE PROFESSIONALS (1995–2008) | 97

It was great then to go on and win the Triple Crown against Scotland in Lansdowne Road. Down through the years, Scotland had given us many a beating in the Six Nations, even in days when we were expected to win. It was such a fantastic feeling once the final whistle went. Nobody wanted to leave afterwards. We felt it was a tangible reward for all the hard work we had put in down the years. The previous year, losing the Grand Slam decider against England had been such a massive disappointment. We felt the distance between us was nowhere near as great as the scoreboard suggested. Jonny Wilkinson [of England] produced the greatest display of rugby I have ever seen that day, and the margin of their victory flattered them, so it was doubly nice to win the Triple Crown in Lansdowne Road twelve months later.

A landmark in Brian O'Driscoll's career came in March 2004 when he captained Ireland to their first Triple Crown in 19 years. According to O'Driscoll,

> even at half-time in the game in Cardiff, when we were 6–0 down, we knew we could win. People said we were a 'nearly team' before we won the Triple Crown. I remember saying, when we beat Australia in 2002, 'Let's not be the nearly team. Let's not get the good win now and again, but let's strive to beat the big guns consistently.' I think we did that winning the Triple Crown. We had beaten France in 2000, England in 2001 and Australia in 2002, but we hadn't strung enough good results together against top opposition. Winning the Triple Crown took that monkey off our back and gave us a base to build on.

Ireland vs Scotland, 2004.

When we went on tour to South Africa after winning the Triple Crown, a good performance was no longer to lose by only ten points: a good performance was nothing less than a win.

We knew that we had a lot of potential in the side, and that's why talk of 'brave old Ireland' had no interest for us. We wanted to win and were not satisfied any more to play heroically but to lose.

In the Scotland game we had to wear them down a bit. These Six Nations aren't easy, and a lot of the time you mightn't pull away till the end, which was the case in this one.

There was another agenda in this game: Scottish coach Matt Williams was coming back to Lansdowne Road. He had a point to prove because Scotland's campaign up to then had been so disastrous. Add to the mix that he literally knows the way the wind blows in Lansdowne from his time as Leinster and Ireland A coach and his intimate knowledge of so many of the players he once coached on the Irish team. We were concentrating on playing to the best of our ability, and we felt that if we were to do that we could and would win the game.

On top of that, Gordon D'Arcy was chosen as northern hemisphere player of the season.

The year 2005 should have been the crowning glory of Brian O'Driscoll's career. He was chosen to captain the Lions in New Zealand. However, just 41 seconds into the first Test at the Jade Stadium in Christchurch, he was spear-tackled by Tana Umaga and Keven Mealamu. The Irish captain was forced to leave the field of play and took no further part in the tour. The tackle created a huge controversy and became known as 'Speargate'.

But the good times returned for O'Driscoll the following year when he led Ireland to more glory. Shane Horgan's dramatic last-gasp try against England saw Ireland seal a thrilling win, 28–24, in Twickenham and claim a second Triple Crown in three years. Paul O'Connell believes that O'Driscoll was pivotal to the team's success.

Drico had a different style of captaincy from Woodie, but when he asked you to do something, you knew that anything he asked you to give he himself would give more. Some players give a hundred per cent, but Drico gave a million per cent. He put his body on the line every time, and I loved that about him. He was not a fancy Dan by any means.

AN UNFORGETTABLE OCCASION

With the announcement in 2006 of the rebuilding of Lansdowne Road, which was set to take two years, a different ground was required to stage Ireland's home internationals. The only stadium capable of holding major rugby internationals was Croke Park. To enable this to happen, the GAA temporarily relaxed its rule governing the playing of so-called foreign games on its property.

The year 2007 brought a defining image not just of Irish rugby but of Irish life. Saturday 24 February, when England came to play in Croke Park, transcended the realm of sports perhaps in a way that no other Irish sporting event has ever done. The French had squashed Ireland's Grand Slam hopes a few weeks previously, and they denied the boys in green a Championship when Elvis Vermeulen got an injury-time try to clinch the title for France. But France did not bring the historical baggage that an English side did.

What is firmly embedded in the national memory is the singing of the anthems. Despite all the anxiety about the playing of 'God Save the Queen' at Croke Park, 87 years after Bloody Sunday, something shifted as soon as the singing started. A rare atmosphere pervaded the crowd: this was a moment in history made palpable. The emotion that day was electric, as was evident in the sight of big John Hayes shedding tears while the anthems were being played.

Fears over the playing of 'God Save the Queen' on such hallowed ground had everybody on edge. There was an attendance of 83,000. Demand for tickets was such that they could have sold ten times that number. Ireland's 43–13 win against England, featuring tries from Girvan Dempsey, David Wallace, Shane Horgan and Isaac Boss will never be forgotten. It was a record defeat over the 'old enemy'.

Ireland claimed their ninth Triple Crown and went to the World Cup in France with great confidence. But their high hopes proved completely misplaced. Two weeks before the tournament, Ireland played a warm-up match against Bayonne that would become known as the 'battle of Bayonne'. Amid the litany of cynical tackles, the most noteworthy was probably a punch from Mikaera Te Whata that put Brian O'Driscoll's participation in the World Cup in jeopardy. O'Driscoll memorably summed up the Bayonne approach to that match: 'They were more interested in kicking the sh*t out of us than putting points on the scoreboard.'

When the tournament began, Ireland's performance was so poor that it prompted Eddie O'Sullivan to describe their opening game against Namibia as like 'watching a horror movie at times', even though they got the victory. Another very unimpressive win followed against Georgia before Ireland lost to France and Argentina. Ireland failed to qualify for the knockout stages.

O'Sullivan needed a great Six Nations campaign in 2008 to save his job, but it was not forthcoming. His replacement, Declan Kidney, arrived with the firm intention of getting the team back on the road to glory.

Ireland vs England at Croke Park, 2007.

TRUE PROFESSIONALS (1995–2008)

Ronan O'Gara scores a drop goal to win the game against Wales, 2009.

5

SHOULDER TO SHOULDER

(2009–24)

It was Ireland against Wales in Cardiff in the Six Nations Championship in 2009.

Both nations held their breath.

The Welsh out-half, Stephen Jones, faced up to a last-gasp penalty with Ireland leading 17–15.

At stake was Ireland's first Grand Slam in 61 years.

In the stand Jack Kyle looked on to see whether another Irish team would enter into sporting immortality, as his team had done in 1948.

Jones's kick looked good.

Spine-tingling tension pervaded the stadium.

GOOD TIMES IN BAD TIMES

After the economic collapse and financial crisis of the preceding years, Ireland was by 2009 in the grips of a severe recession that would see the country lose its economic sovereignty. That spring, as it had done in the 1980s, the Irish rugby team lifted the spirits of a demoralised nation.

Ireland began their Six Nations campaign with a thrilling 30–21 win over France at Croke Park and a facile victory over Italy. Then came England. The match was a showcase for the brilliance of Brian O'Driscoll. With the scores tied at 3–3 at half-time, the captain sent a beautiful kick clean between the posts for a drop goal after a nice pass from Paul O'Connell. Ronan O'Gara later sent a smart chip into space, and O'Driscoll gathered, only to be absolutely flattened in the tackle by Riki Flutey. Drico was out for a couple of minutes but chose to soldier on, and three minutes later he showed his true grit and scored Ireland's only try. Ireland won 14–13 and followed it up with an uninspiring 22–15 win over Scotland.

The high point of O'Driscoll's career, perhaps surpassing even the honour of captaining the Lions on the ill-fated 2005 tour, came when he led Ireland to win against Wales in 2009 and claim the Grand Slam. Was he nervous before the game? 'I was probably more nervous going into that game than others because the stakes were so high, but I was determined not to let my teammates see that.'

Ireland overturned a 6–0 interval deficit with tries early in the second half from O'Driscoll and Tommy Bowe. Stephen Jones thought he had won the match for the Welsh with a drop goal in the 76th minute.

The drama went up another notch.

But cometh the hour, cometh Ronan O'Gara. With two minutes to go he conjured up a drop goal of his own.

Although Ireland conceded a last-minute penalty, Jones's kick fell just short.

Cue delirium.

The Grand Slam-winning team, 2009.

SHOULDER TO SHOULDER (2009–24) | 105

The Irish team that made history that day was:

15.	Rob Kearney
14.	Tommy Bowe
13.	Brian O'Driscoll
12.	Gordon D'Arcy
11.	Luke Fitzgerald
10.	Ronan O'Gara
9.	Tomás O'Leary
8.	Jamie Heaslip
7.	David Wallace
6.	Stephen Ferris
5.	Paul O'Connell
4.	Donncha O'Callaghan
3.	John Hayes
2.	Jerry Flannery
1.	Marcus Horan

Replacements: Tom Court, Rory Best, Mick O'Driscoll, Denis Leamy, Peter Stringer, Paddy Wallace and Geordan Murphy.

One unforgettable moment of the celebrations was when Jack Kyle congratulated Brian O'Driscoll minutes after the match. The party continued the following day, and Tommy Bowe took the stage at the Dawson Street homecoming to sing 'Black Velvet Band' with all the team looking on in amusement – with one exception: John Hayes had slipped away from the official celebrations and was watching Bowe's performance on television back home at his family farm. To nobody's surprise, O'Driscoll was chosen as player of the tournament.

The good news for the Irish players continued when Paul O'Connell was chosen to captain the Lions tour to South Africa that summer. O'Connell was one of 14 Irish players selected, and for him it was

> a fabulous honour, considering the captains that had gone before me, some of them legends of the game. I and a few of the players had had a bad Lions experience in 2005, losing 3–0 to New Zealand. [O'Connell had won three Lions caps against New Zealand in 2005 and was one of only two tourists to play in every minute of each Test, except for a stint in the sin bin.]
>
> That old-school cliché of leaving the jersey in a better place kicked in. We had the experience where we had gone on a Lions tour and we had left it in a far worse place. When you have spent all your rugby career dreaming of playing for the Lions and that happens it's a horrible feeling ... Although we lost the series 2–1 in 2009, I would like to think we left the jersey in a slightly better place. The players are from four countries, but there is one team, one philosophy, one jersey, and I loved that.

In 2010 Ireland left a Triple Crown behind them with a home defeat to Scotland in their final game. Later that summer things took a turn for the worse with a 66–28 defeat to the All Blacks in New Plymouth.

Following Ireland's disappointing defeat to France in 2011, Declan Kidney's patience was sorely tested in the defeat to Wales, with Mike Phillips scoring the decisive try after an illegal quick Welsh throw from a line-out. However, Ireland prevailed against an English side seeking the Grand Slam. Ireland were rampant and won 24–8.

After that, Ireland headed back to New Zealand for the World Cup. First up was an unimpressive 22–10 win over the USA, now being coached by Eddie O'Sullivan.

Then came Ireland's best performance in the World Cup: an emphatic 15–6 win over Australia. Such was the elation afterwards that Ronan O'Gara went so far as to suggest that he would consider retiring. The management were quick to shoot down that suggestion.

Having topped their group, Ireland faced Wales in the quarter-final. But Warren Gatland came back to haunt Ireland, and his Welsh team dispatched his former employers 22–10.

Seán O'Brien is tackled in the Six Nations match against England, 2011.

Declan Kidney trains the Ireland Rugby squad, 2008.

GONE TOO SOON

The year 2012 was a disappointing year for Ireland on the field – and a tragic one off it. Ireland finished mid-table in the Six Nations, beating Scotland and Italy and drawing with France. Summer brought defeats in all three Tests against New Zealand, Ireland finishing with a humiliating 60–0 loss in the final Test.

Then came news that put everything else into harsh perspective.

At just 22 years of age Nevin Spence was on the cusp of making the Irish team. The rugby world was his oyster. But on 15 September 2012 tragedy struck, and he lost his life. In the worst farming accident in Ulster in over twenty years Nevin was taken from the family he adored in an attempt to rescue a beloved dog after it had fallen into a slurry tank on the family farm in Hillsborough, Co. Down. His father, Noel, and his brother Graham also died in the tragedy. Nevin's sister Emma put her life on the line in an attempt to rescue her father and brothers before being overcome by the fumes. She would survive the incident.

Grief is unending, but so is hope. Somehow the family found the resources they needed. With characteristic insight, Emma observed, 'Courage does not always manifest in the roar of the lion.' The Irish rugby family rallied behind the family as a pall settled on this tightly knit community.

In 2023 Ulster Rugby unveiled the Nevin Spence Memorial Stand before their United Rugby Championship game with Edinburgh just ahead of what would have been Nevin's 33rd birthday on 26 April. It was a proud occasion for Emma and the Spence family.

> When we lost Nevin, Ulster Rugby said he would never be forgotten, and the club has been very true to their word. From teammates he played with, coaches, physios and staff to supporters from near and far, the warm-hearted and unconditional support has been a real lifeline to our family.

Ulster players during a minute's silence in remembrance of Nevin Spence.

KUKRI
Bank of Irela
KUKRI
Bank of Ire
KUKRI
Bank of Irel
Bank of Ire
KUKRI
Bank of Irel

SO THIS IS CHRISTMAS?

Not for the first time, Warren Gatland ruffled the feathers of Irish rugby fans when he dropped Brian O'Driscoll for the third Lions Test in Australia in 2013. To add fuel to the flames, O'Driscoll was not even selected for a place on the bench. The Lions won the game and the series 2–1.

After the tour O'Driscoll told Shane Horgan in a TV interview that Gatland would not be on his Christmas card list. O'Driscoll's comments created a furore and he realised that he was going to have meet Gatland at a function in a few weeks' time. Not wanting the supposed feud to develop further, O'Driscoll presented Gatty with a Christmas card even though it was only September.

That Lions tour also showcased the courage of Paul O'Connell. He fractured his arm in the final 15 minutes of the first Test. The Wallabies captain, James Horwill, was amazed, having heard the snap, that the Irish lock played on.

NO ORDINARY JOE

Declan Kidney needed a good Six Nations campaign in 2013. He got the opposite.

It began well enough with a 30–22 away win against Wales – a match noteworthy because it featured Brian O'Driscoll's 46th and final try for Ireland. Although Ireland drew 13–13 with France, they lost to Scotland and England. To the shock of most Irish fans, they lost to Italy 23–15. It was the end of the road for Kidney. He who was replaced by Joe Schmidt, who had established his credentials as a top coach by leading Leinster to two Heineken Cups. His appointment was greatly welcomed by Jack McGrath.

> I owe so much of my career – first with Leinster and later with Ireland – to Joe. His attention to detail is phenomenal. Say when we were playing France we all got a two-minute video clip of thirty of the French players, showing their strengths and weaknesses – what foot they like to kick with, the hand they pass off with – and this kind of detail is invaluable ... The amount of work that goes into producing those video clips is unreal. I know people are always going on about how brutal his video analysis was. Certainly, new players coming into the squad were a little apprehensive about them.
>
> Joe would not criticise you if you made a mistake. What drove him mad, though, was when you made the same mistake a few times when he had told you about it and that you needed to avoid it. In international rugby the margins are so small that a small mistake can cost you a match, and that is why Joe was so keen on the minute detail. He had a way of making you think differently, like saying, 'It's not how quickly you run that's important: it's how quickly you think.'

On the pitch the Schmidt era almost got off to a spectacular start. With less than half a minute remaining, Ireland were leading the All Blacks 22–17 and seemingly on course for their own page of rugby immortality. Ireland had led 19–0 after an incredible opening 18 minutes. But Ireland became less dominant and a late converted try crushed the dream that day. As Schmidt, himself a New Zealander, noted, 'To be a minute away from history and have the ball in your hands on their 10-metre line … it was devastating.'

Schmidt used the match as a learning opportunity.

> One area that I will admit to being behind the likes of New Zealand then was the quality of their bench. If I list off all the guys who came on as a sub against us they would have started for pretty much every other team in the world. I resolved to try and have a squad of 30 to 35 players, where one could replace another seamlessly, without any weakness to the overall team. We had not reached that stage in 2013, but when we played them in Chicago [in 2016] we were a lot further on that journey, with young players like Joey Carbery slotting in, and that's one of the reasons why we finally beat them.

Schmidt would lead Ireland to consecutive wins in the Six Nations in 2014 and 2015. The World Cup in 2015, though, would be a disappointment, with an injury-ravaged Ireland again going out at the quarter-final stage to Argentina. The tournament marked the end of Paul O'Connell's playing career: he sustained a serious injury in an emphatic 24–9 victory over France.

New Zealand's Ryan Crotty scores the last try of the game, 2013.

Schmidt got the show back on the road when Ireland claimed a historic first Test win in South Africa in Cape Town in 2016. The merchants of doom had predicted a tough time for Ireland on their summer tour after a disappointing Six Nations and on foot of several high-profile absences from the touring party, notably Johnny Sexton.

Few saw Ireland's 26–20 win coming. That number shrank still further when C.J. Stander, who was born and raised in South Africa, was sent off on his first overseas tour for Ireland for striking the head of Pat Lambie after only 23 minutes. But Ireland would ultimately prevail. For Schmidt it was a special performance.

> We knew to go there and get a victory would be unbelievably tough and require a massive physical performance. If we had sat back and kept giving them ball we would have eventually run out of steam, so we had to take the game to them. There were a lot of tired bodies afterwards, but because we had made history we were in a state of euphoria after the win.

HISTORY IN THE WINDY CITY

More history was made in November 2016 in Chicago. Ireland produced a thrilling display to record a first win over New Zealand, at the 29th attempt, ending the All Blacks' run of 18 straight wins.

The game was shrouded in emotion. From the outset the Irish effort appeared to be fuelled by the memory of Anthony 'Axel' Foley, who had died suddenly the previous month at the age of 42. Prior to kick-off, Ireland lined up in the shape of a number 8, the jersey worn with pride by Foley for many years, while their opponents performed their traditional pre-match haka.

Back home across the Atlantic Ocean, Anthony's father, Brendan, was watching and was still

> probably traumatised from Anthony's sudden death. It was like an earthquake hit the family.

The Ireland team face the Haka in the shape of an eight in memory of Anthony 'Axel' Foley.

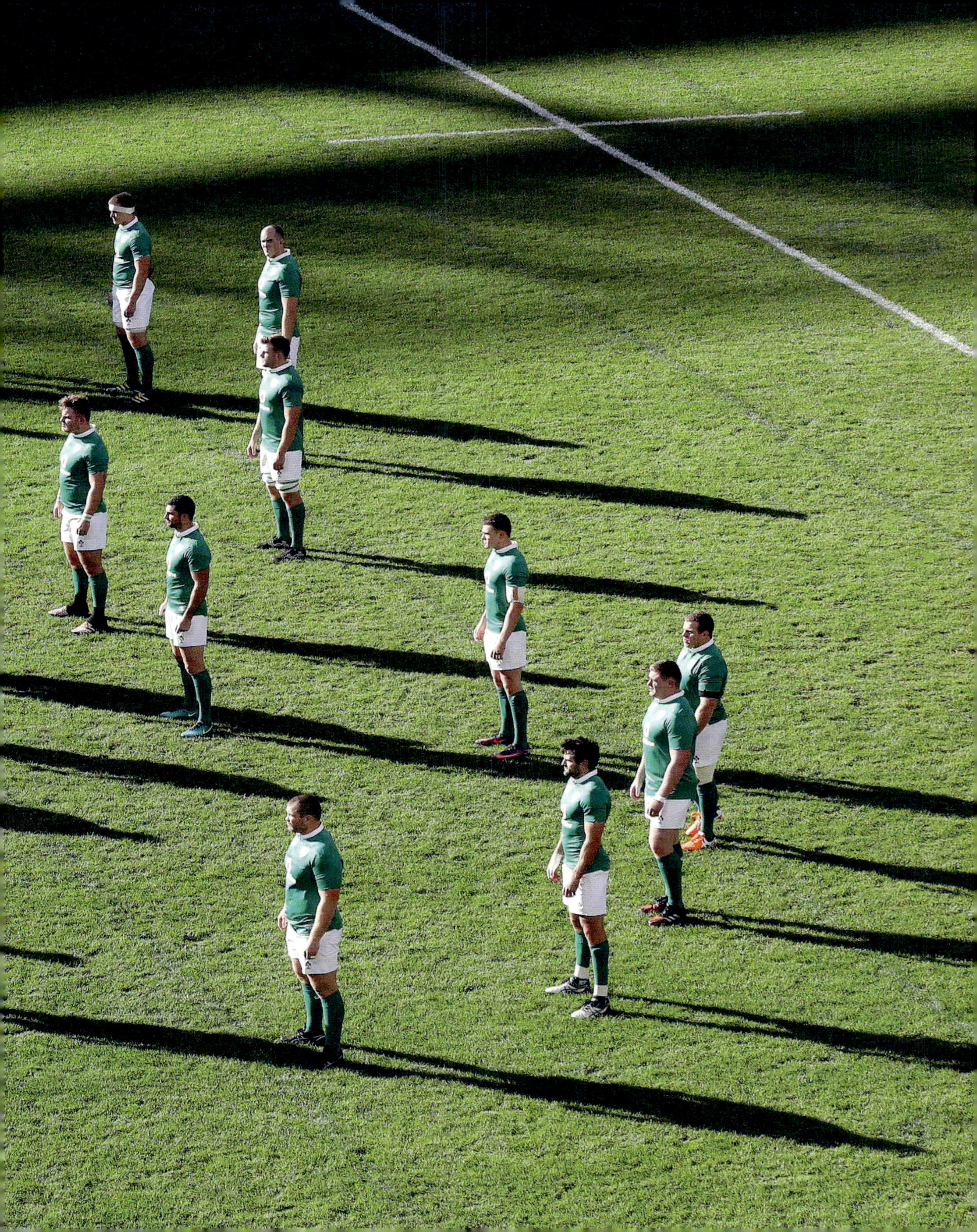

All my early caps were won away from home. Finally, I made my home debut against Wales in 1980, and I was given two tickets for the game and for a small reception afterwards. I gave them to my wife, Sheila, and Anthony, who was seven.

Before the game, Willie Duggan came up to us. Willie was always trying to wrangle extra tickets for friends. He asked me if I had any spare tickets. When Willie saw that one of my tickets was for Anthony he said that a child like him would not need a ticket. I begged to differ, but Willie hoisted Anthony up on his shoulders and brought him to the turnstiles.

There they were greeted by a stony-faced man who said it was not possible for a child to get in without a ticket. Willie unleashed a tirade of ... colourful language and the man had a change of heart.

We won the match 21–7, which was a then record victory over the Welsh, and as we were celebrating afterwards, word came down to us that Anthony was not able to get into the reception because he didn't have a ticket. Willie went up to retrieve Anthony and brought him down into the dressing room. It was a much bigger deal for Anthony to get into the Irish dressing room than to get a glass of orange and a bar of chocolate at the reception.

Afterwards, Willie took a great interest in Anthony's career. They were both number 8s, and I think Willie saw Anthony as the same type of warrior as he had been himself.

So I watched that game in Chicago at home with Willie. It was a very proud and poignant occasion – made all the more poignant in retrospect because Willie himself died suddenly shortly afterwards.

For Jack McGrath, winning the game 40–29 was one of the high points of his career.

To end a 111-year wait and be part of the first Irish team to defeat the aristocrats of rugby was stupendous. The match was played in front of a capacity crowd of sixty thousand at Soldier Field in Chicago, a venue chosen in an attempt to increase the exposure of the sport. It was right and fitting that the win came only three days after the Chicago Cubs ended a 108-year drought to land baseball's World Series. Five million

Conor Murray celebrates Robbie Henshaw's try against New Zealand, 2016.

SHOULDER TO SHOULDER (2009–24) | 115

Joe Schmidt, 2016.

people flocked to the Cubs' victory parade on Friday, and after beating the All Blacks the scores of Irish fans in town were fully able to join the party – and they brought a real Irish tinge to it. A great sporting occasion and a wonderful party.

NO SHOW LIKE A JOE SHOW

The year 2018 would mark the high point of the Joe Schmidt era. This was reflected in the end of the year World Rugby awards. World Player of the Year: Johnny Sexton. World Team of the Year: Ireland. World Coach of the Year: Joe Schmidt.

It all began with a Grand Slam. Schmidt pinpoints the key moments of the season:

> We were completely in control for most of the opening match against France, to such an extent that we thought, 'This is getting boring,' so we decided to allow Teddy Thomas to waltz through for a try just to make it interesting!

For Schmidt the decisive score in the match was Sexton's drop goal.

> We did it the opposite way to 2009, when the Grand Slam was won by [Ronan O'Gara's] drop goal at the very end. But in 2018 Johnny's score was the critical one that everyone remembers, and it came in the very first match.
>
> Johnny rightly gets the credit for his nerves of steel in such a big moment – but it wasn't just Johnny. As most rugby fans know, there were 41 phases before his drop goal.
>
> After the match was over we showed a version of the move to the squad, and we broke it down to show a clip of each player on the pitch doing something well. Johnny was involved three times, and everyone also remembers Keith Earls's catch from Johnny's cross kick – if Keith missed that very difficult catch we could forget the Grand Slam. Likewise, if Iain Henderson had not caught the ball at the start of the move we were beaten. It was so tense that most people have forgotten that Fergus McFadden made the most fabulous clear-out from a ruck.

It was nothing as eye-catching as Johnny's kick, but it was absolutely critical.

There was one painful moment for the coach that season.

> Before he touched down against Italy I was shouting at Robbie [Henshaw] not to score that try, which saw him have to leave the pitch with that serious arm injury. I have seen that type of injury happen often, and I was pleading with him ... because I could see what was going to happen. I knew that meant that he was out for the rest of the campaign, and I was devastated because he is such a quality player, and I felt he was going to be a huge loss for us.
>
> So what happens next? We bring in Chris Farrell to replace him for the Wales game, and in his first competitive match for us he wins man of the match. It seems that he is in fairytale land, but then he gets injured and is out for the next two matches. So we have to bring back Garry Ringrose, who had played little or no serious rugby for months, earlier than we would have wished. Garry played superbly against Scotland and England and looked as if he was never away.
>
> Sometimes you can be lucky, but other times, as in this case, you have acquired habits that make you look lucky. I would refer people to the consistency of our performances just before and after half-time against Wales, Scotland and England. People might think they were coincidences, but they weren't.

But there was some unpleasant business before the ultimate glory. The England head coach, Eddie Jones, and the Rugby Football Union both issued apologies after video footage emerged of Jones referring to the 'scummy Irish' and to Wales as a 'little sh*t place' during a speech the previous year. Jones said he was 'very sorry' for remarks he conceded were inexcusable. Schmidt was not unduly bothered.

> I was not going to get distracted by anything Eddie said. I know Eddie of old, and the idea of him saying controversial things is nothing new at this stage. I am very thankful to Eddie, though. Eddie had tried to play it clever and had extended the dead-ball line by two metres behind the goalposts, thinking it would suit England. That is where the luck came in, because without those extra two metres Jacob Stockdale would not have scored his try. It was a delicious irony, which I loved, but Eddie? Not so much.
>
> There was another irony ... [They] changed the lines – they had to change the colour of those lines – but the referee was colour blind! You could not make it up!
>
> Everybody remembers that we beat England in Twickenham on St Patrick's Day, but what some people forget is that it was played during an unseasonal snowstorm both here and in England. It was Arctic cold and there was a vicious wind. Our forwards coach, Simon Easterby, had prepared our line-out calls and had them on a table in our dugout before the game on three sheets of paper, but this huge gust of wind came and blew two of them into the English dugout, which meant that the English had most of our line-out calls – except the short ones. So we used our short ones for most of the game, and in the weather conditions it was the right strategy. So that was a case of something that might seem to be a big disadvantage for us working in our favour.

Schmidt was as gratified by the performance.

> There are a lot of things we can't control. Injuries are an obvious example. You don't choose to go and play some of the best teams in the world with some of your world-class players watching in the stands. All we can do is prepare well and work hard to give the best performance we possibly can.
>
> For some games there is a big burden of expectation. People forget that the week before we won the Grand Slam in 2018 we had won the Six Nations. The fact that we won the tournament for the third time in five years should have been a big deal, but nobody cared. The week before the England game the only thing people were saying was, 'Will ye win the Grand Slam?' So although it was minus five degrees, it was a red-hot atmosphere in Twickenham, because if we lost, winning the Six Nations would have been a total anticlimax.
>
> I think 2018 was an important year for the team because it showed that the higher the stakes, the better we performed – which was not always the case with Irish teams in the past.

It was a campaign never to be forgotten for Jacob Stockdale. The 21-year-old Ulster winger scored seven

Jacob Stockdale scores a try against England, 2018.

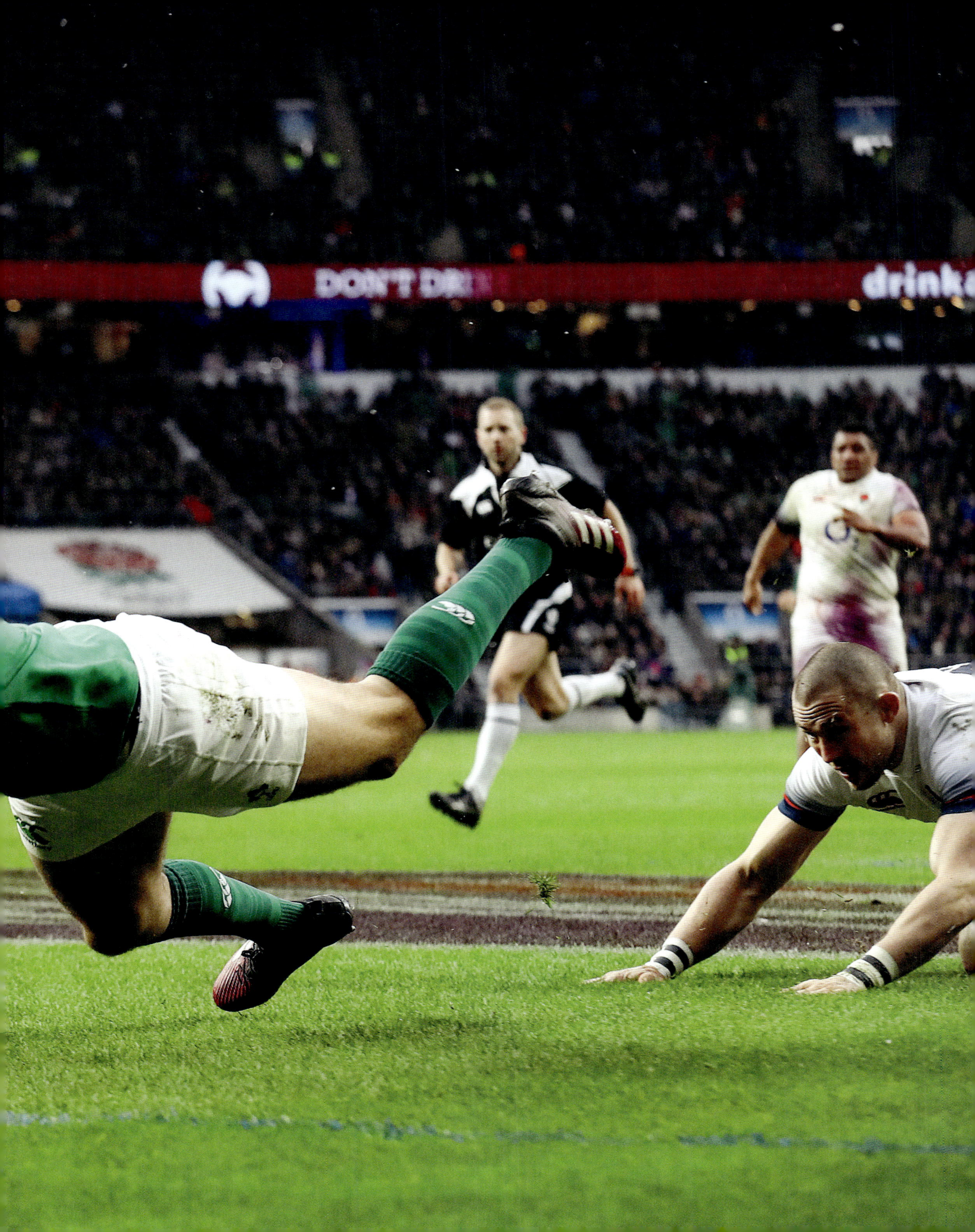
DON'T

Joe Schmidt in Japan, 2019.

tries in five games, setting a new record for an individual during a Six Nations Championship.

The good vibes continued that summer when Ireland had their first Test series win in Australia in 39 years. Then came the icing on the cake: a second win over the All Blacks, but this time at home in Dublin amid hype that took even Schmidt by surprise.

> Our win in Chicago [in 2016] really heightened the demand for tickets when we played the All Blacks in 2018. I have never seen anything like it. I played against their coach, Kevin 'Smiley' Barrett, whose three sons played for the All Blacks, and he is a lovely guy. A few weeks before the match he rang me and asked me if I could get him eight extra tickets because the family have such strong Irish roots. The ones I had been allocated I had already given away, so I couldn't help him, but it really brought home to me how crazy the demand for tickets was.

The hype was merited: it was a pulsating contest. Even before the game started, Ireland signalled their intent by taking a step forward during the haka. On the day, Ireland's passion and will to win – their accuracy and aggression – was encapsulated by the warrior-king of Irish rugby, Peter O'Mahony. Bruised and battered but not broken, barely walking because of injury, he forced himself through the pain barrier, like the greatest combatant on the battlefield, to make a crucial try-saving interception. Jacob Stockdale had a chip-and-chase try that proved the difference between the sides.

It was a day when heroes abounded all round the field. Devin Toner ruled the roost in the line-out, Cian Healy tore into the opposition like a man possessed and everyone in the green jersey appeared to play the game of their lives. The match had been billed as a showdown between Johnny Sexton and Beauden Barrett of New Zealand for World Player of the Year. It would be the Irishman who would win the duel on the day. James Ryan, with no fewer than 17 carries and 20 tackles, played like a seasoned veteran at the age of 22. That it was the first time since 1995 that the All Blacks had failed to score a try in a game against a Northern Hemisphere side was a massive affirmation of the Irish defence.

Fans can still picture the cascade of disbelief and elation that washed over their faces in that moment. As soon as the final whistle blew, the entire human mass erupted with a volcanic burst of applause.

These were heady times, after all. Gregor Paul's verdict on the 16–9 win in the *New Zealand Herald* was that Ireland could

> now claim to be the best team in the world after producing a stunning performance that was brave, creative and relentless. They deserved the win and with it, they deserve to be seen as world rugby's best team.

TIME TO SAY GOODBYE

After suffering heavy losses to England and Wales in the Six Nations, Ireland went to the World Cup in Japan in 2019

Jacob Stockdale scores a try against New Zealand, 2018

as the world's number one side. The tournament began brightly with an emphatic 27–3 win over Scotland. But that was as good as it got. After a shock defeat to Japan, Ireland crashed out of a World Cup at the quarter-final stage for the seventh time in a grim 46–14 defeat to New Zealand.

After the game Joe Schmidt spoke in the dressing room and said a few words to the players. He talked about how proud of them he was and about how much he enjoyed working with them, not just as a team but as people. Rory Best stood up as captain and thanked him for everything he had done for the team. Schmidt got a bit emotional, which was something the players weren't used to seeing. It was the end of an era.

Schmidt was succeeded by his assistant, Andy Farrell. It took time for him to find his feet, but once he hit his stride the team got back to their winning ways.

Farrell's first Six Nations campaign was interrupted by the global pandemic in 2020. Prior to the arrival of COVID-19, Ireland secured wins against Scotland (19–12) and Wales (24–14) before losing to England (12–24). Ireland's fourth-round game against Italy was delayed until October 2020, with Ireland recording a 50–17 win before an empty Aviva Stadium. They went on to a 27–35 defeat against France, finishing the tournament in third place.

In an attempt to keep the international rugby show on the road, the Autumn Nations Cup was conceived to raise desperately needed money through television revenue. In it Ireland again defeated Wales (32–9) and Scotland (31–16) but were beaten once again by England (7–18). Their performance in the game against minnows Georgia, a somewhat flattering 23–10 win, did not inspire huge confidence. Ireland were at first struggling in their set plays, but one of Farrell's masterstrokes was to add the legendary Paul O'Connell to the coaching ticket.

In his second year Farrell's philosophy of leadership became apparent. He understood that players can be led only where they want to go. A leader rides the waves and understands the deepest yearnings of their charges, and their purpose must resonate with the mood of their team. Farrell believes that the coach's task is to focus the players'

Ireland and Italy play to an empty stadium, 2020.

AVIVA STADIUM
AVIVA STADIUM
AVIVA
AVIVA
YOU'RE SAFE IN THE HANDS OF AVIVA
YOU'RE SAFE IN THE HANDS OF AVIVA
4
1
19
9

Andy Farrell, 2021.

aspirations, to articulate them in simple terms, to enthuse, to make the goal people already want seem achievable. He explained to the players that he could do nothing on his own: ultimately, it was all about them. He created a more relaxed atmosphere in camp, a contrast with the intensity that had prevailed under Joe Schmidt. The tight bond he nurtured among the squad off the field increasingly became manifest on it.

The 2021 Six Nations took place during the ongoing pandemic and with an absence of fans. In these eerie surroundings Ireland had a difficult opening, losing their first two matches to France (13–15) and eventual champions Wales (16–21). There were by now some mutterings about the direction of the team but wins over Italy (48–10) and Scotland (27–24) steadied the ship. But the mood changed dramatically in the final game of the Six Nations, when Ireland comprehensively beat England 32–18. It was a real lift for Farrell's reign. That Christmas, Paschal Donohoe, then Minister for Finance, claimed that Ireland's first half against England was the best forty minutes of the year.

Not for the first time, Warren Gatland created a controversy, in the summer of 2021, when he chose not to select Johnny Sexton for the Lions tour to South Africa. Conor Murray was appointed Lions captain after Alun Wyn Jones was initially ruled out by a dislocated shoulder. Against the odds, Wyn Jones flew out to resume the captaincy just three weeks after his injury. The hosts won the series 2–1, with Robbie Henshaw emerging as one of the standout stars on the tour.

Meanwhile, that summer Ireland beat Japan (39–31) and the USA (71–10), a match memorable for Rónan Kelleher scoring four tries. Ireland followed up in the Autumn Nations series with wins over Japan (60–5) and Argentina (53–7).

The high point, though, was a 29–20 win over the All Blacks – the third time Ireland beat New Zealand and

Bundee Aki breaks through during the Lions Tour, 2021.

also the third time in five years. It was another outstanding Test match between the sides and a fitting testament to Ireland's apparent newfound willingness to attack with ball in hand – powered by a dynamic pack. The player of the match was Co. Mayo native Caelan Doris, who scored a brilliant solo try in the second half and dominated the All Blacks in contact for the entire evening. (In keeping with the proliferation of family ties in Irish rugby, Caelan's uncle Connell had played centre for Leinster under-19s with Ollie Campbell until his career was prematurely ended by a shoulder injury.) James Lowe and Rónan Kelleher also chipped in with tries, and after captain Johnny Sexton departed injured, Joey Carbery came off the bench and kicked three penalties to steer Ireland home, including one from the halfway line. With 'Olé, olé, olé' ringing all around the Aviva, this was a game to make all who watched it feel better about life.

Ireland began their 2022 Six Nations campaign with a crushing 29–7 win over Wales. A loss to France of 30–24 the next week at the Stade de France would ultimately deprive them of the Grand Slam. But Ireland got back to winning ways in Dublin with an easy 57–6 win over Italy. They would then show their class with their biggest victory over England at Twickenham since 1964 (31–15).

On the last day of the tournament, Ireland had to win against Scotland – and France had to lose against England – in order for Ireland to win the Championship. Unfortunately for Ireland, France beat England 25–13. However, Ireland had the not insignificant consolation prize of winning the Triple Crown on the final day of the tournament, beating Scotland 26–5 in Dublin, with hooker Dan Sheehan really catching the eye and Conor Murray claiming a bonus point with a fourth try at the death.

The sense was that this Irish team were going places, and a tour down under confirmed that impression.

Caelan Doris celebrate his try against New Zealand, 2021.

Mike Lowry, Robert Baloucoune, James Lowe, Mack Hansen, Andrew Conway and Hugo Keenan celebrate winning with the Triple Crown trophy, 2022.

New Zealand's Brodie Retallick with James Lowe, 2022.

HISTORY IN THE MAKING

In the summer of 2022 Ireland headed to New Zealand to face the greatest superpower the rugby world has ever known.

The tour began badly with a 32–17 loss to the Māori All Blacks. Then the scourge of Covid produced high drama and, as if it were written in the stars, a reunion with an old friend. The All Blacks coach, Ian Foster, and his assistant coaches, John Plumtree and Scott McLeod, were forced to isolate at home after positive tests for the disease, which also forced centres David Havili and Jack Goodhue out of the squad camp in Auckland. In their time of crisis, who did they call? The New Zealander who coached the Irish for six years from 2013 and whose reign included Ireland's first two wins over the All Blacks: Joe Schmidt. Ireland also had a Covid case in their squad, with the Australia-born winger Mack Hansen forced into isolation.

New Zealand won the first Test 42–19 against Ireland at Eden Park. Ireland started well in Auckland, Keith Earls scoring in the sixth minute to put the visitors ahead, but a blitz of three tries in ten minutes at the end of the first period gave the All Blacks a comfortable 28–5 half-time lead. Garry Ringrose reduced the deficit with a try at the start of the second half, and Bundee Aki scored in the closing minutes.

The Irish won the second Test 12–23 in Dunedin – the first time they had beaten the All Blacks on New Zealand soil – to level things up at 1–1. Andrew Porter scored two tries and Johnny Sexton kicked 13 points in the famous victory.

Both teams headed to Wellington for the decider a week later. Victory and the series went to Ireland, who beat the All Blacks 22–32. It was the first time they had achieved back-to-back victories over New Zealand, and the result meant they went to number one in the world rankings. Moreover, they did it in style, scoring three tries to lead 22–3 at the break. Josh van der Flier scored for Ireland after a maul early on, and Hugo Keenan and Robbie Henshaw also grabbed well-worked tries in the first half. New Zealand fought back to

New Zealand perform the haka, 2022.

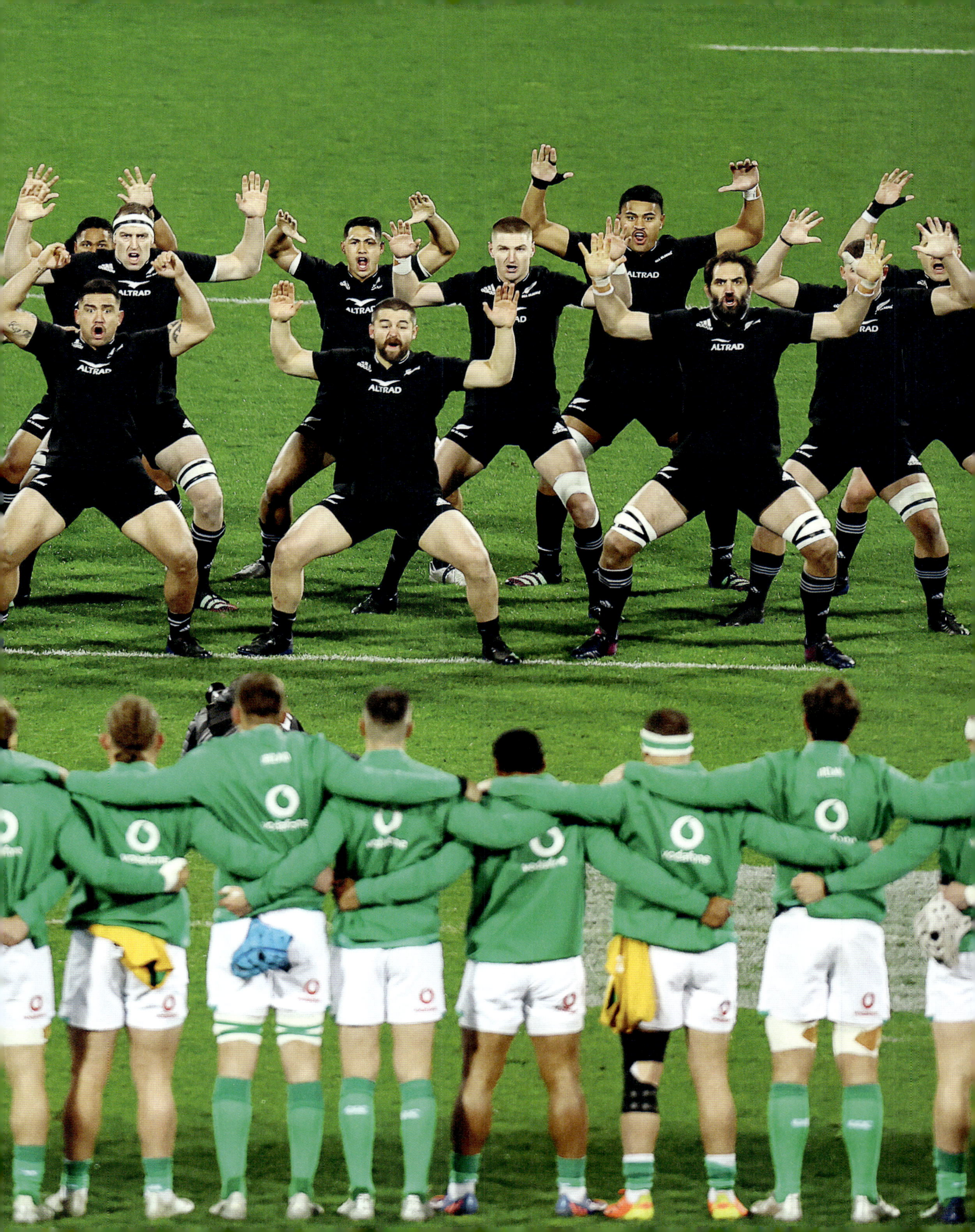
ALTRAD

Josh van der Flier during the Six Nations campaign, 2024.

The Irish team celebrate winning with the Guinness Six Nations and Triple Crown trophies, 2023.

reduce the deficit to three points going into the final quarter. As usual Johnny Sexton led by example and brought the game plan to life. In many ways the pack were the architects of the success, driving the team forward as the All Blacks tried to assert themselves. Rob Herring scored a try, and Ireland managed to hold off waves of pressure in the closing minutes to make yet more history. As the clock ticked down into the final minute, Peter O'Mahony was in tears – the extent of the achievement setting in.

'I bet you we have four million at home up for breakfast, probably having a couple of pints watching us,' said Johnny Sexton immediately afterwards. 'We speak about them all of the time. We want to do them proud, and we certainly did that.'

'This has never been done before,' added Peter O'Mahony. 'It's something I never thought was possible as a young fella, but now the young fellas back home will know this can be done.'

The way the players, notably O'Mahony, engaged with the fans – and the players' accessibility after the Test series was secured – showed that high-performance athletes today can still be themselves and have fun.

Ireland followed their successful New Zealand tour with three victories, over South Africa, Fiji and Australia, in the autumn series. Their win over Australia was their 12th successive home triumph and completed a clean sweep of successes over the southern hemisphere's big three in a calendar year.

The flanker Josh van der Flier was at the forefront of Ireland's play throughout 2022, including in their historic series victory over the All Blacks in New Zealand. He was a constant threat to opposing defences and started all 11 of Ireland's tests in 2022, scoring four tries. A powerful ball carrier in attack, he was equally impressive in defence with his relentless tackling and tireless work at the breakdown. He was named World Rugby Men's Player of the Year 2022 at the World Rugby Awards in Monaco. He became the third Irish winner after Keith Wood (2001) and Johnny Sexton (2018). He received the award ahead of three other nominees: Lukhanyo Am (South Africa), Antoine Dupont (France) and Johnny Sexton.

Frank O'Driscoll receives his cap, 2023.

Ireland's success that year was also reflected in the fact that four Irish players were chosen for the World Rugby Men's 15s Dream Team of the Year: Tadhg Furlong, Tadhg Beirne, Josh van der Flier and Johnny Sexton.

The good times continued in 2023. Ireland came into the Six Nations Championship as favourites and swept through it, making a huge statement six months out from the World Cup. A month after beating defending champions and second-ranked France at home, Ireland dispatched England in a 29–16 victory in front of a raucous crowd at the Aviva Stadium, winning their fourth Six Nations Grand Slam. It confirmed their status as the world's top-ranked rugby union side heading into the forthcoming World Cup.

Ireland were well worthy of their clean sweep, having won all their matches by 13 points or more and, notably, ending France's 14-game unbeaten run along the way in one of the best Championship games in recent memory. Two tries from Dan Sheehan and one each from Robbie Henshaw and Rob Herring ensured that Ireland finished ahead of France in second place. Johnny Sexton was given the perfect send-off in his final Six Nations match, with a second Grand Slam and the Championship's all-time point-scoring record. He moved on to 560 points to surpass Ronan O'Gara, in what was his 60th and final Six Nations Test. He limped off with just minutes to go, to a well-deserved standing ovation. Even the hard-to-impress Sexton was dizzy with delight and uncharacteristically raised his arms aloft as he kicked a touchline conversion.

Elation once again.

'The Fields of Athenry' was booming out all around the Aviva Stadium as the crowd felt the hand of rugby history firmly on their shoulders. A total of 1.45 million viewers were tuned in live on television screens throughout the country. It was the most-watched live television event of 2023 at that point and the highest-rating sporting event since 2017.

Best of all for home fans in the middle of St Patrick's weekend celebrations was that it was the first time Ireland had sealed the Grand Slam in Dublin after doing it in Twickenham (2018), Cardiff (2009) and Ravenhill (1948).

CAP IN HAND

The year 2023 was also noteworthy because the IRFU decided to award caps to 17 players (from 1946 to 1989) who featured for Ireland but were not awarded caps for games that were not then recognised as international Test matches. Among their number was Brian O'Driscoll's father, Frank. The full list of players is:

FLIGHT OF THE EARLS

Ireland warmed up for the 2023 World Cup in France with the 'summer series', in which they had victories over Italy (33–17), England (29–10) and Samoa (17–13). A highlight of the series came in the England game when the much-loved Keith Earls became the ninth Irish player to win 100 caps – joining Cian Healy, Johnny Sexton, Paul O'Connell, Brian O'Driscoll, Ronan O'Gara, Rory Best, Conor Murray and John Hayes. It was written in the stars that the new centurion would mark the occasion with a swan dive in the corner for his try.

IRELAND CAP NO.	PLAYER	CLUB	YEAR CAPPED
1142	Jack Belton	Old Belvedere	1946
1143	Hugh Dolan	UCD	1946
1144	Hugh Greer	NIFC	1946
1145	Jack Guiney	Bective Rangers	1946
1146	Des Thorpe	Old Belvedere	1946
1147	Paul Traynor	Clontarf	1952
1148	John Birch	Ballymena	1970
1149	Frank O'Driscoll	UCD	1970
1150	Leo Galvin	Athlone	1973
1151	Emmet O'Rafferty	Wanderers	1976
1152	Rab Brady	Ballymena	1985
1153	Paul Clinch	Lansdowne	1989
1154	Gerry Quinn	Old Belvedere	1946
1155	Terry Coveney	St Mary's College	1946
1156	Rev. Austin Curry	Old Wesley	1946
1157	Hugh 'Gordon' Dudgeon	Collegians	1946
1158	Edward 'Teddy' Coolican	Dublin University	1946

Keith Earls scores a try while making his hundredth cap, 2023.

Mack Hansen scores a try against South Africa, 2023.

FOREVER YOUNG

Ireland eased into the 2023 World Cup, scoring 12 tries in an 82–8 trouncing of Romania, their highest tournament points tally and margin of victory, with captain Johnny Sexton in his 39th year replacing John Hayes as Ireland's oldest international. The captain, playing his first match in six months because of injury and suspension, marked the occasion by scoring 24 points, including two tries. In the process he equalled Humphreys' record of 24 points in a single World Cup game.

Sexton continued his record-breaking form into Ireland's second match, a 59–16 win over Tonga. He replaced Ronan O'Gara as Ireland's top points scorer when he brought his total to 1,090 career points. It clearly meant a lot to him: he did an uncharacteristic hop and skip before punching the air in celebration when he scored the try that broke the record.

Ireland's third match in the tournament was the definitive arm-wrestle. They beat world champions South Africa 13–8 (although South Africa would regroup and win the tournament). A try from Mack Hansen, five points from the boot of Johnny Sexton and three points from sub Jack Crowley were sufficient to steer Ireland to victory.

On the night on which Peter O'Mahony won his 100th cap Ireland beat Scotland convincingly, 36–14, in a vibrant atmosphere, topping Pool B and securing a quarter-final clash with New Zealand. Unbeaten in 17 Tests, Ireland experienced an agonising eighth quarter-final exit in their history and are still waiting to make a World Cup semi-final.

The All Blacks raced into a 13–0 lead, but Ireland recovered well to narrow the half-time gap to a single point, 18–17, with tries from Jamison Gibson-Park and Ireland's player of the tournament, Bundee Aki. An absorbing match went right down to the final play as Ireland died on their shields, throwing everything they had at their opponents for 37 phases over 5 minutes and 17 seconds, but the clinical All Blacks held on for a 28–24 victory.

The enduring image of the evening will always be of Johnny Sexton playing his last match in the green jersey, with his young son, Luca, on the pitch after the final whistle. Both were in tears. Yet in the whirlwind of emotion Luca still struck the right note when he said, 'You're still the best, Dad.'

As the Rolling Stones sang with characteristic insouciance, you can't always get what you want. Not even when you're Johnny Sexton.

Recognition of Ireland's achievements came when Andy Farrell was named World Rugby Coach of the Year and five Irish players – Dan Sheehan, Tadhg Furlong, Caelan Doris, Bundee Aki and Garry Ringrose – were selected on the World Rugby Team of the Year, the joint highest, alongside France.

CHAMPIONS

After their World Cup disappointment Ireland began their 2024 Grand Slam defence with an emphatic 38-17 win against France in Marseille. Under new captain Peter O'Mahony they tore the French apart with the bonus-point win – just Ireland's fourth victory away to the French in 40 years. Joe McCarthy was Player of the Match on his Six Nations debut. It was Ireland's biggest ever victory over France, on their own soil.

An injury to Peter O'Mahony saw Caelan Doris captaining Ireland for the first time as Ireland scored six tries to win their second game against Italy 36-0. A 31-7 victory over Wales followed before Ireland's dream of becoming the first team to win consecutive Grand Slams was thwarted in Twickenham. Marcus Smith scored a drop goal in the last play of the game to secure a compelling 23-22 win for England. On Saint Patrick's weekend in Dublin, Ireland won their nineteenth consecutive home match in a 17-13 victory over Scotland to win their second consecutive Six Nations Championship. It was their fifth title in 11 years. In retaining the championship, Ireland reaffirmed their status as the northern hemisphere's leading team.

Johnny Sexton after the Rugby World Cup quarter final loss, 2023.

REGION ILE DE France
COUPE DU MONDE DE RUGBY 2023
#RWC2023
Emirates FLY BETTER
SOCIETE GENERALE
mastercard
SUPER TRY
Orange
LOXAM

RBS Women's Six Nations Championship, 2015.

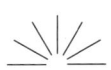

6

ALL IN THE GAME

The story of women's rugby begins in Ireland.

Portora Royal School in Enniskillen, which boasts alumni such as Samuel Beckett, Oscar Wilde and Neil Hannon, was founded by Royal Charter in 1608, with the motto 'Honour all men'. However, 270 years later a young female student would be the catalyst to ensure that women would be forever honoured in rugby.

In 1883 the school was on a downward curve after the departure of a headteacher who took many pupils with him to a new school, a problem compounded by a decision to stop taking on boarders. Enter a new assistant headteacher, William Valentine. He brought three new rugby disciples: his children William, John and Emily. Although the school did not have an official team, intraschool matches were played every Saturday.

Happily, unlike for the case of William Webb Ellis, we have documentary evidence of Emily's immersion in the sport. In 1887 a shortage of male players meant that she got the call, and the 10-year-old answered with gusto, making her the first female to play rugby officially, as she recorded in her diary.

> At last, my chance came. I got the ball. I can still feel the damp leather and the smell of it and see the tag of lacing at the opening. I grasped it and ran dodging, darting, but I was so keen to score that try that I did not pass it, perhaps when I should. I still raced on, I could see the boy coming towards me; I dodged, yes I could and breathless, with my heart thumping, my knees shaking a bit, I ran. Yes, I had done it; one last spurt and I touched down, right on the line. I had scored my try. I lay flat on my face, for a moment everything went black. I scrambled up, gave a hasty rub down to my knees. A ragged cheer went up from the spectators. I grinned at my brothers. It was all I had hoped for.

ON THE OUTSIDE LOOKING IN

It was more than a century after Emily Valentine's first rugby game that Ireland played its first women's international. So why did it take so long? The reasons were many and complex. The underrepresentation of women was by no means confined to rugby, of course: sport is a microcosm of society.

Michael Cusack, founder of the GAA, has claimed that the association spread like a 'prairie fire'. However, women did not play a central role in the early decades of the GAA. Although the tide of change was affecting women, much of the establishment continued to have prejudices. It is instructive to consider the institutional Church's attitude to the newly established Ladies' Land League as an indication of its attitude to women. The organisation was set up in January 1881, and by May it had 321 branches. The women became responsible for a detailed register known as the 'Book of Kells'. This was a record of every estate, the number of tenants, the rent paid, the official valuations, the name of the landlord or agent, the number of evictions that had taken place and the number that were pending. The register was compiled from weekly reports sent in by the country branches. The League was also active in relief work: when notice of a pending eviction was received, a member travelled to the area with money for assistance.

The League quickly fell foul of the Church. This was not perhaps surprising, given that the involvement of women in such a group was entirely new. Archbishop Edward McCabe of Dublin denounced the organisation and in the same breath recalled the supposed traditional modesty of Irishwomen and the 'splendid purity' of St Brigid. He went on to state that the proper place for women was the 'seclusion of the home'. In a letter read at all Masses in the Archdiocese of Dublin in March 1881 he stated:

> But all this to be laid aside and the daughters of our Catholic people are called forth, under the flimsy pretext of charity, to take their stand in the noisy arena of public life. They are asked to forget the modesty of their sex and the high dignity of their womanhood by leaders who seem utterly reckless of consequences.

The influential Archbishop John Charles McQuaid considered the athletics fields detrimental to women's physical condition and potentially damaging to future motherhood.

It is difficult to quantify the extent to which these religious influences hindered women's participation in sport in general and rugby in particular; but given the pervasiveness of religion for the next seventy years it is reasonable to assume that they were a forbidding impediment. The Church reflected the stratified, paternalistic society of the time. Rugby flourished among men in the late nineteenth century through the universities and professions such as medicine at a time when women were largely excluded from these professions.

Even though by this juncture the women's suffrage movement had carved its place into public consciousness, it is noteworthy that on 5 December 1921 the Council of the Football Association officially recorded:

> Complaints having been made as to football being played by women, the FA Council feel impelled to express their strong opinions that the game of football is quite unsuitable for females and ought not to be encouraged ... the council request clubs belonging to the Football Association to refuse the use of their grounds, for such matches.

Those attitudes were not restricted to soccer. The celebrated British athlete Harold Abrahams, one of the subjects of the Academy Award-winning film *Chariots of Fire*, was for many years an outspoken critic of women participating in athletics.

The marriage bar that was in place in the Irish civil service until 1973 meant that women were legally required to retire from employment after marriage. Even though sport was by this time embracing historic cultural change, it would not be until the 1970s that women began to really make their mark in the GAA. As we have seen, Ireland's first men's rugby international came in 1875, but it would be 118 years before Ireland played their first women's international.

A breakthrough for women in Ireland came with the election of Mary Robinson as president in 1990.

Ruth McKeown, 1999.

However, in her inauguration speech, she signalled that there was still much to be done to achieve full equality. 'As a woman I want women who have felt themselves outside of history to be written back into history, in the words of Eavan Boland, finding a voice where they found a vision.'

FROM SMALL OAKS

Women's rugby was growing slowly in the early 1990s in Ireland. Although Ireland did not participate in the inaugural Women's Rugby World Cup in 1991, there were teams emerging. In 1992 players were seeking wider horizons and were exploring the possibility of starting an Irish team. A pioneering woman in this respect was the Blackrock player Mary O'Beirne, who formed the Irish Women's Rugby Football Union.

On Valentine's Day in 1993 the Irish women played their first international, against Scotland at Raeburn Place – the world's second-oldest rugby ground, on which the first men's rugby international took place in 1871. The Irish women's team was captained by Jill Henderson, who was playing for Waterloo in the north-west of England. Scotland won 10–0. The following year Ireland competed in the World Cup in Scotland, winning one match against Japan.

Another milestone came two years later when Ireland was one of the first four teams to play in the women's Home Nations competition, losing to Scotland 0–21, beating Wales 22–6 and losing to England 12–8. It would be another eight years before they recorded their second win in the competition, although they did not take part in 2000 and 2001, focusing their efforts on growing participation.

Stephanie Dowling, 1999.

One of the pioneers of that era was Fiona Steed.

I was studying physiotherapy between 1990 and 1993 [in the north of England] and I started playing in college there, in my second year. I would have played camogie for Tipperary up until I finished my Leaving Certificate, but at that time there wouldn't have been many opportunities to play Gaelic games in the north-east of England. I did try hockey in first year, but I kept getting pinged because I was just too physical and I kept raising the stick too high, so it really wasn't the sport for me.

My flatmate and I tried soccer and rugby in second year, and I just absolutely loved the rugby. I kept thinking, 'Wow, this is fantastic!' I would have watched rugby at home – the Five Nations as it was at the time – but I wasn't really into it.

In the 1993/4 season I left college and started playing with Novocastrians RFC in Newcastle. We were playing in the equivalent of the third division in England but we'd an incredible coaching set-up and we went through the season undefeated. I don't think we even conceded a point at all that first season. I remember Rugby World had us up as Team of the

Month because we'd done so well. We eventually went all the way up to division one.

At 21 Steed found herself playing in Ireland's second Test match in Ravenhill.

I'd only played one real season of club rugby and wasn't really thinking about Ireland, especially as there had only been one Irish international at that time. But in 1994 there was a match against Scotland, and I got picked for that through playing for the Exiles [Irish players based abroad] and became an international, playing 61 more times after that. I think we lost that game 5–0, and I was playing at 13, where I got the ball twice and dropped it once. I remember vividly there was a girl playing at inside centre and she didn't really pass the ball. I don't know if I could have done any more with it if she did, to be honest – the whole thing just passed me by.

After spending years flying over and back from England, Steed decided to move home to Ireland.

In the 1999/2000 season the IRFU pulled us out of the Five Nations. I'm still not sure why, but I think it might have been because of the huge reliance on Exiles, and they wanted to grow the game at home. I suppose they had to have a look at the grass roots. We still had Irish training sessions, but ... I ended up travelling home 11 out of 16 weekends for training and in 2000 we played in the European Championships. We flew back into Heathrow after that tournament and everyone else was flying back to Dublin, and I was the only one staying in England and decided to move home.

When I returned I started playing for Shannon – I'd already been flying home to play for Munster. I was really lucky because I'd done a post-grad diploma with the University of Northumbria

Fiona Steed, 2002.

and, because I was an international, they treated me as one of their elite players, so they paid for all my flights that year, which made it feasible to fly over and back. I played for Munster and Shannon and we won the AIL [All-Ireland League] the following season [2001], and I stayed playing until 2004.

At the end of the 2004 Six Nations I'd done it for ten years, and I was mentally and physically worn from it, so I just retired. I was getting married in July, and I just thought, 'Do I go on to the next World Cup in 2006, or do I stop now?' And after ten years it had been a hard slog – not that it's easy now: it's hard in a different way for the current squad – but we lost all three home matches in Thomond Park to Wales, Spain and Scotland. And even though I scored two tries against Wales, I just couldn't physically give any more of myself at that stage.

After she retired Steed became one half of Irish rugby's ultimate power couple when she married John Hayes. How many husbands and wives have 167 caps between them? It is noteworthy that their romance was carefully nurtured by Rosie and Anthony Foley.

One of the GAA immortals, Sue Ramsbottom, also played for Ireland. The Laois legend is in the conversation, with players like Cora Staunton, as the greatest women's footballer of all time. Ramsbottom

> never knew about women's rugby growing up as a kid. I guess like for most women my age, women's rugby was never accessible, was never something that you ... aspired to be like, because you never had role models like that to look up to.
>
> Early in my army career, while I was based in Athlone, I did a degree in computers in UCG. To give myself something to do for the winter I started playing rugby for Galwegians. Then I was selected to play in the interprovincials, and after that I was asked if I would take part in an Irish trial. I did and went on to win three caps against England, Scotland and Wales. Unfortunately, I had to miss out on the World Cup in Holland in 1998 because it came immediately before my final exams. I would have been back in time, but the exams were my priority. I was a kicking full-back: any time I saw a big one charging at me I got rid of it as fast as I could!

The year 2008 was a significant one for Irish rugby off the pitch. The integration process was completed as the Irish Women's Rugby Football Union was dissolved at its last AGM in Naas and women's rugby came fully under IRFU stewardship. On the pitch a glorious new era was about to emerge.

CAPTAIN FANTASTIC

Fiona Coghlan was not born with a rugby silver spoon in her mouth, though she did have a very personal link with one of the doyens of Irish rugby.

> The first person ever to touch me was Karl Mullen! I can't say I have any memory of it: he was the doctor who delivered me in the maternity ward. As an obstetrician it is claimed that in his life he delivered enough babies to fill Lansdowne Road.
>
> I grew up in Clontarf about a hundred metres from the rugby club. Back then there weren't many sports for girls. There certainly wasn't any rugby. At the time people thought it was a mad decision for a Dubliner to go to college in Limerick. But that was the only place to study PE teaching, so I had no option. Freshers week in UL you sign up for everything, especially whoever is giving out the free stuff! So I signed up for the rugby.

But it was not love at first sight.

> At my first training session I was put in the forwards. I didn't really love it, standing round, doing line-outs. I didn't know what I was at, so I said, 'I'm not going back to that again.'
>
> Three weeks later I got an email to say that they were stuck for numbers, and I'd never like to see a team stuck, so I went down to help out. They weren't stuck for numbers – the opposition were – so I ended up playing for DCU. Once I started to play I fell in love with the game.
>
> UL Bohs started a women's team in 2001, and it became my life. Before that it was a case of 'Go to college on a Monday morning and come home on a Friday evening. I'm not staying in Limerick for the weekend.' Once I was on the UL Bohs team my parents had to take trips down to visit me, or see me at matches in Dublin, because I was so committed.

Having made the Irish team and become the team's captain in 2008 (taking on the role permanently in 2010), Coghlan would have to wait for success. The year 2012 was an important one.

> We had some galvanising moments. We had a horrible trip to France: we flew into Paris and then had an overnight train down to Pau. We played that game and only lost 8–7. When we came back everyone was just talking about our travel arrangements, and the girls were really annoyed, and I was like, 'Why is no one talking about the game?' I said we've basically just got to win something to improve things, but I certainly didn't think it would happen the next year. Things kind of just came together. I think it was a merging of some new young talent and some older heads and a great management team as well.

The year 2013 was a watershed.

It was when we beat England that the media sat up and started to take notice.

> England weren't a professional team, but they were better resourced than us. That was when the bandwagon started. In the first game, against Wales, we robbed them, basically, winning 12–10. Ali Miller got a toe under a Welsh try to stop them scoring, and then we scored one of our best tries of the tournament, a real team try, to win the game.

The match was not without drama.

> When we got back to the dressing room Joy Neville couldn't open the door. We asked one of the officials to resolve the issue, but he was unable to. So our coach, Philip Doyle, kung-fu kicked the door open and we ended up having our showers while the door was open. Afterwards we discovered that we were not actually locked out but that Joy hadn't opened the door the right way!

Joanne O'Sullivan, Fiona Coghlan and Joy Neville sing the national anthem, 2010.

Jenny Murray is tackled during the Women's Six Nations, 2013.

Nobody was paying much attention, but then we played England next, and when you beat them 25–0 I think people sit up and take notice, particularly in Ireland. That was just a brilliant game. We played out of our skin that day. England's pack was really strong and we fronted up really well.

Alison Miller scored a hat-trick of tries as England were beaten by Ireland for the first time in women's rugby. Then Ireland faced Scotland away. According to Coghlan,

> everyone had jumped on the bandwagon, and we were going for the Triple Crown. We were poor in the first half, really sloppy, but we got it together at half-time and performed really well in the second half. People were asking where the Triple Crown trophy was, but there wasn't one for the Women's Six Nations. Scotland give you this little quaich [drinking vessel], so we were drinking out of that instead, pretending it was the trophy.

By now Ireland were just two wins away from the Grand Slam.

> The French game was International Women's Day [8 March], and for the first time the Irish President came to one of our games. It was a night game in Ashbourne, really misty and kind of eerie. It's a small venue with only one tiny stand, and you couldn't see from one side of the pitch to the other. That was a brilliant game and we won that one after kicking on from a slow start. We knew then that we had the Championship won that weekend because of other results going our way, but we didn't want to finish there: we wanted the Grand Slam.

Ireland ground out a 6–3 win against Italy in their final game.

The sun was cracking stones the day before the game and we were out having coffee, and it was beautiful. But when we woke up the next day there was snow and rain. It went from sun splitting the stones to an absolute mud fest in the rain. We had to change our game plan on the morning of the game. It was a slog – a dog fight. Yes, we had the shiny trophy at the end, but we didn't do ourselves justice without a performance. It was a real leveller and it was not a great game of rugby but I suppose compelling in that it was touch and go right until the end, when Joy Neville won a turnover under our posts and we kicked for touch and won the line-out, and that was it: the game was over.

It was such a historic and memorable moment for the women's game in Ireland. There wasn't much about us before that year. That whole journey was amazing. I knew we were getting better every year.

The final game against Italy was the first live women's game on RTÉ. Coghlan's own personal contribution was rewarded that December when she was chosen as the Irish Times/Irish Sports Council Sportswoman of the Year. The team was determined that this would be a stepping stone to further success, and that indeed would be the case, as Coghlan recalls with eyes gleaming:

> We knew then that we needed to continue the momentum. We weren't going to be a one-hit wonder. It set us up for the 2014 Women's Rugby World Cup – our chance to shine on the world stage. A lot of people didn't speak about us because New Zealand were in our pool. Unless you win your pool it's very difficult to make it to the semi-finals.
>
> The day we played New Zealand was a phenomenal occasion. You could feel the energy the girls had in the warm-up. The way the crowd sang 'Ireland's Call' before the game was on a level I had never experienced before. It was one of those moments that makes the hairs stand up on the back of your neck. We knew New Zealand were doing the haka, and Philip

Ashleigh Baxter, Nora Stapleton and Niamh Briggs celebrate a famous win over New Zealand, 2014.

The Ireland team celebrate their Grand Slam in the Women's Six Nations, 2013.

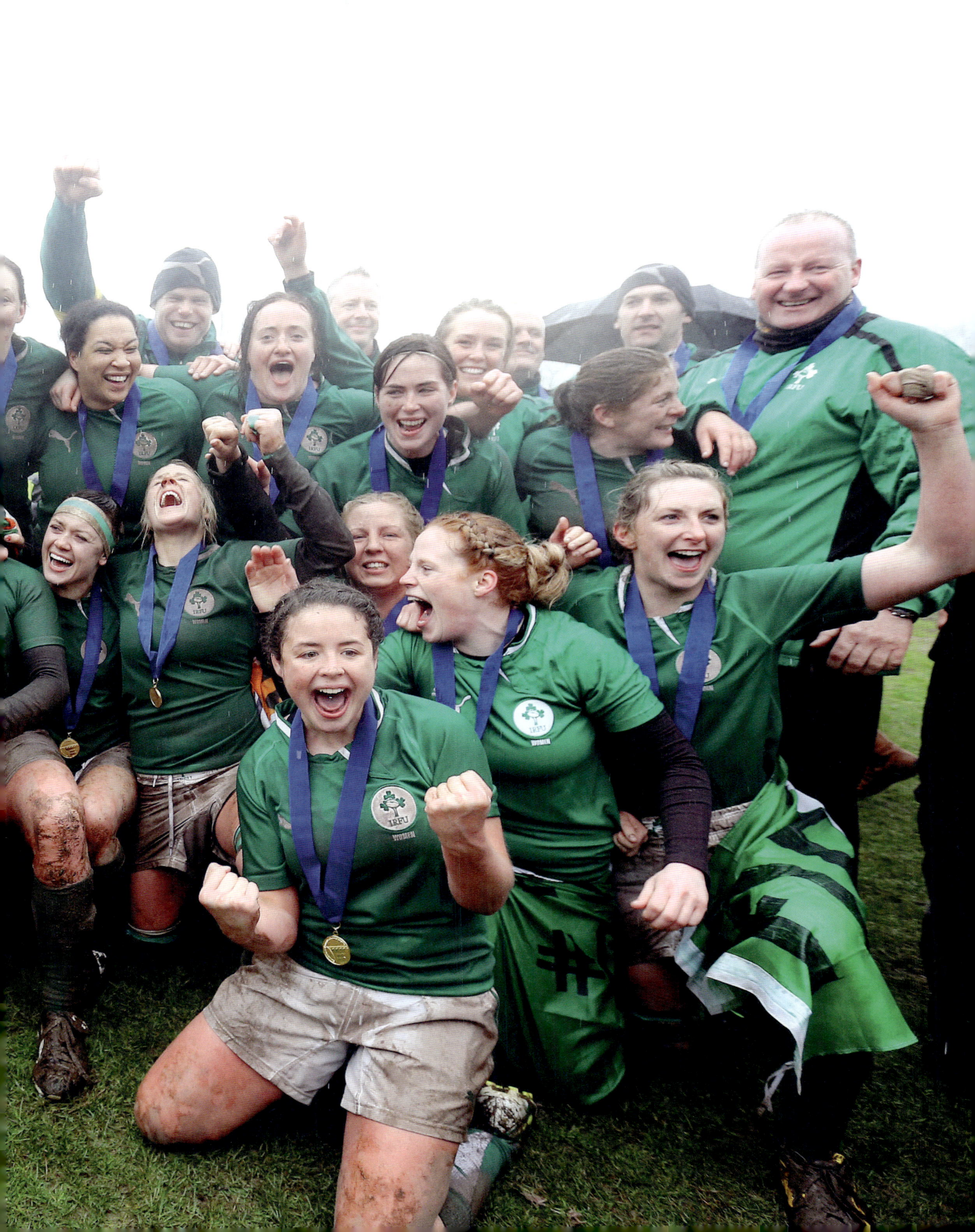
IRFU

Ireland Women's squad, 2014.

[Doyle] asked us if we wanted to do something beforehand to counter it. I said no because I knew we would not be fazed by it.

After the haka the Irish team had their customary huddle. The captain knew that no *Braveheart*-style speech was required. Her message was short and sharp: 'Let's go f***ing mental.' The talking had already been done.

> We were really well prepared and had a game plan in place to beat New Zealand. Heading out to the pitch, Joe Schmidt was there showing his support. That was hugely symbolic. Tania Rosser, who's a Kiwi, led us out for her 50th cap. It ended 17–14 and that was the first time New Zealand had been beaten in the Women's Rugby World Cup. We blew the competition open.

It was a shock of seismic proportions that reverberated around the rugby world. The Black Ferns, who came into the fixture with a 20-match unbeaten World Cup run since the 1991 semi-finals, led 8–7 at half-time thanks to a Selica Winiata try that even they would probably have conceded went against the run of play. Ireland's scores in the first half came from a Heather O'Brien try and a Niamh Briggs conversion. Kelly Brazier's second penalty of the evening extended New Zealand's advantage to 11–7 under the watchful eye of Johnny Sexton in the crowd. Irish coach Philip Doyle had clearly imbued the Irish with great resilience, and in a tight third quarter Briggs countered brilliantly to set up Alison Miller for a wonderful try. To rub salt into the New Zealand wounds, Briggs aced a stunning conversion from the touchline. Brazier managed to bring New Zealand level at 14–14 with another penalty, but a final penalty from Briggs with ten minutes left sealed the Irish victory.

Ireland's second successive triumph in Pool B meant they effectively qualified for the semi-finals for the first time. But England would bring an end to the fairytale story for Ireland in the semi-final before convincingly beating Canada to claim the World Cup. The Irish team for that historic semi-final was:

Niamh Briggs	UL Bohemians/Munster
Ashleigh Baxter	Belfast Harlequins/Ulster
Lynne Cantwell	Richmond/Exile
Grace Davitt	Cooke/Ulster
Alison Miller	Portlaoise/Connacht
Nora Stapleton	Old Belvedere/Leinster
Tania Rosser	Blackrock/Leinster
Fiona Coghlan (capt.)	UL Bohemians/Leinster
Gillian Bourke	UL Bohemians/Munster
Ailis Egan	Old Belvedere/Leinster
Sophie Spence	Old Belvedere/Leinster
Marie Louise Reilly	Old Belvedere/Leinster
Paula Fitzpatrick	St Mary's College/Leinster
Claire Molloy	Bristol/Connacht
Heather O'Brien	Highfield/Munster

REPLACEMENTS

Sharon Lynch	Old Belvedere/Leinster
Fiona Hayes	UL Bohemians/Munster
Laura Guest	Highfield/Munster
Siobhan Fleming	Tralee/Munster
Larissa Muldoon	Bristol/Exile
Jenny Murphy	Old Belvedere Leinster
Vikki McGinn	Blackrock/Leinster

It is evident that Coghlan still regrets the way the tournament ended.

> We drew England in the semi-final, and it proved a bridge too far. We had injuries. We'd fix one thing and something else would go wrong. It just wasn't happening for us on the day. But England were also in top form and just were not going to be beaten.
>
> Four days later the third-place play-off was a cracker of a game. We lost and maybe we shouldn't have. It was a huge honour for me to lead that group. Successful leaders recognise their strengths and their weaknesses. I was playing to be the best that I could be, the most successful I could be. In 11 years I never missed a training session.
>
> We expected high standards. We had a saying on the team, 'The winning qualities of this team will be determined by the standards we set.' That wasn't just on the pitch: it was the standards set off the pitch too, how we conducted ourselves. We had to live by those standards. People throw the word 'culture' around easily nowadays. For us our culture was our standards.
>
> For me no one is greater than the team. In my role as a captain and as a leader I relied hugely on the squad and management around me. I really valued our senior leadership group, with the likes of Joy Neville and Lynne Cantwell. They'd been there through the highs and lows from 2003. If they felt any decision I made was wrong, they'd come to me. I'd go to them for advice. It was an open communication, for the whole team. Everyone's opinion was valid. For any successful leader they need that cohort of people around them to help them. We had a great bunch of girls who put their heart and soul and body on the line for everyone, whether or not they were playing. So we got the job done. But we also had a great time with a lot of fun doing it as well.

Fiona Coghlan retired after the World Cup and was succeeded by Niamh Briggs as Irish captain. In 2015 Briggs would lead Ireland to the Triple Crown and Championship.

GROWING THE FAN BASE

Brendan Foley had watched his daughter Rosie win 39 caps for Ireland in the noughties. He was excited about the progress of the game.

> It was a real feather in the cap for the women's game that they beat New Zealand before our men did, and of course they also won the Grand Slam. They were a golden generation, and the hope is that they inspire the next generation to take up the game. Unfortunately, there is a drop-off in participation among young women from the mid-teens on in sport generally, and hopefully the great players we have seen and are seeing will inspire others. I would love to see the interest and participation that there is in rugby boys' schools replicated in girls' schools.

Niamh Briggs talks to her team before their match against England in the Women's Autumn International, 2015.

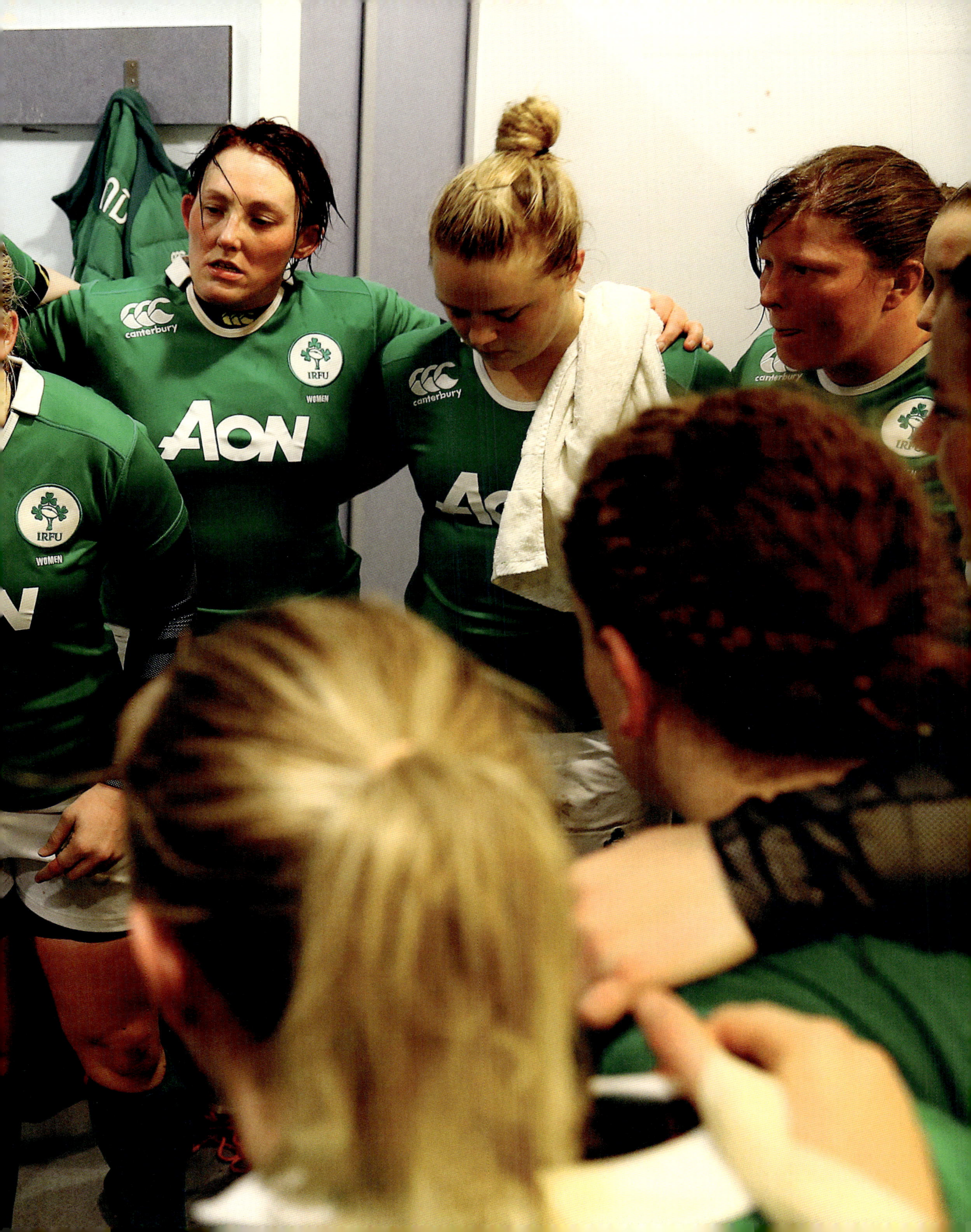
canterbury
IRFU
WOMEN
AON

Rosie Foley, 2004.

I saw Rosie and her teammates, who were so dedicated and so talented. They didn't get the profile they deserved, but things are slowly changing for the better. They just needed to get their place in the shop window. It would be nice to think that they get the recognition their tremendous talent deserves.

Ollie Campbell was thrilled by the success.

When I started playing, the only acknowledgment of women in the game generally came in after-dinner speeches when some dignitary would invariably say something patronising like 'And of course we must thank the ladies in the kitchen for all their hard work.' Thankfully, those old attitudes are gone out with the ark. Now women's rugby has become an important feature of Irish sporting life. I certainly see the evidence of that in my own club, Old Belvedere, where the women's game is thriving.

Everybody loves a winner and when Ireland beat the Black Ferns in 2014, following up on their Grand Slam win the year before, the Irish sporting nation sat up and took notice. The fact that the Black Ferns enjoy such dominance in World Rugby makes Ireland's victory over them in the 2014 Rugby World Cup all the more remarkable. When Sophie Spence was nominated for World Player of the Year it was a sign of how far the game has come in this country.

Thankfully, on foot of those great triumphs, Ireland's matches are now shown on television. Young people get their heroes from television, and it is great that the stars of the team – like Niamh Briggs, Joy Neville, Fiona Coghlan and Lynne Cantwell – have become household names.

SOUND AND VISION

The American tennis player Billie Jean King famously said, 'You have to see it to be it.' Female role models act as massive inspiration for girls and women by showing what is possible. It is vital that girls learn about exemplary women, but it is perhaps just as critical that boys see

Niamh Kavanagh, Lynne Cantwell, Joy Neville and Gillian Burke celebrate their win against France, 2013.

women as role models. Giving boys this exposure combats gender stereotypes, and highlighting the achievements and stories of historical and present-day female role models can go a long way towards advancing gender equality for future generations of rugby players.

Seamus Heaney claimed: 'If you have the words, there's always the chance that you'll find the way.' The media's role is critical. Historically, the media, like sport, has always held up a mirror to society. It is telling that it was not a GAA fixture but the Kingstown (Dún Laoghaire) Regatta in July 1898 that was the first Irish sporting event to be reported live on radio. It reflected the sensibilities of the mainstream media at the time.

The media has played a huge role in bringing Irish rugby to the hearts and minds of so many Irish people. The famous commentaries, such as those of Fred Cogley, Tom Rooney and Michael Corcoran; the many brilliant print journalists, such as Ned Van Esbeck and Con Houlihan; and a new generation of pundits, such as Jenny Murphy, Grace Davitt, Ciara Griffin, Lindsay Peat and Fiona Hayes – all have been pivotal to the enduring and growing popularity of the game. RTÉ, Virgin Media, TG4, Newstalk and independent radio stations have all featured women's rugby prominently in their schedules in recent years, and this has hugely added to the profile of the game. The print media, too, has played a massive part in bringing the women's game to a national audience.

As one of RTÉ's most prominent rugby pundits on the men's game as well as on the women's game, Fiona Coghlan is keenly aware of the critical importance of the media to the women's game.

> As a secondary teacher I see it with my students. To them it is absolutely normal for a woman to be talking about the Irish men's team on national television. That's the way it should be. It is the same game, after all, for men and women.

Joy Neville referees the Ulster vs Benneton Rugby Pro-14 match, 2020.

Ireland vs Fiji, Rugby Sevens Series, 2023.

Given his own career in the media, Tony Ward has watched the increasing spotlight on women's rugby with more than a passing interest.

> In 2017, when the Black Ferns were selected by an elite group of eight giants of the game – like Brian O'Driscoll and Richie McCaw – ahead of the All Blacks in Monaco to the gong for the team of the year, and when Limerick's Joy Neville won referee of the year, it represented two powerful affirmations of the growing prominence of the women's game internationally.
>
> That year the Black Ferns won their fifth World Cup, in Ireland, compared to the All Blacks' three. It was great to witness all the hype here before the World Cup in Ireland in 2017 and to see the main Irish games now on television. When my own daughters were teenagers they were looking for female role models in sport, but now the women's game is in the shop window, and that will help to grow the game still further. If we are to grow, to be relevant and attract new audiences we have superb role models to draw from. By being accessible on social media, the next generation of players and fans can relate to them.

SETBACKS

Unfortunately, despite winning the Championship again in 2015, the Irish women's team were unable to emulate that success in the years that followed. The rolling wave of retirements of the Grand Slam-winning side within a few years of each other was always going to be a problem.

The year 2015 would be a milestone for the women's game in Ireland on a number of levels. The IRFU's Union Committee approved the co-option of its first female member, Mary Quinn, at their meeting on 29 September. The first meeting of the Union Committee that Mary attended was on 5 November. It was a seminal moment on the journey to an inclusive rugby community.

That same year Ireland were chosen to host the 2017 Women's Rugby World Cup. The World Rugby chairperson, Bernard Lapasset, making the announcement, observed that

> the Women's Rugby World Cup continues to go from strength

to strength, proving a hit with fans, broadcasters and sponsors around the globe, with its compelling, competitive action and global profile. With impressive results on and off the field, the IRFU is a leader in driving forward the promotion and development of women's rugby and the union's passion, dedication and expertise in women's rugby was reflected in an impressive and forward thinking bid. The awarding of the Women's Rugby World Cup 2017 to Ireland is great news for teams and fans as the sport continues to reach out and inspire new participants in our great game.

The pool stages were held at UCD before the world's top female rugby players moved north to Belfast for the positional play-offs, semi-finals and the Women's Rugby World Cup Final at Kingspan Stadium. Although it was envisaged that the tournament would be an excellent opportunity to promote women's sport and to further raise the profile of women's rugby in Ireland, the team did not do as well as hoped. After the pool stages Ireland were ranked sixth and failed to make the semi-finals – a disappointing outcome not least in terms of promoting the game.

A nice moment came in 2018 when the IRFU awarded caps to more than one hundred female internationals who played in competitive Test fixtures in 1993 to 2006 but who were never awarded caps.

A low point was the failure to qualify for the 2021 World Cup in New Zealand (delayed because of Covid). Sixty-two former and current players signed a letter to the government calling for 'meaningful change' in the administration of the women's game.

Another huge disappointment came in the 2023 Six Nations Championship, in which Ireland failed to win a single game.

GREEN SHOOTS

Learning curves need to be navigated better than has always been apparent. Part of the issue has been juggling resources – players and financial – at both sevens and 15s rugby. The former were seen as vital in attracting

Nora Stapleton dodges a tackle, 2017.

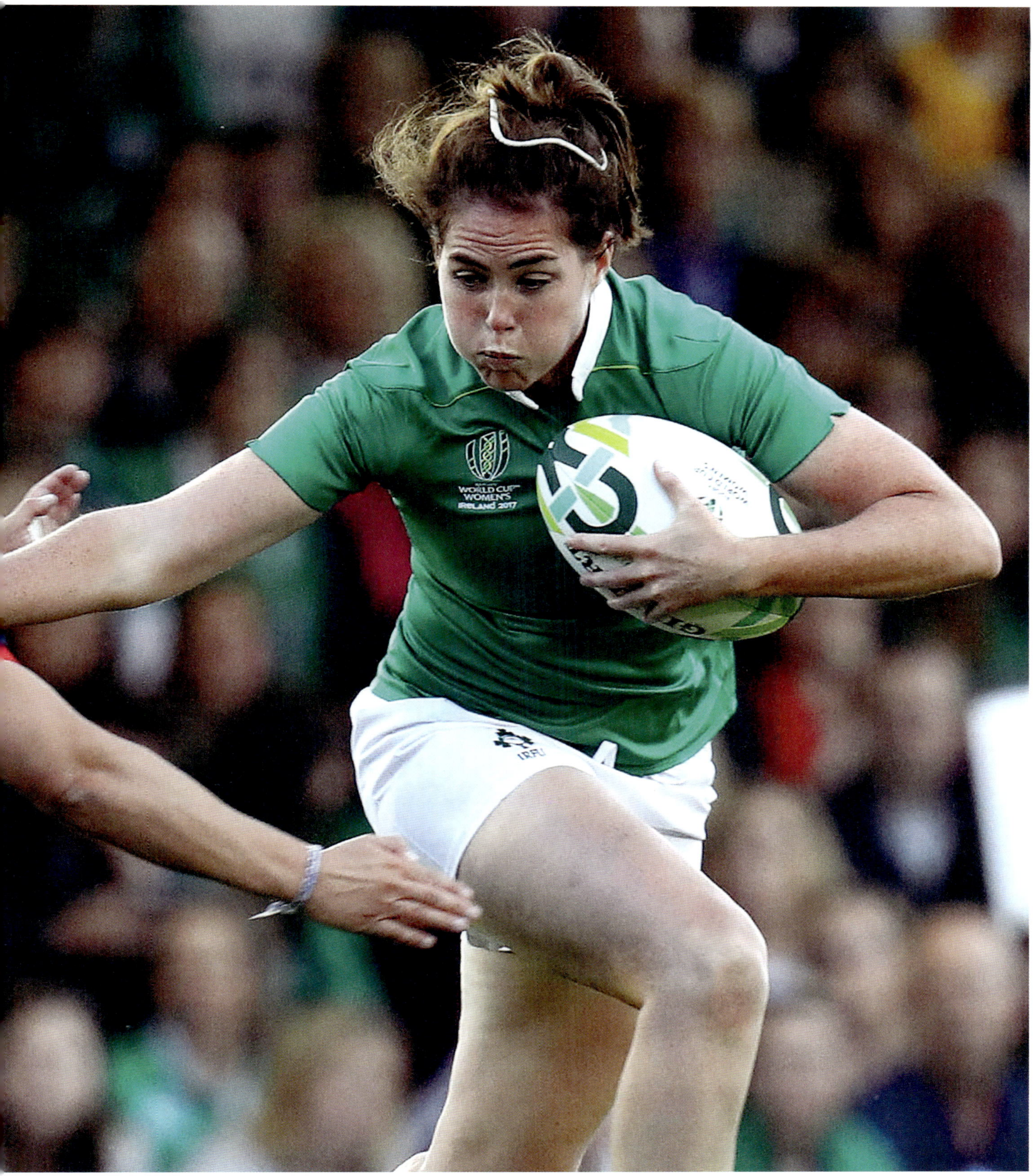
WORLD CUP
WOMEN'S
IRELAND 2017
IRFU

new players to the sport. In 2009 the game of sevens was made an Olympic sport, thus becoming a new opportunity for countries to grow the sport. In an Irish context the commitment to sevens has presented a major challenge for the 15s side because of the relatively small number of players available. Fighting on two fronts in any arena is not easy.

The Women's Sevens squad first embarked on their quest for Olympic qualification back in 2015. There followed near misses for the Rio and Tokyo Games. In 2023 the squad realised their Olympic dream by securing the fourth and final automatic qualification berth through the HSBC World Rugby Sevens Series.

The side, skippered by Lucy Mulhall, beat Fiji 10–5 at the France Sevens in Toulouse, ensuring that they finished in fifth position in the overall 2023 Women's World Series standings and joining Australia, New Zealand, the USA and hosts France as the fifth team to book their place at the 2024 Games in Paris. It was another milestone for the National Sevens Programme, following on from the Ireland men's qualification for Tokyo 2020 and a World Cup bronze medal in 2022.

The 2023 squad, coached by Allan Temple-Jones, was:

Kathy Baker	Blackrock College
Claire Boles	Railway Union
Megan Burns	Blackrock College
Amee-Leigh Murphy Crowe	Railway Union
Stacey Flood	Railway Union
Katie Heffernan	Railway Union
Eve Higgins	Railway Union
Erin King	Old Belvedere
Emily Lane	Blackrock College
Kate Farrell McCabe	Suttonians
Anna McGann	Railway Union
Lucy Mulhall (capt.)	Wicklow
Béibhinn Parsons	Blackrock College

The future of this team, with thrilling players such Béibhinn Parsons and Amee-Leigh Murphy Crowe, brims with possibility.

Another significant boost came at the same time when Joy Neville was chosen on merit as the first woman to officiate at a men's Rugby World Cup in France in 2023. She was selected as part of a seven-member television match official (TMO) panel for the tournament. Neville was part of the team that won the Grand Slam in 2013 before she took up refereeing in retirement. She refereed the Women's Rugby World Cup final in 2017, and in 2020 she became the first female TMO for a top-level men's Test match. Her philosophy is 'To tell a woman what she cannot do is to tell her what she can.'

BUILDING BLOCKS

There is a recognition that, while a lot has been done, more needs to happen for Ireland to reclaim its place at the top table of women's rugby at 15s level. After the disappointment of missing out on qualification for the 2021 World Cup the IRFU introduced a suite of measures to revive the fortunes of the 15s game: to maximise performance, access and participation in the game and to modernise its governance. In October 2022 it was announced that 29 Irish women's players had accepted professional contracts, with players receiving bonuses for match appearances and wins and tournament fees. All players on IRFU contracts will train full time at the union's high-performance centre in Dublin.

Following the success of the policy in the men's game of keeping players at home, the IRFU is keen to convince female players not to move to the English Premiership. Mindful of concerns about the quality of the domestic tournaments, and with a view to raising standards, it was also confirmed that a new women's Celtic Challenge competition would be introduced. This cross-border club competition organised by the IRFU, Scottish Rugby and the Welsh Rugby Union with financial support from World Rugby began in January 2023. It ran for a second year spanning an 11-week period from December 2023 to March, 2024. This time two Irish teams – The Wolfhounds and The Clovers – participated.

Ireland Sevens players celebrate qualification for the 2024 Paris Olympic Game.

Two important positions have been created by the IRFU. The first, Head of Women's Performance and Pathways is a pivotal role, according to Fiona Coghlan.

> We need to have an Irish women's team at a World Cup – that it's on TV, that young girls can see it. But what's more important is the pathways. I think the Head of Women's Performance and Pathways role is huge. It is crucial that a young girl can start at four and see the pathway all the way up, no matter where she wants to play – whether it's just club, interpros or international … It's going to be interesting going forward to see what model they take … The contracts for players are absolutely amazing, but more important is that we have those pathways developed, that we have the players that are able to step up to the necessary standard and that they're getting competitive game time week in, week out.

The second important new IRFU position is Head of Equity, Diversity and Inclusivity. This role aims to develop, train and implement best-practice policies and protocols so as to ensure that Irish rugby is as safe, inclusive and welcoming as possible. Unconscious bias and all instances of exclusion are unacceptable. In building rugby in the long term, there is a keen awareness in the IRFU that it is important to include a cross-section of voices from diverse backgrounds, from within and outside the game.

In 2023 the IRFU doubled its direct investment in Women's Rugby, to €6.4 million. Eight coaches, including former internationals Niamh Briggs and Larissa Muldoon, were recruited to work with players aged between 18 and 23 at five new centres of excellence based in universities in Carlow, Dublin, Galway, Belfast and Limerick. Two more centres in Sligo and Cork are planned.

In 2023 the IRFU also announced the launch of a women's under-20s programme, beginning with a training camp and games against Italy and Scotland. It is a significant new strand of the Women's Pathway programme and an opportunity to nurture promising young talent.

Fiona Steed feels that there are both challenges and seeds of hope for women's rugby.

> One of the big challenges is that there has been so much negativity about the senior team in recent years. The senior team is where the visibility is. If the senior team is struggling all the other good things that are happening around the country

are not seen. My concern is that all the negativity creates a narrative which becomes a self-fulfilling prophecy. We have had a high turnover of players and coaches in the space of a few years and that has not been without difficulty.

The changes in governance are significant. In 2021 I was appointed to the IRFU Committee as a representative from the Munster Branch. Now we have 40 per cent female membership. As chair of the Women's Sub-Committee I have seen all the new developments at first hand.

With great new coaches, the new centres of excellence and the many other steps that are in place I really believe that we are creating new pathways that will give more women and girls the opportunity to play rugby in Ireland to the best of their ability – and to equip them with the expertise they need in areas like nutrition, strength and conditioning as well as the skills development they need. I take hope from the fact that we will be following international best practice in these areas. This will enable increasing numbers of girls to play in schools, clubs and colleges and then ultimately to represent Ireland. It is important that a Women's All-Ireland League is established as a sustainable high-performance competition.

The year 2023 was a seismic moment for the game in Ireland: the IRFU achieved 40 per cent female representation on its committee. The writer Zadie Smith has said that 'progress is never permanent, will always be threatened, must be redoubled, restated and reimagined if it is to survive.'

Things took a turn for the better when Ireland secured qualification for the 2025 Women's Rugby Cup by finishing third in the 2024 Six Nations.

LOVE STORY

January 2023 saw one of the most joyful moments in Irish sport. Despite the intensity of a critical women's interprovincial game between Leinster and Munster, Clodagh O'Halloran could feel it in her fingers and in her toes that love was all around her. The previous Monday, Clodagh rang the Munster head coach, Niamh Briggs, to tell her that she was going to propose to her partner and teammate Chloe Pearse – if the team won – after the game at Musgrave Park. Clodagh and Chloe had first met seven years before at Munster provincial training.

Clodagh got the idea of proposing at the fixture before Christmas and had bought the ring a few weeks earlier. She asked Chloe's parents for permission, told her own parents about her plan and recruited Niamh to look after the ring during the game.

Clodagh had no intention of proposing if they lost. She scored Munster's third try two minutes into the second half to help secure a 26–17 victory. Chloe, who came on as a substitute after 48 minutes, had no idea what was coming until Clodagh made a beeline for her. Many tears of joy were shed, not just by the happy couple but by many of those watching on.

Munster rugby was their northern star, guiding the couple on their way, into each other's loving arms.

Clodagh O'Halloran proposes to Chloe Pearse at Musgrave Park, 2023.

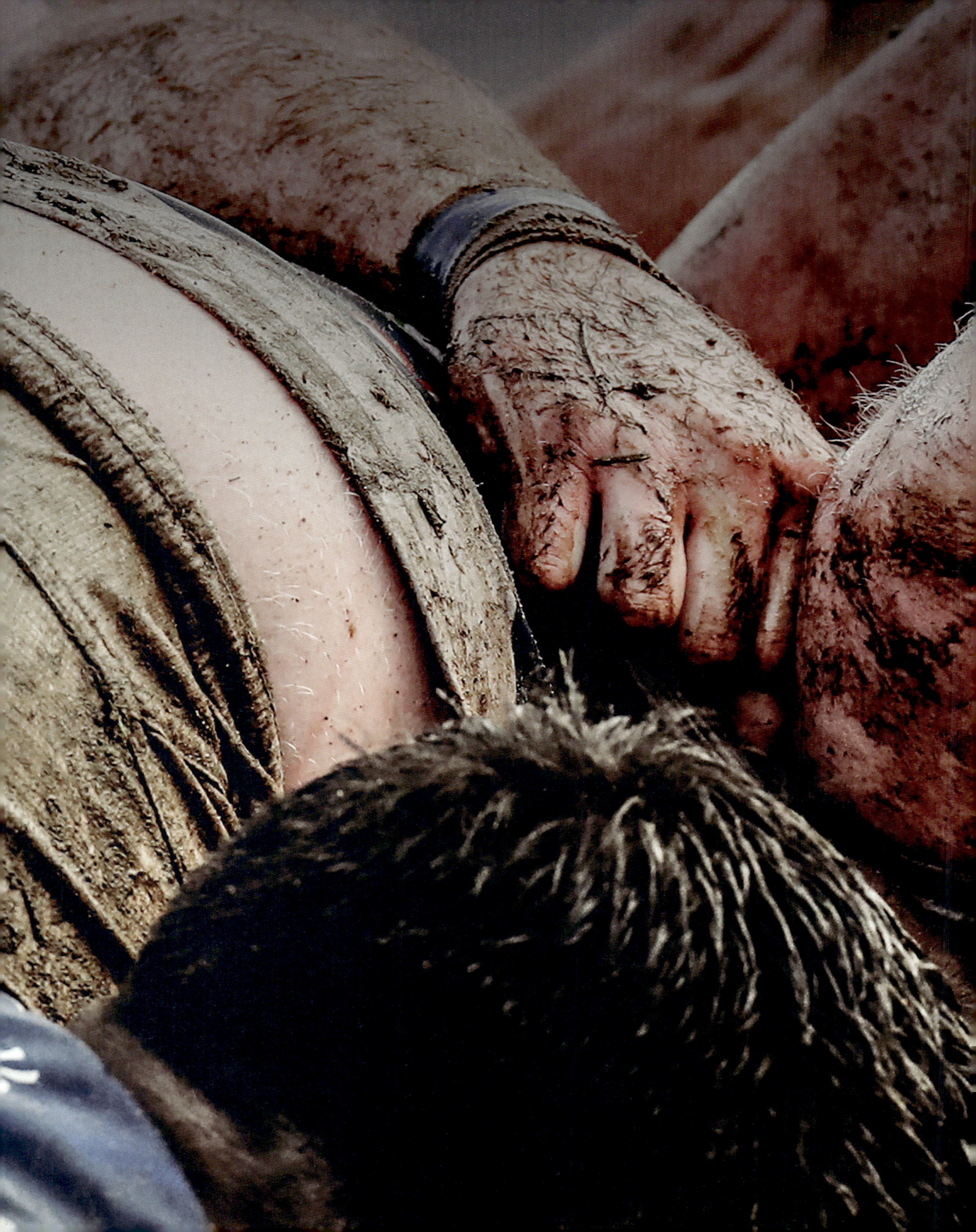

PART TWO:

PILLARS OF THE IRISH RUGBY COMMUNITY

The Ireland rugby flag.

7

THE FOUR PROUD PROVINCES

It is fair to say that not all sporting organisations in Ireland and beyond have been equally well served by their administrators. No administrative system is perfect, and not all decisions stand the test of time. However, broadly speaking, Irish rugby has been well served in this respect. Moreover, the IRFU has shrewdly got the benefit of outside expertise on its committees, including giants of the corporate world such as Feargal O'Rourke. Together they have given much time, energy and wisdom to skilfully navigating Irish rugby through often choppy waters, from global recessions to a devastating pandemic.

One of the biggest challenges facing the administrators was the advent of professionalism in 1995. Never were imagination and creativity more needed to forge a path through the brave new world. Some recalibration of the traditional structures was necessary. Difficult, even painful, decisions had to be made to serve the common good.

Irish rugby today is supported by four pillars: the provinces, the clubs, the schools and the underage structure. These are the focus of the remaining chapters of this book.

ACCORDING TO PLAN

The success of Irish rugby was based on a recognition that the way forward could be built only by mutual acceptance by all parties, not by domination. This required dexterity and flexibility, and compromise was therefore not a dirty word but a potent strategy. To take one example, for much of the past century one of the home matches for the Five Nations Championship was played annually in Belfast and the other in Dublin, and the Irish team stood for 'God Save the King' or 'God Save the Queen' in Belfast. Another example is that the IRFU designed its own flag in 1925 and, after some rumblings, the IRFU decided in 1932 that the Tricolour would fly beside the IRFU flag at all international matches in Dublin. Accommodations were made to ensure that neither religion nor politics would rupture the carefully nurtured harmony.

When rugby crossed the Rubicon of professionalism in 1995, it became increasingly obvious that the needs of Irish rugby required the consideration of a new structure that would see it not merely intact but flourishing.

Of course, to move forward in such circumstances necessitated some degree of letting go, and that is not always easy. To decide about principles is one thing: to make a fundamental decision determining the game's future is something very different. This journey towards a shared narrative inevitably would not be painless. It was a delicate moment in a transition from insights to practice, from vision to formal commitment, in search of the appropriate structure to express, promote and sustain the bonds of the past.

The IRFU decided to convert the four representative provincial sides into club teams, with the financial muscle to keep top talent in Ireland, while retaining strong links with amateur clubs and schools in order to enable young talent to be brought up through the ranks. It would ultimately prove to be a winning formula – but there would be some bumps on the way.

MARCHING TO THE BEAT OF THE CONNACHT DRUM

The provinces have a long rugby history, and their story has been one of innovation. In 1990 Tom Kiernan was appointed chairperson of the Irish Exiles committee. He set up a structure for getting players in the UK with Irish qualifications to play for the Exiles and then for having those of appropriate standard progress to the Irish team. It was agreed that the Exiles would participate in the Interprovincial Championship, and in September 1992 the Exiles played their first match against Munster.

Interprovincial games were played irregularly but starting in the 1946/7 season the provinces played against each other in the annual Interprovincial Championship. An important change happened in 1998/9, when a format was introduced to the Championship involving a double programme of games, with each province facing each other twice.

The Connacht Branch of the IRFU dates back to 1885, when Connacht played their first interprovincial match against Leinster. The clubs represented at the founding meeting were Ballinasloe, Castlebar, Galway Grammar School, Galway Town, Queen's College Galway and Ranelagh School, Athlone. Henry J. Anderson was the first Connacht person to play for Ireland, in 1903. He later became president of Connacht Rugby and, in 1927, opened a sports facility called the Sportsground, which remains the home of rugby in Connacht today.

Inevitably, as Irish rugby adjusted to the new realities of professionalism after 1995, there were teething problems for the provinces. Most of the big stars of the Irish game, such as Keith Wood, moved to English clubs. Although the IRFU's strategy of getting most of its top players back to Ireland worked brilliantly, the problem was that there was a huge additional financial burden in running the four provinces – and it appeared that Connacht was going to suffer most.

One proposal for balancing the books amid the financial crisis after professionalism was to discontinue the Connacht professional team, as the IRFU faced multimillion annual losses. This prompted the establishment of Friends of Connacht, which aimed to secure the future of rugby in the province. A crowd of six hundred assembled in the Radisson Hotel in Galway in January 2003 to begin the resistance. The outcome was a decision to march on Lansdowne Road.

According to Garda estimates, 1,200 people participated in the march, mostly fans connected with Connacht but also, in a show of solidarity, former internationals from outside the province, such as Jim Glennon and Mick Quinn. The West was awake and plans to diminish the status of Connacht rugby were shelved.

No one quite appreciates, and recognises, the light like rugby fans who have lived in darkness. It might have been difficult to foresee then, but just 13 years later Connacht rugby would roar out of the wilderness. For the first time in their 121-year history Connacht won a major trophy as they brilliantly claimed the Guinness Pro12 title in May 2016 in front of a record final crowd of almost 35,000. Moreover, Pat Lam's side utterly deserved their 20–10 win as they outclassed Leinster with a scintillating display of attacking rugby in Murrayfield. The Westerners had booked their place in the play-offs by topping the league table, but before the game few gave Ireland's least successful province much hope against the aristocrats from across the Shannon.

Connacht's team were poster boys for the new multicultural, multiethnic Ireland: the forwards powered by Portumna's minor hurling All-Ireland winner, John Muldoon; the backs led by Nigerian-born and Dublin-raised match-winner, Niyi Adeolokun; and the team coached by the talismanic Pat Lam, a New Zealander of Samoan descent from Auckland.

In 2023 Bundee Aki was one of four nominees for the World Rugby Player of the Year award following his outstanding displays at the World Cup. Aki arrived in Galway as a 24-year-old who had spurned a chance of representing the All Blacks. He was an instant fan

Niyi Adeolokun scores a try in the Guinness Pro12 final, 2016.

The Connacht team celebrate their victory in the Pro12 final, 2016.

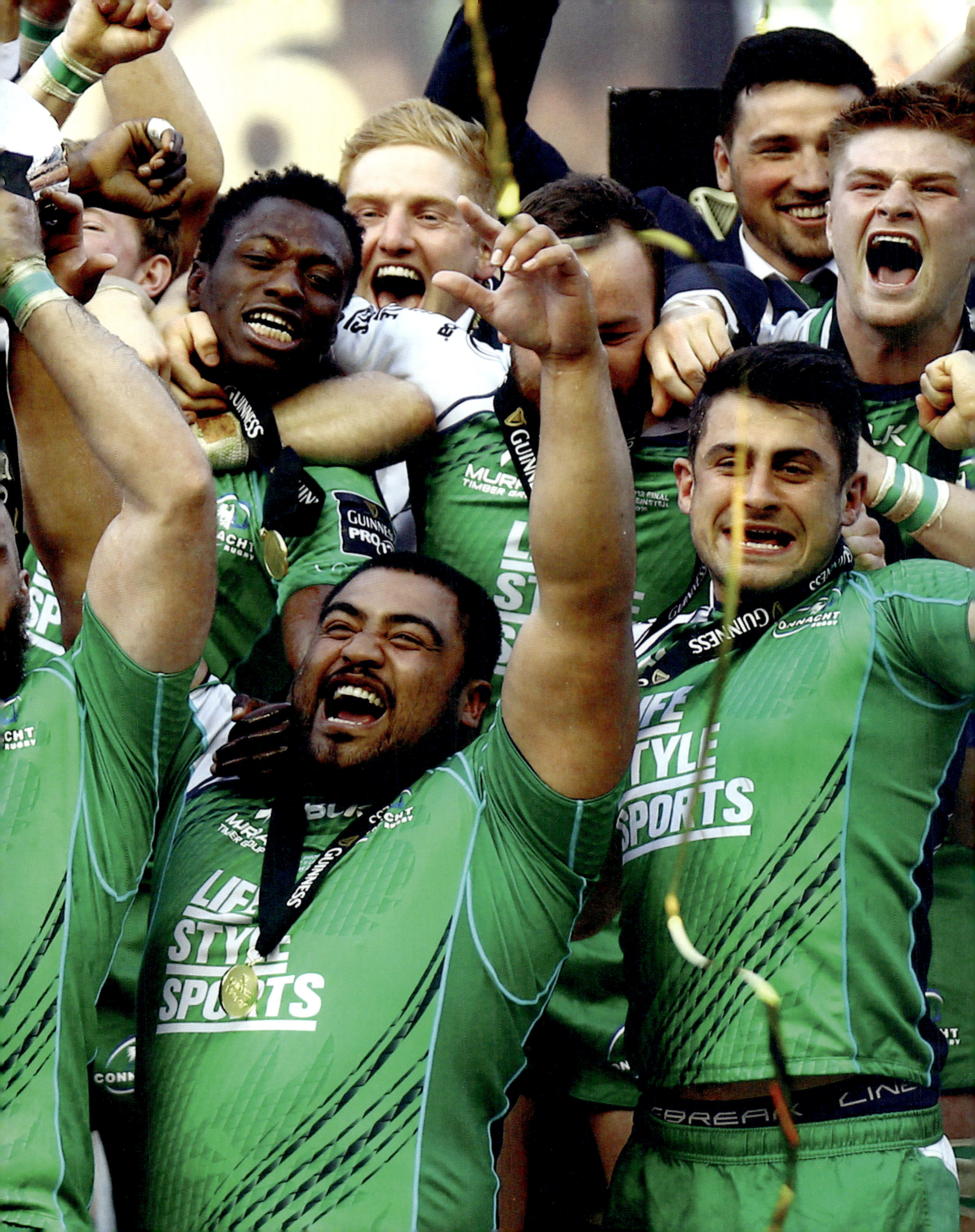

LIFE STYLE SPORTS
LIFE STYLE SPORTS
GUINNESS
GUINNESS

Bundee Aki with his family after Ireland's win over South Africa at the 2023 World Cup.

favourite, tearing into defences and bringing Connacht to the cusp of the Champions Cup. By the end of his second season he had not only been the inspiration for Connacht to win the Guinness Pro12 title but was also named the league's best player.

Aki's journey to Galway was a fascinating one. His parents named him Fua Leiofi, but he was called Bundellu after the family doctor who delivered him (he picked up the nickname 'Bundee' at the under-age level). He followed in the famous footsteps of Jonah Lomu by playing junior rugby, barefooted at times, for the Weymouth club in South Auckland. At the age of 18 he worked as a bank teller, earning the cash to raise his firstborn child. One day Tana Umaga, the former All Blacks centre, having learnt that Aki worked there, walked into the bank and asked him along to training. There followed a Super Rugby title in 2013 with the Chiefs, leading Pat Lam to bring him to Galway in 2014. Aki's success with Connacht enabled his debut for Ireland against South Africa in 2017. He was nervous before the game – but not about the rugby.

It was obvious that the camera was going to linger on the new boy and, sure enough, there was a ten- or fifteen-second close-up of me! Did I know the words to 'Ireland's Call' before I was called up? Honestly, no, I didn't! I had to be coached in the kitchen one night by my little girl, Adrianna, who was pretty stoked about me playing for Ireland. Having learnt it at school, she was able to sing me the song and then brought the lyrics up on her phone so we could have a go at it together. 'That's awful, Daddy. That's not quite so awful … That'll have to do!' She's mad into her Irish as well, so if I've got a question about the language, I ask her.

It was a proud moment for Aki.

The first people I told when I got named in the squad were my parents. I rang them up in the middle of the night and all they did was cry.

I am proud to be representing Connacht, as well as my family, and Ireland. When I first arrived with my family the overwhelming welcome I received from Connacht people was unbelievable. They have been so supportive from day one. You can see how close and tight this community is, even putting up signs. I am so grateful to be part of this small community.

UNREST IN ULSTER

The first Irish interprovincial game took place in 1875 and was between Ulster and Leinster, with Ulster being the victors. Ulster's greatest period of success in the interprovincial tournament was in the 1980s and '90s, when they won ten titles in a row.

The story of rugby in Ulster could not but be affected by the enduring legacy of almost thirty years of the Troubles. Ulster rugby could not be immune to this darkness.

In April 1987 one of Northern Ireland's most senior judges, Lord Justice Gibson, and his wife, Lady Cecily Gibson, were killed by an IRA landmine at Killeen, between Newry and Dundalk, as they drove home to Drumbo, Co. Down. Three Irish rugby internationals – Nigel Carr, Philip 'Chipper' Rainey and David Irwin – were in a car travelling in the opposite direction to attend a squad training session and were caught in the blast. Carr, a flanker, was one of the stars of Ireland's Triple Crown triumph in 1985, playing a role similar to the one Jim McCarthy had played so brilliantly for Ireland in the Jack Kyle era – and with similar aplomb. He would never play rugby seriously again.

The three players were great friends from university and were going on a journey that they had taken many times. It had been a mixed season for the Irish team: better than the year before but not as good as the Triple Crown-winning one before that.

The year 1987 was a unique one from a rugby standpoint, with the inaugural World Cup, and the trio were terribly excited about it. So as they drove south there was lots of banter and rugby talk. David Irwin takes up the story.

> The day began early because we were driving south for a session at 10:30 ... I was driving along chatting to the two guys when suddenly there was a massive thud and also a giant explosion of light. It was like facing a hundred flashbulbs going off at once. I was aware enough to think that a bomb had actually gone off underneath our car. My first thought was that the IRA were trying to kill somebody else and they have made a mistake and we've got mixed up in it. That sense lasted several seconds.
>
> Having experienced what I thought was a bomb in my own car, I then realised that it was literally stopped in the same lane and still pointing in the same way ... My first thought was to feel my own body, just to check that everything was still there, and when I established that was in fact the case, I remember looking to my right and noting that there was a massive crater in the Belfast side of the road. And at the same time I turned round to the left and I realised that Nigel had been bleeding quite badly and that the blood was coming out profusely from a neck wound. He seemed to be semi-conscious.
>
> The whole front of the car had been pushed in but particularly over on Nigel's side, and I said to him, but he probably doesn't remember it, 'We've been in a bomb. You're okay. You're bleeding from your head, but you're fine.'
>
> While I was saying this to Nigel, as I looked past him through the passenger window, I could see another car, parallel to our own, pointing to Dublin, and there was a huge inferno of flames in that car, with two vague shadows of people and fire in the front seat. I assumed that it was possibly an RUC car and then, as I panned round, I saw Philip lying sort of across the back seat – motionless.
>
> Initially, I thought he might be dead, but I wasn't sure. I felt I had to get out of the car and get the guys out in case the petrol tank would explode. I wasn't totally aware of what was going on around me. As I managed to get out of the driver's door, one of the things that struck me was that two or three of the cars that had been behind us driving south actually drove round my car and passed us and drove down the road a bit, and I remember thinking at the time, 'How could people drive past this?' But in retrospect they were that bit outside the incident and were probably in shock themselves, and the natural thing was to drive round it and get to safety.
>
> As I walked round the front of my car I was aware of two or three females running up and down the road screaming hysterically.

I found out afterwards that they were part of a group of nurses that were driving north, and they were actually behind Judge Gibson's car, and that car had gone into the ditch. They were distraught. Again, this all happened within several seconds. A large juggernaut or lorry was driving up the road, and I stopped it and told the driver to go up to the garage and ring the police and for an ambulance.

It was then that Irwin's expertise as a medical doctor proved invaluable.

I went round to Nigel and tried to get the passenger seat open, which was a wee bit difficult because it sort of buckled with the impact. Once I got the door open again, Nigel was coming round a bit but was still very groggy. I told him I had to get him out of the car because there was a danger the car might explode and create a further explosion. I asked him if he was in pain. He told me he was very uncomfortable in one of his thighs. I suppose, being a doctor, I would have been aware that a common road accident type of injury is where the dashboard is pushed in under the passenger's knees, and that can cause you to fracture your femur. My initial thought was: 'Oh, my goodness, Nigel has to miss the World Cup because he's fractured his femur.'

As I tried to get him out on the passenger's side, I realised his ankles and feet were caught underneath the dashboard, and between me pulling and Nigel giving some assistance I managed to drag him out. I think one of his trainers was left stuck in the car. I half-carried him and he half-walked as we went up the road, and then I set him down on the grass verge. I took my belt off and tied his knees together again, assuming he had a fracture of his leg.

Nigel Carr, 1982.

I went back and spoke to Philip. He had started to come round, though he was still groggy ... He was able to get out by himself with just a little bit of assistance from me. I took him up and sat him beside Nigel.

At that point the traffic had stopped about fifty yards either side, and people were getting out of their cars and looking round. It seemed fairly clear to me by then what had happened, but I wasn't sure why it had happened. A plain-clothes detective came along, and I asked if it had been a police car that had been blown up. He told me that it was a High Court judge and his wife. It became clear that the police had been waiting to escort him the rest of the journey, and the gardaí had escorted him up to the south side of the border, but the car was in no man's land where the bomb had gone off. Then I saw that Philip had got up and was walking round obviously concussed and not sure what was going on.

Irwin handed over the care to others at that point.

Shortly after that the ambulance had arrived to take Philip and Nigel away. One of our rugby bags was about forty yards up the road from the impact of the explosion from the car. I couldn't work out how this had happened. The explanation was that the bag flew out with the force of the explosion, and then the boot had closed again.

At that stage the objective was to get the two guys to Daisy Hill Hospital [in Newry], and I recall feeling so disappointed that Nigel was going to miss the World Cup. I gathered our valuables and bits and pieces from the car. I was told that I was going to be escorted back to Newry police station in a police car. I remember thinking, 'Jeepers, we've all come through that and I'm alive, but now I have to get into a police car.' I knew from living in the North that sometimes when bombs were set off and the police came on the scene, a second bomb was sometimes set off. I was thinking, 'I hope this doesn't happen to me on the way back.'

He maintained his medical vigilance even after the ambulance had arrived.

Once I got to Newry police station my first job was to ring our families, who needed to know. Then the police car brought me to the hospital. I met the doctor in the corridor, and my first question was about Nigel's leg. I was so relieved and felt, 'Great, he will be okay for the World Cup', but it turned out later that he had a fracture in his ankle and had what is known as a rigid abdomen, which meant internal injuries. I then found out that, although Philip had taken a bad blow to the head and was unconscious, he was basically okay.

I must have been given some sort of pain-killing injection when I was en route. I don't recall feeling that sore. I didn't think things were that bad. I knew I had cuts and bruises, but I also had twisted joints, chipped bones, five broken ribs and internal bleeding. For the next few days I was in acute pain. I would hold on for as long as I could and then get an injection into my backside to give me relief.

Irwin then started to piece the chain of events together.

I became more aware of what had happened. Lord Gibson had gone to the same school as me, and over the following days I learnt that he and his wife were a very nice couple. The intelligence was that the man responsible for planting the bomb was killed somewhere else a few years later.

After their 'success' with the Gibson assassinations, the IRA sought to repeat their coup the following year. Three members of the Hanna family from Hillsborough (Robert; his wife, Maureen; and their six-year-old son, James) were killed by a bomb in Killeen when the IRA mistook their jeep for one owned by another senior member of the judiciary, Sir Eoin Higgins.

Although the father, mother and youngest child were killed, there were two teenage children in the Hanna family who were not in the car that day, and they needed to be consoled.

Irwin was deeply touched by the tragedy.

In my own role as a family doctor I come across death frequently, but the big difference in the Hanna incident was the loss of a six-year-old child. There's an inevitability when a person gets older that they will die, but when a child of that age dies it is much harder to comprehend. Those who are left behind are left uncertain, worrying did they suffer, and after I heard the news I felt an urge to write to the remaining members of the Hanna family and try to put into words what we had been through ... I was trying to get across to them that their family would not have suffered, because things happen so fast in a car bomb. It happened to the Hannas in nearly exactly the same spot – literally fifty or a hundred yards from where our incident happened. It gave me a closer empathy with what transpired.

Years later the three players went together to meet the Rev. John Dinnen, the rector in Hillsborough who had been badly affected by the deaths of the Hanna family.

GIVE PEACE A CHANCE

In 1994 the IRA claimed to have ended their campaign of death and destruction when they announced a ceasefire. After twenty-five years of the staggering weight of despair, the amazement was intense when it was lifted. However, the IRA broke the ceasefire on 9 February 1995 with the Canary Wharf bombings in London, killing 29-year-old Inam Bashir and 31-year-old John Jefferies and leaving many others with life-changing injuries.

Two former Irish internationals who won Triple Crowns together in 1982 and 1985 – Trevor Ringland and Hugo MacNeill, from different sides of the border and raised in different traditions – decided that action was called for as Northern Ireland headed back to the brink of the abyss.

On 18 May 1996 Lansdowne Road hosted a special fixture between Ireland and the Barbarians called the Peace International. The game had been organised by Ringland and MacNeill to express the wish of the rugby community for peace. In the programme notes Tony O'Reilly spoke of the 'overwhelming desire in Ireland and beyond for peace in our country'. This was bigger than sport – an attempt to channel the opposition to violence into a force of beauty, of vitality, of meaning.

The Barbarians team included David Campese of Australia, Philippe Sella of France, Francois Pienaar of South Africa and Rory Underwood of England, and they won 70–38.

DAVID AND GOLIATH

On the field Ulster were the first province to climb the European summit. David Humphreys amassed a number of records, becoming Ireland's record point-scorer and Ireland's most prolific drop-goal scorer. He received an honorary doctorate from the University of Ulster for services to the game. The highlight of his career came in January 1999 when he captained the team to victory in the European Cup, Ulster thus becoming the first Irish province to become European champions. According to Humphreys,

> we didn't have a very good team, but we got on a roll. There were just a few hundred people at our first match, but our success struck a chord initially across the province and then throughout the whole of Ireland. When we drove down to Dublin for the final in Lansdowne Road, all the flags of support for us really inspired us.
>
> All of Ireland got behind us as we were bidding to become the first Irish side to win the competition. I suppose it was all the sweeter for me as I was captain. Mark McCall was captain for the opening match, but he got injured, and the captaincy fell onto my shoulders by default. The whole day was an incredible experience.

Ulster beat Colomiers 21–6, and their full-back, Simon Mason, was in inspired form from the tee. He kicked four first-half penalties. Humphreys kicked a drop goal in the second half before Mason kicked two more penalties to put the game beyond the French side. The Ulster centre, Jonny Bell, was named man of the match after the win.

Another highlight for Ulster came in 2002 when Humphreys scored a record 37 points in a European Cup tie against Wasps in a 42–3 victory, scoring a try and four drop goals in the process.

In 2006, at the end of a glorious week for Irish rugby, seven days after Munster won the Heineken Cup, Ulster claimed their first Celtic League title. Given his great service to the province, it was appropriate that the victory was sealed by a dramatic late kick by Humphreys against the defending champions, the Ospreys, in Wales. Humphreys slotted over a 40-metre drop goal just two minutes from time

Peter Sella of Barbarians is tackled by Jonathon Bell of Ireland during the Peace International, 1996.

David Humphreys with the Rugby European Cup trophy, 1999.

Ulster players celebrate as the final whistle is blown in the Celtic League, 2006.

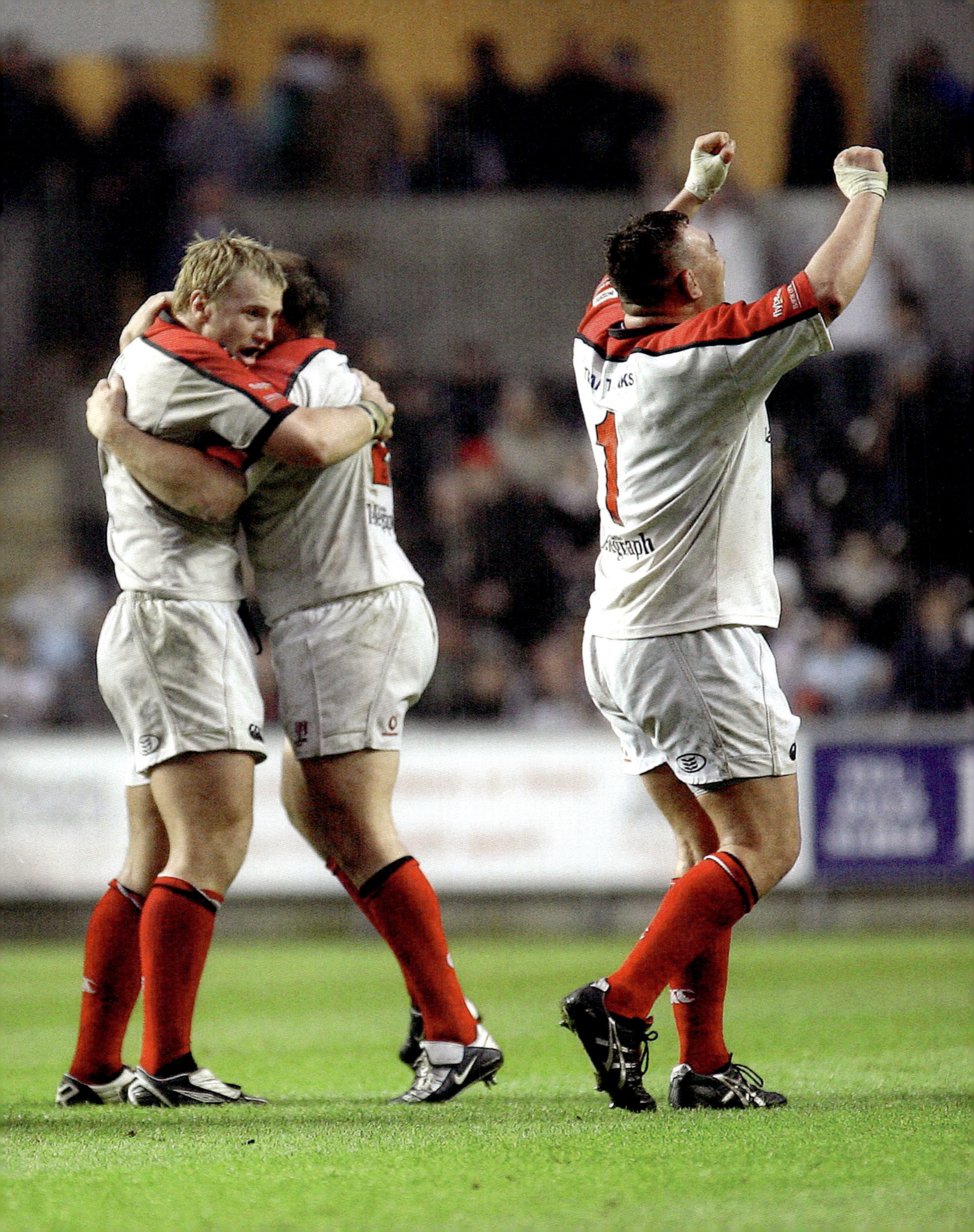

to snatch the title from Leinster. What rugby fans didn't know was that Leinster were about to embark on an era of unprecedented success and become kings of Europe.

LEINSTER LIONS

Leinster's first Heineken Cup trophy came in a 19–16 win over the kingpins of England, Leicester, in 2009.

Leinster had a team of great talent, but it was not maximised until Michael Cheika was appointed coach. The number 10 is the player who reflects the attitude and the potential of the team they play in, and nobody personified Leinster's exuberant new running style under Cheika better than Felipe Contepomi. His game was based on his ability to create space for others and by his awareness, typified in his role in the try that Brian O'Driscoll scored against Toulouse in the Heineken Cup quarter-final. Contepomi had a temperament that made him prepared to attack from anywhere. Some people saw it as a failing in his game, but Cheika saw it as a strength. He did outrageous things, and sometimes they backfired, but when they worked they opened up defences. He often came up with something outlandish, be it a chip under his own posts, a sidestep on his own 22 or an outrageous dummy, and no opposing coach can legislate for that. Contepomi credits Cheika with changing Leinster.

> Culture is something that you can destroy overnight, but it takes a long time to build. You have to work on it every day and get everybody to buy in. You get people to change, then the behaviour becomes a habit and eventually it changes into a culture, and that's what Michael Cheika has to take much of the plaudits for.

Cheika brought Leinster to the top table in European rugby through a unique amalgam of flair, a vibrant team spirit and his newly created work ethic in a province that had previously relied on skill. His other unique contribution – one that was critical to the success in 2009 and to all of Leinster's big wins through to the unique double in 2018 – was to persuade Isa Nacewa to sign for the province.

Rocky Elsom, Isa Nacewa and Leo Cullen rejoice after Leinster's first Heineken Cup victory in 2009.

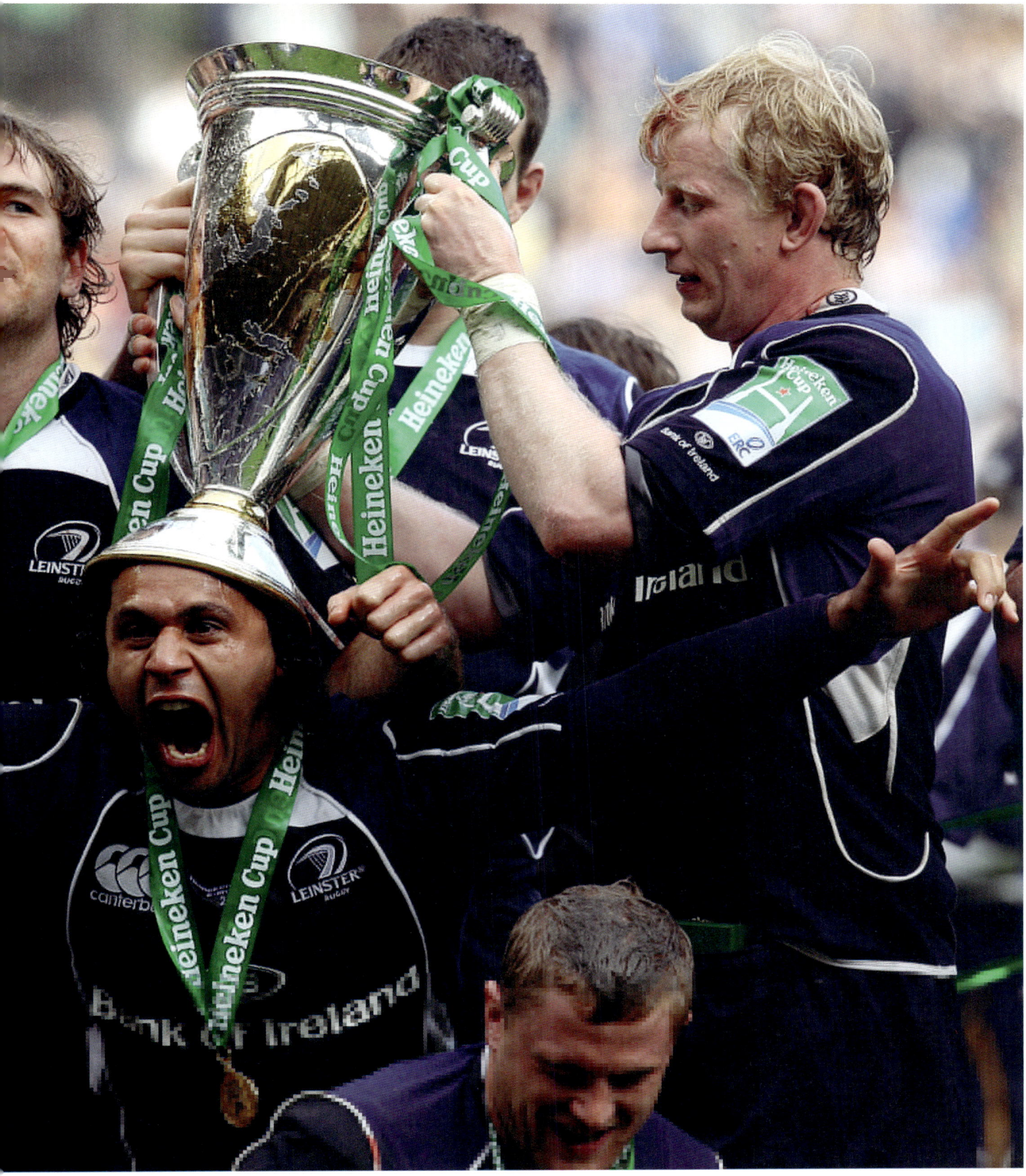
Heineken Cup
Heineken
LEINSTER
Ireland

Brian O'Driscoll celebrates Leinster's victory in the 2012 Heineken Cup final.

Nacewa was indirectly responsible for the appointment of Cheika's successor. Joe Schmidt had been talking to Nacewa to see if he could tempt him to play at Clermont, but Nacewa ended up persuading Schmidt to apply for the job at Leinster instead.

Schmidt took over as Leinster head coach for the 2010/11 season and guided the province to their second Heineken Cup title in his first campaign. One young Leinster player at the time was Ian McKinley, who recalls that

> Joe just demanded the utmost in concentration both in training and in games. His attention to detail is incredible ... I was going to be picked for a game against Cardiff, and I went into his office to point out where we could attack. I gave him an example, via video. He just turned and said, 'Good work, but go look at these clips and tell me what you see.' In those you saw different spaces to attack. He was always one step ahead. His knowledge of the game was on a different level.

> If you were a workhorse, doing your stuff unseen by almost everyone, Joe knew you'd done the work. If there was a professional game of rugby going on, Joe had seen it. If you called him and told him about a play you saw, Joe knew about it. Joe has a photographic memory about rugby. I've never seen a coach show such massive attention to detail or one with such a smart rugby brain. He made little tweaks, and all of a sudden an opposition defence opened up in front of you.

Leinster won back-to-back European titles in 2012 despite trailing Northampton 22–6 at half-time. Johnny Sexton's half-time speech is credited with changing the outcome of the game.

Schmidt saw events differently from the accepted narrative. He shares the accolades that were given to Sexton but not the accepted wisdom that has emerged about the game.

Johnny's speech was good, but in my memory it was Jenno [Shane Jennings] who gave the most forceful speech. The thing about Johnny, though, was that he delivered on the pitch immediately after half-time, and that is what really mattered.

In 2012 Leinster crushed a spirited Ulster by a record Heineken Cup final-winning margin to become the first side to win three titles in four years.

Leinster set a new final record of five tries and became only the second team, after Leicester ten years previously, to successfully defend the Heineken Cup – and also the second, after Toulouse, to win more than two European titles. Leinster's style in winning those finals saw them acclaimed in some quarters of the rugby press as the best Heineken Cup team ever.

Schmidt gives the credit to something he read in a book about Aristotle: 'We are what we repeatedly do. Excellence is not an act but a habit.' The European triumphs would be testimony to this wisdom. Schmidt did not

> want to dictate to the players. If it was going to work it was not going to be the management telling them what to do. It had to come from them and be driven by them, not us. They had to have ownership and, to be fair to them, they did take ownership of it, and that is one of the main reasons why we were so successful.
>
> The one specific area we did give them direction was on the importance of discipline – both on and off the field. The need for discipline on the field was obvious in terms of not giving away penalties or, worse, stupid yellow cards, which could cost

Johnny Sexton scores a try on the way to a man-of-the-match performance against Northampton in the Heineken Cup final, 2011.

us dearly. The discipline off the field was in relation to diet and 'sleep hygiene'. I have to confess that these were two new words to me. We wanted, even needed, all of them to get plenty of sleep. Sleep hygiene refers to creating the right conditions for sleep, which means shutting off all computers and electronic devices before trying to sleep. We encouraged them to read a book instead.

He recalls that Lee Child was a particularly popular author with many of the Leinster players.

In 2018 Leinster went one step further with a Champions Cup and League double under the guidance of Leo Cullen and Stuart Lancaster and their 'comfortable in chaos' philosophy, aimed at encouraging players to be prepared for any scenario that might develop during a game. They inspired, and they played brilliant rugby.

STAND UP AND FIGHT LIKE HELL

In May 2023 Munster won their first silverware in 12 years when they beat the Stormers 19–14 in the BKT United Rugby Championship final in Cape Town. Munster had already sprung a shock at the Aviva Stadium in the semifinal when they stunned the red-hot favourites, Leinster, with Jack Crowley's decisive late drop goal evoking memories of Ronan O'Gara at his imperious best.

Crowley's finger-wag celebration even echoed ROG's famous reaction to his Grand Slam-winning kick in 2009. Munster fans had been worked up after seeing video of the Stormers players and staff deliriously celebrating Munster's win against Leinster, including hooker Joseph Dweba's ebullient yelps of 'We're gonna f*** them up!'

The most striking thing about the occasion was that about five thousand Munster fans made the journey to South Africa despite the short notice and the fact that Ireland was in the throes of a cost-of-living crisis. It was a reminder, if any were needed, of the depth of passion the Munster team generates and why they are, in an Irish context, arguably the 'people's team'. To understand this, it is necessary to probe the province's rich rugby story a little more deeply.

THE MIRACLE MATCH

The rugby public were gripped by Munster rugby because of matches such as the one on 18 January 2003, which has entered folklore as the 'miracle match'.

In a Heineken Cup pool game in Thomond Park in Limerick, Munster faced mission impossible: they needed to beat Gloucester by no fewer than 27 points to qualify for the quarter-final. They also needed to score four tries. Surely it couldn't be done.

As if there were not enough tension, a copy of the Gloucester game plan was found in the back of a taxi in Limerick. It was rushed to the Munster coach, Alan Gaffney. Was this the real thing, or could it be a double bluff? In the end, Munster won 33–6, meeting the points requirement. Surprisingly, Ronan O'Gara gives the credit for the victory to one of the subs that day.

> I suppose the two greatest characters of Munster rugby in my time were Mick Galwey and Peter Clohessy. They were old school and are a huge loss to the game, and the freshness they brought to the game and to the Munster squad was very uplifting. Probably my most abiding memory of my days in the Irish squad was when the players and management made a presentation to Peter to mark his fiftieth cap. Peter responded by singing the Frank Sinatra song 'I Did It My Way'. What an appropriate song! He did things his way or no way. That's why I liked him and admired him so much. Without the Claw [Clohessy] and Gaillimh [Galwey], Munster would never have become the force it did.
>
> Gaillimh was on the bench that day. The night before, he really got us going with a great speech about what it meant to play for Munster. It got us all in exactly the right frame of mind. He was the spark we needed to win the miracle match.

The 'extra man' is part of the mythology of sports, but the role of the fans – and the volume of their support – cannot be underestimated on that day. It highlights the special connection the team has with their supporters – a connection that reframes Munster rugby not just as a game but as a movement.

John Kelly scores a try for Munster against Gloucester, 2003.

Despite his success with Ireland and the Lions, Jim McCarthy's fondest memories are of playing in the famous red jersey of Munster.

> When I look back, it's the matches with Munster that stand out for me. Bill Shankly's famous saying ['Some people believe football is a matter of life and death ... I can assure you it is much, much more important than that'] applies to rugby in Munster, especially in Limerick. For me, the person that encapsulated that feeling was the late, great Tom Clifford. He was the character among characters.
>
> I'll never forget his funeral. The church was teeming with rugby folk. The priest giving the homily had been a lifelong friend of Tom's and told us how he had invited the giant of Irish rugby to his ordination Mass. After the ceremony he asked Tom what he thought of it. Tom replied, 'You spoke too long. The next time if you go on for longer than ten minutes I'll set off an alarm clock in the church.' The next Sunday the priest saw Tom arriving in at the church and noticed he had a bulge in his overcoat. When Tom caught his eye, he pulled out an alarm clock!
>
> My clearest memory is of Tom playing for Munster against the Wallabies in 1948. Munster had a very simple way of dealing with touring sides: that was as soon as possible to bring them down to our level, and then it was an even match! Tom was in the front row packing against Nick Shehadie, one of the stars of the Australian side, and said, 'Come in here, son. You may as well die here as in fu**in' Sydney!'

HUNT OR BE HUNTED

Never was Munster's fighting spirit better exemplified than in Seamus Dennison's bone-crunching hit on the All Blacks legend Stu Wilson in the opening minutes of their never-to-be-forgotten 12–0 victory over the All Blacks in 1978. It sent a clear message: we shall not be moved.

Brendan Foley believes that the team were helped by a stroke of luck.

> What some people forget is that it was the first year there had been a bank holiday on the last Monday in October, so we had three days of preparation for the match the previous weekend, which was more than we ever had with the international side. Tom Kiernan had us really well prepared. In fact, I and some of the Limerick lads worked the morning of the match before meeting with the team at lunchtime.

Tony Ward recalls the build-up to the match:

> I do not exaggerate when I say that we trained in mud-bath conditions before one, maybe two men and a dog in Corbally while on the other side of town, in Crescent College, across the road from Dooradoyle [Garryowen FC], there were massive traffic and crowd issues as rugby-daft Limerick made its way to see the mighty All Blacks train in the flesh.
>
> Our coach, Tom Kiernan, brought us up to the lakes between Killaloe and Lough Derg and organised two sizeable boats and loaded each with buckets, water pistols and hoses. As if the rain wasn't enough – it pumped down incessantly from Saturday through to Tuesday morning – we spent I couldn't tell you how long conducting our own naval battle on the lakes. You couldn't make it up! Yet in those few hours we had succeeded in releasing the shackles and hitting a unifying sweet point that even our pre-season tour to London (where we got hammered by Middlesex before scraping a draw at Sunbury against an Exiles XV) failed to come even close to replicating.
>
> Therein lay the greatest pressure and I believe the biggest single reason we did what we did, when we did, on the High Altar at the then spiritual home of Munster and Irish rugby. We didn't expect to beat the mighty All Blacks, but did we believe we could? Yes, yes and yes again.
>
> And that was the theme from Kiernan at every get-together in the build-up to the match. It was about honouring the jersey, respecting the legacy and, however clichéd it might sound, dying for that cause. The individual components were of course covered in great detail, but never did he (or we) stray from that central plank in our build-up.
>
> There is something special about putting on the red Munster jersey and beating the All Blacks ... a historic achievement. Nobody who played that day will ever forget the feeling. The All Blacks were godlike figures, with a reputation for invincibility. The atmosphere that day in Thomond Park was incredible.
>
> We had won convincingly and left the pitch in a state of bliss. However, the crowd demanded that we come out again. It was the only time that I've witnessed a sporting occasion when all around people were crying. To be able to say you were there was great, but to have been at the centre of the action was just fantastic.

The victory was overshadowed by the news that, while the team captain, Donal Canniffe, was leading the Munster team to the historic win, his father, Dan, collapsed and died in Cork while listening to the match. At the banquet in honour of the team's victory, a minute's silence was observed, and Pat Whelan, vice-captain, stood in for Donal.

The Munster 22 that day was:

Larry Moloney	Garryowen
Moss Finn	UCC
Seamus Dennison	Garryowen
Greg Barrett	Cork Con
Jimmy Bowen	Cork Con
Tony Ward	St Mary's/Garryowen
Donal Canniffe (capt.)	Lansdowne
Gerry 'Ginger' McLoughlin	Shannon
Pat Whelan	Garryowen
Les White	London Irish
Moss Keane	Lansdowne
Brendan Foley	Shannon
Christy Cantillon	Cork Con
Colm Tucker	Shannon

Donal Spring	Trinity
Mickey O'Sullivan	Cork Con
Barry McGann	Cork Con
Olann Kelleher	Dolphin
Ted Mulcahy	Bohemians
Gerry Hurley	Sundays Well
Anthony O'Leary	London Irish/Cork Con
Declan Smith	Cork Con

One of the bonuses of that win was that many of the Munster team were offered invitations to play in enjoyable exhibitions – none more so than Moss Keane. Moss was once playing for the Wolfhounds, and in the side was Charlie Kent, the big blond English centre. Charlie is a diabetic, and at half-time a rather puffed-up ambulance man arrived in the players' huddle and tapped Moss on the shoulder. He asked Moss whether he was the man who wanted a sugar lump. Moss replied, 'Arra Jaysus, who do you think I am, Shergar?'

GLORY, GLORY MUNSTER

If Seamus Dennison's tackle is the defining symbol of the victory over the All Blacks, the next enduring image of Munster's dominance came in the 2006 Heineken Cup semi-final at Lansdowne Road as they crushed the bookies' favourites, Leinster. The final nail in the coffin for Leinster came when Ronan O'Gara raised an arm in celebration before he even crossed the try-line. After he placed the ball down he cleared the hurdle of the advertising board towards the south terrace to join the Munster faithful in celebration after Munster's 30–6 triumph. It was a gesture that conveyed a powerful message: absolute supremacy.

Saturday 20 May 2006 became the new high point of Munster rugby. The red army finally claimed the holy grail of European rugby by defeating Biarritz 23–19 in the Heineken Cup final at Millennium Stadium in Cardiff. Despite conceding seven points in the opening few minutes, Munster went on to outscore Biarritz 17–3 in the remainder of the half. It was their most convincing half of rugby in the three finals to date. The difference was that they were now converting pressure into points, unlike in their previous finals. They pushed the bounds of fitness, conditioning and, most of all, commitment beyond anything they had in the past.

A great weight had been lifted from some of the sturdiest shoulders in world rugby. For so long it had seemed to be the destiny of that Munster team always to fall at the last hurdle. Each year since 1998/9 they had reached the knockout stages of the competition, losing three semi-finals, to Stade Français, Toulouse and Wasps, and, heartbreakingly, two finals, to Northampton and Leicester.

Two years later, in 2008, Munster won their second Heineken Cup title in three seasons with a nail-biting 16–13 triumph over Toulouse. Denis Leamy's first-half try was complemented by 11 points from Ronan O'Gara.

The sweetness of the wins was intensified for Paul O'Connell by the fact that there had been so many disappointments on the journey.

> I picked up a shoulder injury playing for Munster in the run-up to the Heineken semi-final against Castres. The morning of the match I had to do a fitness test. That is a test I will never forget, because my shoulder was standing up well, and I was hitting a tackle bag which Declan Kidney was holding. The problem was that I hit it so hard at one stage that I knocked out one of Declan's teeth! He was due to do a TV interview three-quarters of an hour later, so he had to go the dentist to get it stuck back in. The shoulder was fine, but I probably wasn't one hundred per cent fit. We won the game, but in a warm-up match before the Heineken Cup final I damaged my ankle ligaments. I did manage to play against Leicester in the final, but with my shoulder and ankle problems I didn't play well.

There was a lot of criticism of the side after that match. According to O'Connell,

> I think criticism is brilliant: it only makes you a better player, if you are mentally strong enough to take it. If someone had a go at me personally in the press and I respected him, I could learn from that. If you don't respect him but he's speaking the truth,

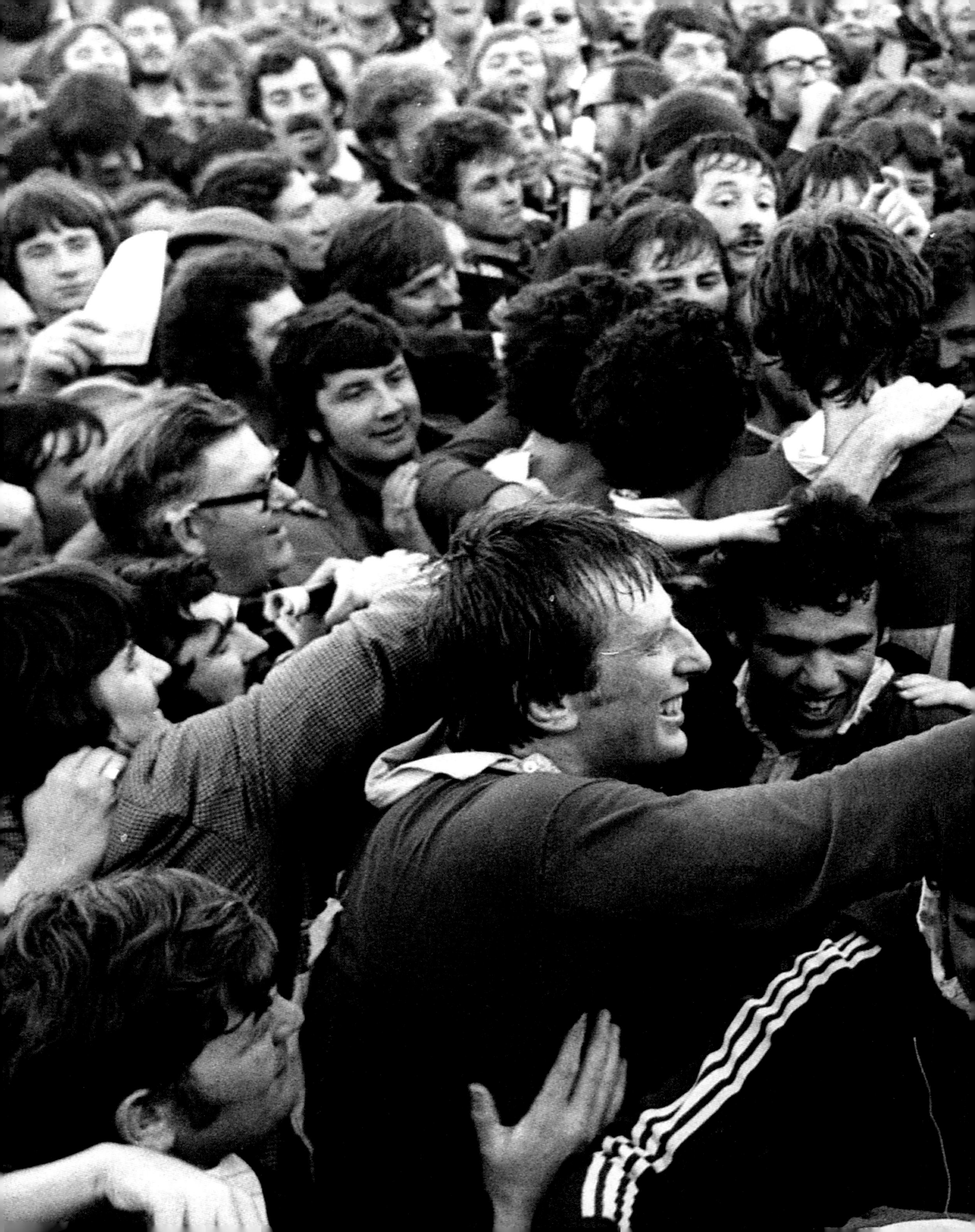

Munster fans and players celebrate their famous win over the All Blacks at Thomond Park, 1978.

you have to take it on board. But if you know it's not the truth you just ignore it.

O'Connell believes that much of the credit for the triumph must go to the coach.

> I am forever indebted to Declan Kidney. He gave me my first big break with Munster. I had a bit of a discipline problem when I was younger, and I suppose I was lucky that he took a chance on me. I was getting too many yellow cards, and if you are doing that you don't get picked, and if you don't play you don't get selected for Ireland and your career goes nowhere.
>
> Declan is a good motivator. He is always looking for the psychological edge. At one stage in Munster we were conceding too many penalties and the odd soft try because of lapses in concentration. Declan got white T-shirts for us to wear in training with Concentration written on the front and Discipline written on the back. You couldn't escape the message wherever you looked on the training pitch.
>
> My favourite story about him, though, goes back to 2000, before I joined the Munster squad. On the way to the Heineken Cup final against Northampton, Munster had to play Saracens away. Saracens were a club without a tradition, and they brought in marketing people to tell them how to bring in the crowds. One of the things they did was to play the *Rocky* music whenever there was a fight or a row. When the team came onto the pitch they played the *A-Team* music. When the opposition came on they played the 'Teddy Bears' Picnic'. When the Saracens place-kicker faced up to a penalty, the crowd put on fez hats and had a little routine to guide the ball over the bar, and the tee came on in a remote-controlled car.

Munster fans watch the Heineken Cup final on a big screen on O'Connell Street, Limerick, 2008.

Peter Stringer scores a try against Biarritz, 2006.

To play against Saracens you had to face a lot of distractions. Before Munster played them the Munster squad were watching a Saracens match as part of their video analysis. With about two minutes to go on the video, Declan turned on a ghetto blaster and had the *A-Team* music blaring, and he put on his fez hat and started playing with the remote control and the lights. After a minute or so Declan turned off the television, took off his hat and turned off the ghetto blaster and he asked, 'What happened in the last sixty seconds of the Saracens game?'

BAND OF BROTHERS

Another trophy came for Munster when Ronan O'Gara converted the late try that sealed the 2011 Celtic League Grand Final just a week after Joe Schmidt led Leinster to their second European title.

Paul O'Connell believes that the Munster jersey is a sacred trust passed on from generation to generation.

I think every player on the Munster team has a bit of a Mick Galwey in him. Gaillimh was very similar to Peter Clohessy in that he was old school. He likes his pints and wasn't very fond of training, but when it came to Saturday there was nobody who put themselves on the line more or gave more on the pitch. He was a great guy to talk to players and to get them up for a match. When you saw a man who had accomplished so much get so emotional and be so committed for every Munster game, it did inspire you to give of your best. He had a great ability to put his finger on the button for every occasion with every guy on the team in a way that got the best out of them.

I learnt a lot from Gaillimh and the Claw because they knew every trick in the game and every shortcut there was to know. Gaillimh had a very good, tight game. He was clever, tactically astute and above all a great leader. When I came into the Munster squad first, Mick O'Driscoll was in the second row for Munster, and he was brilliant in the line-out. I learnt so much about line-out play from him. I was lucky enough to get his place on the Munster team, and he was so helpful.

Woodie [Keith Wood] was a great leader as well. When he pointed his finger at you and said he needed a big game from you, you wanted to give it to him because he was one of the greatest players in the world and had done it all himself. Our job was to leave the jersey in a better state for the next guy.

Those who wear the Munster jersey are not just players but curators of a rich legacy. Munster rugby is less a geographical entity than it is a state of mind.

Shaun Payne, Ronan O'Gara and Alan Quinlan celebrate the final whistle of the Heineken Cup, 2006.

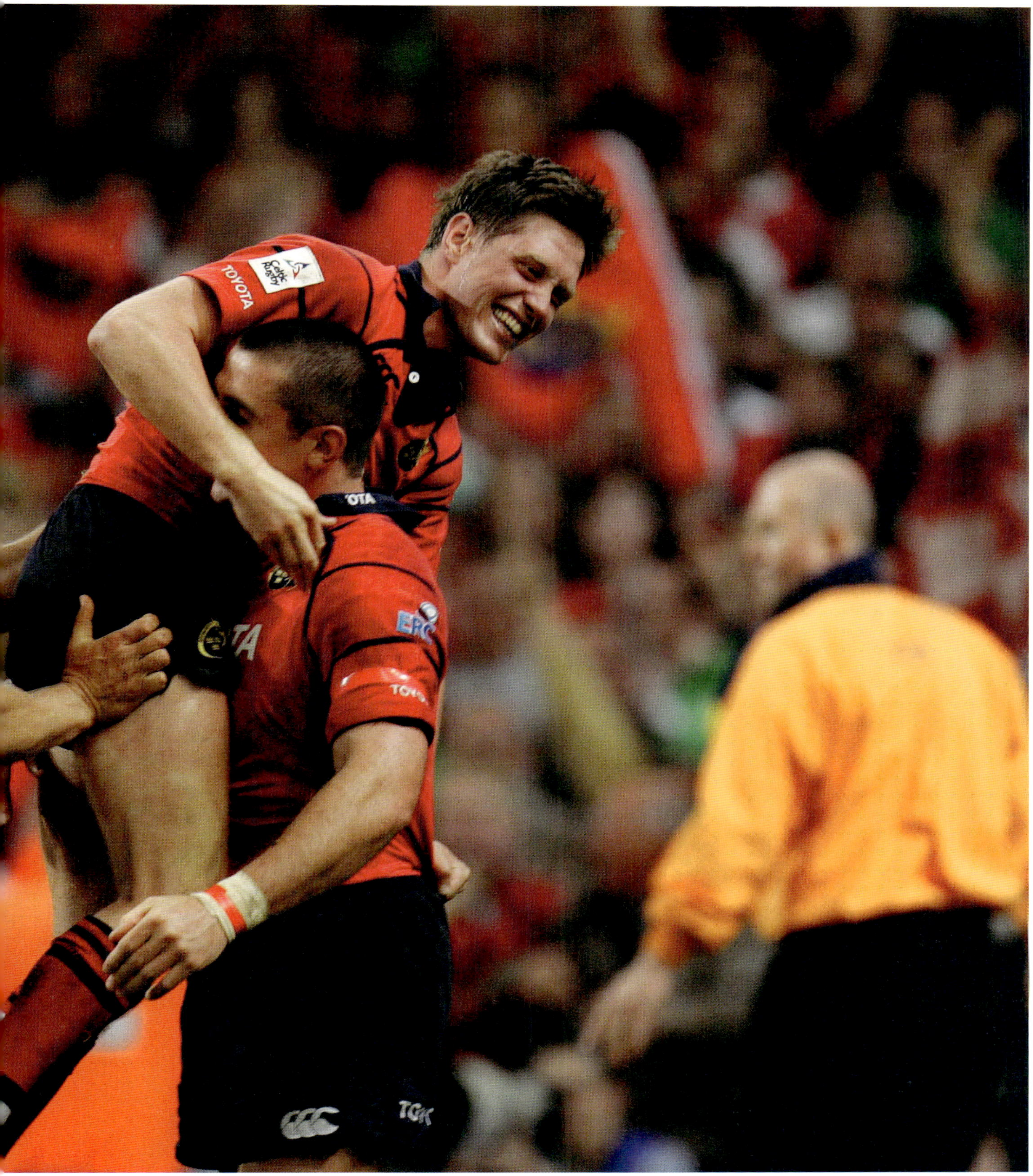
TOYOTA

Lansdowne vs Cork Constitution, 2017.

8

IN THE CLUB

The foundation stones on which Irish rugby has been built in the past 150 years have been, to a major extent, the clubs. Without them the sport would not have extended to so many facets of Irish society. This chapter explains how they have inducted women and men, girls and boys, into the joys of this beautiful game. For example, one of the most celebrated partnerships in Irish rugby was that between Peter Stringer and Ronan O'Gara, and their incredible bond was first nurtured when they were 12-year-olds in Cork Constitution.

The debt that Irish rugby owes the clubs is incalculable because of the assembly line of players they have produced for the Irish national sides. In addition they have provided an invaluable nursery for some of Ireland's finest coaches and administrators.

Historically, clubs in Limerick have introduced boys and girls to the game who did not attend the traditional rugby-playing schools. Clubs in the provinces have done much to attract a new audience for the game. A case in point has been the huge success of mini rugby, which has drawn huge numbers of children to the game – and often their parents. This is particularly important in growing the game in new areas.

THE LIMERICK LEADERS

If Munster was different, Limerick was unique.

Mick English had three claims to fame. Firstly, he was an accomplished Irish out-half, succeeding no less a person than Jack Kyle in the number 10 jersey.

Secondly, he has been immortalised around the world in after-dinner speeches by Tony O'Reilly. After playing against Phil Horrocks-Taylor during a Wolfhounds match in Limerick, English was asked what he thought of his opponent, who had scored a try that day. English replied, 'Well, Horrocks went one way, Taylor the other, and I was left with the hyphen.'

Thirdly, he acquired cult status for his performances at the home of Munster rugby, Thomond Park. The old ground was famous for the twenty-foot wall that was from time to time insufficient to prevent the ball from leaving the grounds. When balls were lost, the crowd were wont to shout, 'Never mind the ball, get on with the game!' English was famous for deliberately kicking the ball over the wall when his side were defending a narrow lead near the end of a game.

In 1952 English began what was to be a very happy 10-year association with Bohemians, and in 1958 he was central to their success in winning their first Munster Cup in 31 years. Part of the gloss was taken off the Bohs' victory when the cup went missing for four days. The strong suspicion was that it was a local job. Eventually, the cup was left outside English's home and discovered by his sister Philomena on her way home from Mass.

English reached an important milestone when he became a Munster player in 1955, and he won Munster Cup medals in 1959 and 1962. He was tickled by a letter written to him by Mai Purcell of the *Limerick Leader* when he won his first Irish cap.

> Mick. I should like to impress on you that I'm spending a whole week's wages to visit Dublin just to see you play and I beseech you not to make an idiot of yourself on this occasion. I furthermore request that on this auspicious occasion mindful of your duties and responsibilities not only to your club and the people of Limerick but to your country as a whole, that you keep your bloody eye on the ball. Good luck and God Bless.

NO CLASS ACT

For its first hundred years, rugby reflected the class divisions in Irish society. In Limerick, though, rugby smashed through the class ceiling.

As we have seen, rugby was a pursuit of the middle and upper-middle classes in Ireland. The vast majority of the rugby-playing population began their careers in the most prestigious fee-paying schools in Ireland, such as Clongowes and Blackrock College. This fact was reflected in Brendan Behan's observations: 'I never heard rugby was a proper game for anyone except bank clerks' and 'It was a game for the Protestant and the shopkeeping Catholic and I never thought it had anything to do with me.'

The exception was Limerick, where rugby was like a religion, touching a nerve in the people of the city's psyche. Limerick is recognised worldwide as one of the great cathedrals of rugby. In the 1970s, when he moved there to train as a PE teacher, Tony Ward began playing rugby with Garryowen. He had no idea what he was getting into.

> I had never heard of the Well [Sundays Well RFC]. In fact I thought [the Limerick club] Young Munster were some team in Kerry. That Cup game was a totally new experience for me as I had only been used to Leinster Schools rugby. The passion and commitment of the players in my first taste of Munster rugby will always remain in my mind.
>
> I remember in my first season, after the Old Crescent game, walking down by the flats in Watergate, and two Corporation workers, bending over the bins, shouted over to me, 'All the best in the cup final, Wardie!' This would never happen in Dublin, as I was then a complete unknown, and I found the experience very strange and moving.
>
> I also recall O'Shaughnessy's florists alongside the Franciscan church, with a full window display of white and blue followers

Shannon players brave the cold conditions, 2010.

for Garryowen. Dublin rugby fans thought I was making up stories when I mentioned these happenings, which are part and parcel of Limerick rugby.

I had been told that rugby was played democratically in only three places: New Zealand, Wales and Limerick. I thought that was just hype before I moved there, but then I saw the doctor playing side by side with the docker, and the banker in the second row linking up with the shop assistant. I probably didn't even understand the meaning of the word at the time, but the ethos of Limerick was best summed up in one word: egalitarian. There were no class boundaries. Rugby is more than recreation in Limerick.

Every rose has its thorn: the price of this republic of rugby is that the highest standards are expected all the time, and no one is safe if they are not reached. Even the legendary Peter Clohessy was to learn this lesson the hard way.

One Tuesday evening after a particularly galling loss to Shannon I was heading onto the field to go training for Young Munster, and there was this old lady – I'd say she was 85 if she was a day – and she called me over to the wire. I knew I was in for an earful straight away. She shouted at me, 'What the hell was wrong with you on Saturday! You were hoisted so high in the scrum I was going to send you a parachute.'

A ROBUST CONSTITUTION

Clubs like Blackrock, Ballymena and UCC have provided many players to the international team. Every club has a unique founding story. Cork Constitution's story is proof of this. Newspapers have always played a huge role in Irish life – nowhere more so than in Cork. Towards the end of the nineteenth century there was intense competition in Cork between the rival papers. The *Skibbereen Eagle* sought to carve out a distinctive identity for itself by focusing on international affairs. Famously, it took a stance against what it saw as Russian oppression. In 1898 it boldly stated that it

will still keep its eye on the Emperor of Russia and all such despotic enemies – whether at home or abroad – of human progression and man's natural rights which undoubtedly include a nation's right to self-government. 'Truth', 'Liberty', 'Justice' and the 'Land for the People' are the solid foundations on which the *Eagle's* policy is based.

The comments were picked up all over the world as an example of resistance to tyranny.

In contrast, the *Cork Constitution* was playing a significant part in the fabric of life in the city but without concerning itself with global politics. It positioned itself as a paper of Cork, for Cork and by Cork. Of more enduring significance was that the staff of the paper were responsible for the formation, in 1892, of what would become one of Irish rugby's most famous rugby clubs. Cork Con joined other clubs in the city at the time: Blackrock, Cork FC, Cork Bankers, Midleton College, Queen's College, Queenstown and the lesser-known Bulldogs. The team would go on to win 30 Munster Cups, 25 Munster Senior League titles and 6 All-Ireland Leagues. It has served Irish rugby faithfully, giving the sport 45 senior internationals, including such giants of the game as Noel Murphy, Barry McGann, Donal Lenihan, Moss Finn, Michael Bradley and Ralph Keyes – right up to recent internationals such as Simon Zebo, Peter O'Mahony and Shane Daly, as well as nine Lions.

One of the club's most noteworthy triumphs came in 1990 in an under-12 European tournament at Roche-la-Molière in France. In a sign of things to come, the team featured a half-back combination of Peter Stringer and Ronan O'Gara. In the International Rugby Experience in Limerick both Strings and ROG speak evocatively of that trip. Tellingly, ROG links their bond – and the telepathic relationship they had developed in the club since they were six years old – directly with the pass to him by Strings for the drop goal in Cardiff to win the Grand Slam in 2009.

It may be unfair to single out an individual, but if there were one person who encapsulates the club it would be Tom Kiernan. One highlight of his career came when Ireland went to Australia for a six-match tour in 1967. The omens for the Test match were not favourable. The previous week Ireland had lost 21–9 to New South Wales at the same Sydney venue. However, tries from Jerry Walsh and Pat McGrath, and a conversion and drop goal

Tom Kiernan, 1969.

from Kiernan, gave Ireland an 11–5 win. They became the first touring team from the northern hemisphere to beat Australia.

Known as the 'Grey Fox', Kiernan won 54 caps for Ireland and played five times for the British and Irish Lions. When he retired he was Ireland's record points scorer, with 158. He kicked the winning score the first time Ireland beat South Africa in 1965. He captained every team he ever played for: UCC, Cork Con, Munster, Ireland and, in 1968, the British and Irish Lions – with fellow Irish internationals Barry Bresnihan, Mike Gibson, Roger Young, Syd Millar, Willie John McBride and Ken Goodall joining him in the touring party.

One vignette sums up Kiernan's love of the game. On holiday in the south of France, Kiernan decided to visit the grave of William Webb Ellis. Shocked at how unkempt it had become, he devoted a day to tidying it up and restoring it to something of its former glory.

Of course, Kiernan was not the only Irish rugby legend to really love his club. Karl Mullen interrupted his honeymoon with his wife, Doreen, to play for Old Belvedere in the Leinster Senior Cup final.

PRIDE

Another feature of Irish rugby is the pride that former internationals who enjoyed great success with Ireland and the Lions retain of their club careers. In 1971 Seán Lynch of St Mary's had a memorable year. After just one season at the international level the prop was chosen by the Lions for what would become a historic tour to New Zealand. He was to play a more central role than anybody could have foreseen at the start of the tour. The week before the first Test in Dunedin, the Lions lost their two first-choice props – the Irish legend Ray McLoughlin and Sandy Carmichael – to long-term injuries suffered in the infamous 'battle of Christchurch'. In this furnace the Lions won the series against all the odds, with Mike Gibson, Fergus Slattery and Mick Hipwell the other Irish players to make the tour.

Lynch is not a player to take himself too seriously. Despite his achievements at the highest level with the Lions, his happiest memories are of club successes with St Mary's.

> From my point of view the pinnacle of my career was captaining St Mary's to our first Leinster Cup in 1969. I had the experience of losing two previous finals, so it was really sweet for me.

Success at the club level provided the platform Lynch needed to step onto the international stage.

Denis Hickie and I were capped for the first time against France in 1971, becoming the first Mary's players to play for Ireland. Jimmy Kelly and George Norton had played for St Mary's and Ireland but were not Mary's players during their international careers. It was a wonderful achievement for the club. When the side was announced there was a great club celebration.

Another international player with fond memories of the club scene is Brendan Foley.

> I was playing for Shannon against Skerries, but our 'medical guy' forgot his kit bag. After twenty minutes I went down with a bad injury on my knee. Our medic went over to his colleague at Skerries and asked him if he could help out. He gave him a bottle and told him to spray it on me. He did, although I thought it had a very strange smell ... I got up and played on.
>
> On the bus home I asked him what sort of magic lotion he had put on my knee. He pulled out the bottle and looked at it closely. It was Easy Start – which is what you use for starting a car in an emergency!

Brendan Foley and John Cantrell, 1981.

Shannon Rugby, 1986.

Phil O'Callaghan, a legend of Irish rugby, is famed for his experiences playing for Dolphin. One story goes back to a match played on a bitterly cold November day. He was lifting one of his forwards, Eoghan Moriarty, in the line-out. The big man shouted down at him, 'Philo, let me down! My hands are frozen.'

Philo once put out his shoulder, and Karl Mullen was to experience his sharp tongue at first hand. When Mullen ran onto the pitch to give him medical care he said, 'I'll put it back, but I warn you it will be painful.' He did, and it was. According to the story, Philo was screaming his head off with the pain. Mullen then turned to him and said, 'You should be ashamed of yourself. I was with a sixteen-year-old girl this morning in the Rotunda as she gave birth, and there was not even a word of complaint from her.'

Philo replied: 'I wonder what she bloody well would have said if you tried putting the f****n' thing back in.'

YOU'LL NEVER WALK ALONE

Family is the motif of rugby in Ireland, particularly club rugby. A case in point is Bruff RFC in Limerick, at which Ireland's first player to win 100 caps, John Hayes, came to prominence. With his wife, Fiona Steed, they have had three children – Sally, Róisín and Bill – who are all playing rugby. But they are not necessarily doing so to follow in their parents' footsteps, as Steed is at pains to point out:

> They weren't pushed in: they asked to play. I started at 19 years of age, and my 8-year-old [girl] was playing on the boy's team because there was no girls' age group for her yet.
>
> I brought them to France in 2014 and we were there when Ireland beat New Zealand. The two girls sang 'Ireland's Call' word perfect and Philippe Saint-André [then head coach of France] was behind us in the stand, and he gave them the thumbs-up when they finished.

Since Bill joined [Bruff RFC] he has become a rugby fanatic. In 2023, after Munster beat Leinster in the URC semi-final, he brought John and myself out in the back garden and had the cones set up for the three of us to re-enact Munster's winning drop goal!

I was roped in to helping out with coaching the underage teams. I do think it is important for the boys to see that a woman is more than capable of coaching them.

The ties that bind rugby clubs in Ireland are even stronger in times of crisis. Despite his 27 caps for Ireland and his record 78 caps for Ulster, Willie Anderson will probably always be remembered as the player who was jailed for months by a military junta. On a tour of Argentina with the Penguins in 1980 he took a shine to the Argentinian flag and decided to claim it as his own.

> Myself and another player were walking home to the hotel around midnight. I liked the look of the flag and its colours. Shortly after that, six guys came through the door with machine guns. They said, 'Someone in here has an Argentinian flag.' I immediately handed it back and said I was sorry. I was quickly told saying sorry was not good enough in this situation. As I was brought down to the jail, two Irish internationals, Dave Irwin and Frank Wilson, volunteered to come with me for moral support. For their consideration they were both thrown in jail with me for three weeks!
>
> I was strip-searched and had thirty sets of fingerprints taken. I was literally in the interrogation chair for a day. Anyone who has seen the film *Midnight Express* will have an idea of the naked terror you can experience when you are in prison and there's a gun to your head.
>
> Things got worse before they got better. I was put into this box, which is the most frightening place in the world, before being taken to my cell. The cell was six foot by four and had nothing but a cement bed in the centre. The people who had been there before me had left their excrement behind ... The only blessing was that I wasn't put in the 'open' cell with a crowd of prisoners, because I would have never survived.
>
> The next day I was taken out in handcuffs, which is the ultimate in degradation. I was taken up the stairs and was stunned to discover that there were about sixty or seventy reporters and journalists waiting for me. For three or four days I was not just front-page news in Argentina: I was the first three pages. To me, the press were not much better than terrorists. As I had a British passport they tried to whip up a nationalistic frenzy and portray me as an imperialist. They didn't print the truth. Some said I had urinated on the flag. Others said I had burnt it. Yet more said I had done both. My lawyer got death threats.

The whole experience was terrifying.

> It was much more serious than anybody realised here at the time. I know for a fact that two or three army generals wanted to have me executed. Others wanted to make sure that I served at least ten years' hard labour. The whole episode cost my parents ten thousand pounds in legal fees, but you can't put a price on the mental anguish that they had to endure. I remember one letter I sent them home that I would hate to have to read again, because I had struck rock bottom.
>
> The two lads and I were taken back to a cell where we came into contact with two South Koreans. They had tried to smuggle some Walkmans into the country. David Irwin taught me how to play chess, and we had the World Chess Championships: South Korea v. Northern Ireland.
>
> One of the guards looked like a ringer for Sergeant Bilko. At one stage he was marching us in the yard and Frank roared out, 'Bilko!' I said, 'For Christ's sake, Frank, just keep your mouth shut.' Thankfully, the guard didn't know who Bilko was.
>
> I think things could have been much worse had the warden not wanted to learn English. His colleagues would have been happy to throw away the keys to our cell. In that country we were guilty until proved innocent.

In adversity Anderson found out who his friends really were.

> After three weeks Frank and David were sent home. It was the loneliest day of my life. I had to wait for a further two months before my trial and release. Someone arranged a hotel room for me. I wouldn't wish what happened to me on my worst enemy. I owe them a lot.

Willie Anderson.

> I wrote to my then girlfriend, now wife, Heather, every day. The following year we got married. I think the Argentinian experience consolidated our relationship. I also learnt a lot about myself. In the beginning I prayed intensely but I gradually realised that I could not leave things to God: I had to take control of things myself. I ran every day and made a great effort to learn something about the culture and the political system. Bad and all as things were for me, it was a real culture shock to visit the town square and see all the women who were frantically looking for their sons. It was part of the way of life there that people disappeared and were lost forever. If you were seen as any kind of threat to the state, you were eliminated.

The story provides not one but two examples of the greatness of club rugby in Ireland: the first is the internal solidarity in a club when a member is in distress, and the second is the solidarity among clubs when there is an SOS. Anderson acknowledges this.

> The members of my own club, Dungannon, rallied round and raised a lot of money to support me. All rugby players contributed via the clubs to a fund to pay for my legal expenses.

GALWAY BOYS HURRAH

Clubs have been the launching pad for hundreds of Irish internationals, and they have also launched some very successful coaches.

As a player Warren Gatland was in the right place at the wrong time in the New Zealand team. Sean Fitzpatrick, one of the all-time greats, was untouchable in the number 2 shirt for the All Blacks, so Gatland, as a hooker, was destined to play second fiddle to him. Gatland then sought a new career in teaching. In 1996 he was head of sports at Hamilton Boys' High School on New Zealand's South Island.

One day the phone rang at 4 a.m. Connacht's Billy Glynn told him that the province needed a coach for twelve weeks and that they were just about to set off on a pre-season trip to Sweden. Gatland discussed the opportunity with the school's headmaster, who encouraged Gatland to grab the chance with both hands. He flew straight to Sweden and then, after three months, was offered a full-time contract as director of rugby at Connacht. At that time it was an amateur set-up, with training on Tuesdays and Thursdays and games on Saturdays. But it would be the stepping stone to a glittering career.

Gatland had come onto Connacht's radar during his time coaching Galwegians. He has spoken movingly about the gratitude he still feels to the club. He was 28 when his daughter Shauna was born in early 1992 in a Galway hospital. Although his wife, Trudi, had a smooth pregnancy, they knew something was seriously wrong when a nurse began crying and specialists rushed into the hospital room. Shauna had spina bifida, a condition in which the spinal cord doesn't develop properly in the womb. A scan confirmed that her condition was severe, and her parents decided against surgical intervention after consulting with the experts.

Galwegians encouraged Gatland to heal with his wife in his native New Zealand. He returned and led the Galway club to promotion. Many sporting bodies talk the talk when it comes to duty of care. Galwegians lived it.

The Cork Constitution Squad – winners of the inaugural All-Ireland League Division 1, 1991.

COMPETITIVE EDGE

Club competitions have been an integral part of Irish rugby for most of its history. The oldest competition is the Leinster Senior Cup, which was first won by Dublin University in 1882. NIFC won the first Ulster Senior Cup in 1885. Bandon were the winners of the first Munster Cup in 1886. Galway Town won the first Connacht Senior Cup in 1896.

The First World War had a hugely detrimental effect on Irish rugby. The 1920s were therefore a time of revival. By the end of the decade 160 clubs and 59 schools were affiliated to the IRFU. Right across the country, playing numbers increased, fuelled by the establishment of new competitions, notably ones for junior clubs. This was most evident in country towns.

An example was Castleisland RFC, founded in 1926. Their most famous player is probably Con Houlihan. Con looked back on his own playing career with typical self-deprecation: 'I was never capped for Ireland, but I was once kneecapped playing for Castleisland.' He brought his love of the game into his journalistic career, once writing about a famous Scotland–Ireland game in which a marauding Moss Keane scored a try despite the best efforts of the Scottish defence. Con's verdict was that 'a rolling Scot gathers no Moss'.

In 1922 a national competition, the Bateman Cup, was introduced. The first winners were Lansdowne, but the competition was shelved in 1939 with the outbreak of the Second World War.

The All-Ireland League was launched in the 1990/91 season. The Division One title was won by Cork Con, with Garryowen as runners-up. Wanderers and Malone were relegated. The Division Two winners were Old Wesley, and Young Munster were runners-up. The competition initially attracted significant media attention and generated a lot of popular support.

As we have seen, the rugby axis tilted the day rugby turned professional in 1995, though few of the clubs appreciated at the time the significance it had for each of them. For generations the clubs had been the indivisible core of Irish rugby, but with the elevation of the provinces they found themselves in a new role. Coaches would be paid, but club players would remain amateurs unless attached to a province. Nonetheless, clubs continue to provide a pathway to the international team. A recent example is Jack Crowley, who became the first full Ireland international to come from Bandon RFC.

THE YOUNG ONES

There is rightly huge emphasis today in leadership studies on the three Es: empathy, engagement and empowerment. Irish rugby would not be in the healthy state it is in today without these attributes. However, perhaps one element of leadership that does not get the central importance it deserves is courage. The IRFU has shown great courage in many ways, such as in developing a provincial structure that is the envy of many countries.

Irish rugby is a theatre of innovation. The spectacular success of mini rugby is one of the many illustrations of this. Watching the tiny tots take up a rugby ball for the first time would melt anyone's heart. The focus here is always on encouragement. The aim of mini rugby is to foster and develop young players of all abilities in a safe, non-competitive, enjoyable environment through activities that ensure progressive skill development, in line

Mini rugby, Shannon vs Abbeyfeale.

with the IRFU Long Term Player Development pathway, Safeguarding and the Spirit of Rugby.

Fiona Coghlan believes that mini rugby is critical to the future of the game in general and women's rugby in particular.

> Our biggest challenge is to grow the numbers playing the game. I was 19 before I realised that women could play rugby. It came as a shock to discover that they did. Today, though, here in Clontarf, I see what is being done in the club to introduce boys and girls from four years up to the game, and there are activities for all the ages … It takes people of all shapes and sizes and abilities, and that has really helped to grow the game.
>
> In the past, rugby was for an elite of Irish society, but mini rugby opens it up to everybody and that is the way to go. There is such a buzz around all the clubs who have mini rugby, and it gives us great hope for the future. As we all know, the GAA is in every parish in the country. Mini rugby gives us the opportunity to get into every corner of Irish society.

Mini rugby brings an egalitarian dimension to rugby today. Despite their legendary status, Brian O'Driscoll and Johnny Sexton are just parents when they watch their sons Billy and Luca, respectively, play mini rugby on the same team. Fiona Steed is an enthusiast for this strategy.

> It is great the way mini rugby brings boys and girls together to play rugby and to have fun together. One of the IRFU's great programmes is that hundreds of young boys and girls from clubs all over Ireland take part in the Aviva Minis Festivals every year. There are four provincial festivals each season, followed by the highlight of the year: the national festival in Aviva Stadium.
>
> One of the big treats at the Aviva Minis Festivals is the regular appearance of Ireland stars like Rory Best, Robbie Henshaw and Jenny Murphy. The children love the chance to meet their rugby heroes and learn new skills in a fun environment.

Mini rugby has established itself in less 'traditional' areas throughout the country, such as Ashbourne, Athy, Ballincollig, Barnhall, Birr, Carlow, City of Armagh, Connemara, Creggs, Holywood, Loughrea, North Kildare, Tullamore and Wicklow, to name just a few

Buccanneers RFC mini rugby.

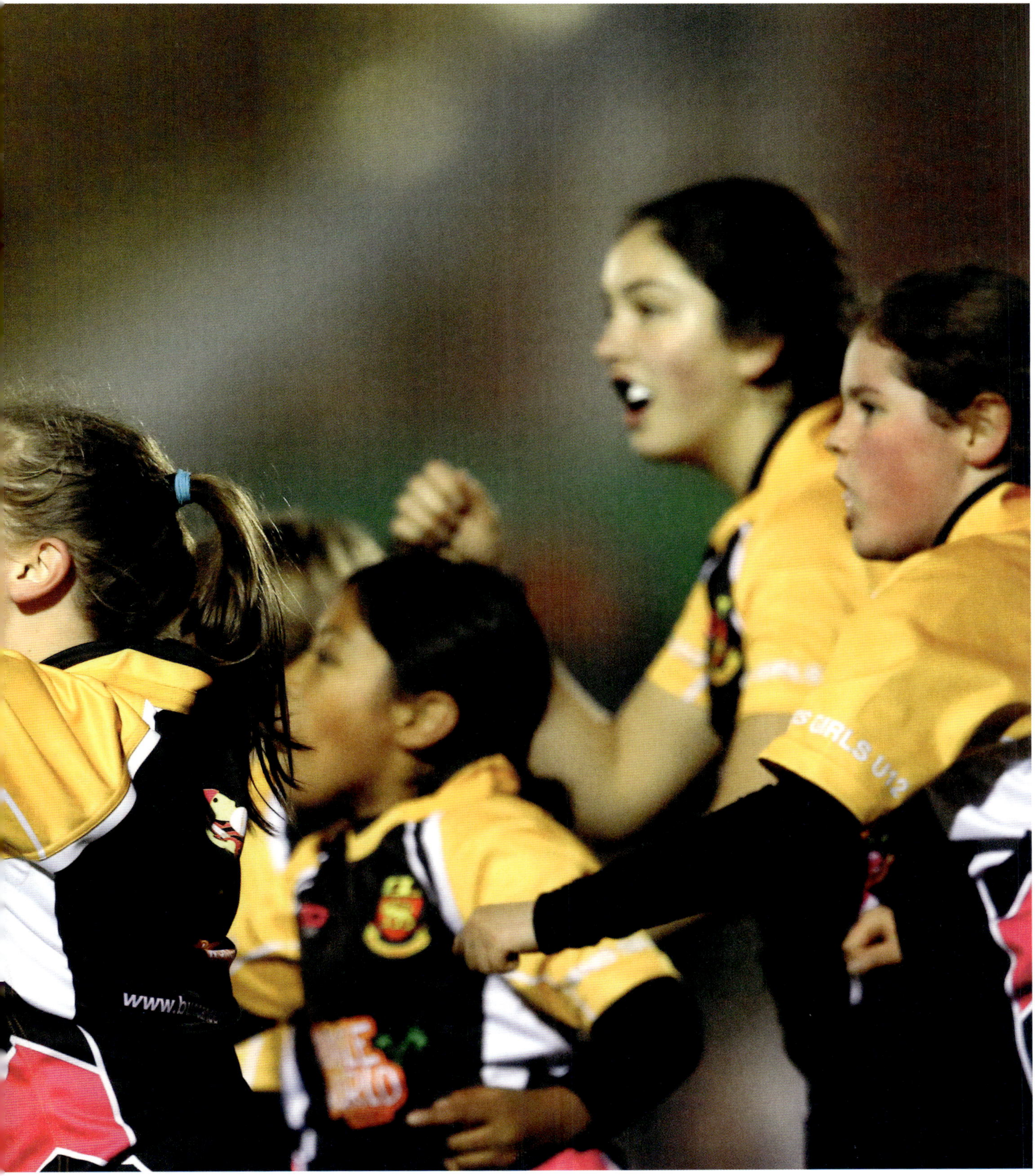

clubs. It is growing a new audience and demographic for Irish rugby.

A CINDERELLA STORY

In recent years the club game has produced a real fairytale story.

In 2023 Clogher Valley Rugby Club made history. The Co. Tyrone club that had been formed just 33 years before beat Richmond 31–17 to win the All-Ireland League play-off final, meaning that Clogher Valley had qualified to play senior all-Ireland rugby for the first time. The area has a population of between five and eight thousand people.

Clogher Valley RFC was formed in 1990. The club was born out of players who had left Fivemiletown High School in June 1980 and came back to play the school side for a Christmas match in December. The rules then changed, and under-18s could not play against over-18s, so a team from the Clogher/Augher area played those from the Fivemiletown/Brookeborough area. Towards the end of the 1980s the two teams combined to play the Prison Service on an Easter Monday.

A plan was hatched to form a team and play within the Ulster league. Clogher Valley entered the bottom league (Minor League 8) in 1990. After winning that league (winning some games by 50–100 points), the team jumped up into Minor League 5. After winning this league (again by quite a margin) it moved up 15 leagues to Junior Qualifying 5.

The Valley kept up the winning streak. They won Qualifying 5, then Q4, then Q3, moving into Q2. A few seasons later they entered Q1 and, despite a wobble in the early 2000s, were in the Junior Q1 League (now the Ulster Championship) for many years.

Clogher Valley players celebrate with the AIL Junior Cup, 2023.

As the club developed, additional teams were added: a 2nd XV, then a 3rd XV, an under-18, an under-16 and an under-14. In 2005 the minis entered the club history books. In 2012 the girls joined the ranks of the club, and in 2021 the first senior women's team played in Valley colours.

One of the club's founding members, Gordon Montgomery, has explained that

> the ethos of Clogher Valley RFC is to be at the centre of the community. While we follow the rugby code and promote fairness, discipline, control and respect – both on and off the pitch – we are a community club in a rural community. Being part of the Clogher Valley community is important to the club, and this can be seen in the club's involvement with mud runs, colour runs, charity events and our involvement with the Fivemiletown Festival.
>
> From a rugby stance, we must promote the culture of respect, fairness, teamwork, sportsmanship, discipline and enjoyment. This is not just among those on the pitch but in the stands, from coaching staff and support staff. We want visitors to leave CVRFC knowing they had a tough game but we were a pleasure to play against and to visit.

Clogher Valley illustrates a subtle shift that has taken place in many clubs. It is apparent in relation to the exercise of power: 'power over' has yielded to 'power with'. A recent innovation is the appointment of a club chaplain. His role is not to preach but to support those in need in times of bereavement, crisis or mental health challenges.

According to the club webmaster Stephen Hetherington, there has been one invaluable resource in establishing the club so firmly in the community. For him, Clogher Valley is

> a club at the heart of the community. Social media helps that hugely. We have 4,500 followers on Facebook, 2,500 on Instagram and up to 150,000 following our TikTok activities, and we have people following us in places as far away as Indonesia, Pakistan and Canada. We have so much exposure in the local community through our posts on social media, and this has cemented our place in the community, particularly among young people – with young females as much as with young males – and that is one of the reasons why we had such an explosion of involvement of women in the club. This is very much reflected in our committees. We have seen that they beat us men hands down in terms of organisational skills.

Inclusion and diversity have become buzzwords in Irish life, but as the former president Bob Beatty explains, they are much more than words in the club.

> None of us have a clue how many Protestants and Catholics are involved in the club. Nobody asks about religion here. One of the most positive developments is that we now have a cross-border dimension because there are a growing number of young girls and boys from Cavan and Monaghan joining us. We transcend barriers of religion, class, gender, politics and the border.

Presentation Brothers College vs
Christian Brothers College, 2024

9

BRICKS IN THE RUGBY WALL

A great democratic revolution has taken place in recent years that has seen rugby played in swathes of schools across the country – for fun and also competitively. The schools and the underage structures are pivotal to the architecture of Irish rugby.

Historically, the schools have been at the heart of Irish rugby. The role of members of the Catholic clergy in schools throughout the Free State and, later, the Republic was crucial to all of this.

Competitive rugby in Ireland began in the schools. Ulster got to the party first with the Ulster Schools Cup in 1876. This was followed by Leinster in 1887, Munster in 1909 and Connacht in 1913. The Leinster Schools Cup has become an essential part of both sporting and social life in Ireland. Tony O'Reilly described it as the 'finest sporting engagement on the face of the earth'.

JUST A LAD OF 18 SUMMERS

A wonderful photograph shows the 15-year-old Kevin Barry playing rugby at Lansdowne Road in 1917. It captures him about to score a try for his school, Belvedere College, and help defeat Blackrock College in the Leinster Schools Rugby Junior Cup final.

Kevin Barry.

Three years later he would be dead, hanged at Mountjoy Jail for his role in a deadly ambush of British soldiers in central Dublin during the War of Independence. Barry was born in Dublin in 1902. His family had a farm in Co. Carlow and a dairy in Fleet Street, Dublin. He attended primary school in Rathvilly, Co. Carlow, and then progressed to St Mary's College in Rathmines before transferring to Belvedere College. At the age of 15 he joined the Dublin Brigade of the Irish Volunteers.

In October 1920 he was convicted by court-martial of killing Private Marshall Whitehead, a 19-year-old from Yorkshire, in a raid in September on a military lorry outside Monk's Bakery in Church Street. Two other soldiers were killed, one aged 20 and the other 15 (although the British thought he was 19). The soldiers were collecting bread for delivery to Collinstown Aerodrome (now Dublin Airport). They were the first military fatalities inflicted by the IRA in Dublin in 1920.

After Barry's court-martial his fate hung in the balance. Tensions in Ireland were already running close to boiling point, especially during the lengthy hunger strike in Brixton Prison of Terence MacSwiney, Lord Mayor of Cork. Calls for mercy for Barry came from unexpected quarters. The Unionist Sir James Campbell, Lord Chancellor of Ireland, who had lost a son in the war, argued that Barry's extreme youth was crucial and that he had clearly been manipulated by older men. A contributory factor to the cross-party support were the pictures of the boy in his distinctive black-and-white hooped Belvedere College rugby jersey. They showed a player who resembled so many British public schoolboys and university students lost during the First World War. It was also significant in headlines across the world that he was a medical student. His execution by hanging, carried out at the prison by John Ellis on 1 November 1920, inflamed Irish public opinion and was a pivotal event in the battle for independence.

It remains a matter of great pride that Barry played for Old Belvedere in the 1919/20 season, and as long as the club has been in existence his photograph has adorned the walls of the clubhouse. He is also memorialised by the annual match between Belvedere College and Old Belvedere under-20s, which is played for the Kevin Barry Trophy.

BELVO

Fr Peter McVerry is one of the best-known people in Irish life because of his campaigning work for the homeless. Before he began this work he taught in Belvedere College, where he was persuaded to coach the rugby team, which included a teenager who was to become one of Ireland's greatest rugby players: Ollie Campbell. The teenage number 10 was a big fan of McVerry's. 'We thought he was great and knew everything about rugby.'

Belvedere celebrate as captain Aoife Ryan lifts the All-Ireland League Division 1 trophy, 2014.

An impressive framed painting of Belvedere College graces Campbell's apartment and is a small sign of the affection he feels for his alma mater.

> To my shame, I mostly associate Belvedere simply with rugby ... When we lost a first-round Junior Cup match 6–3 against Newbridge I cried for three days. When I became an adult and played for Ireland I was much more mature about the whole thing: whenever we lost an international I only cried for one day!

For Campbell, the Leinster Cup wins

> in both 1971 and 1972 were incredible thrills. After the first victory I took ... the mud from Lansdowne Road from my boots and kept it in a plastic bag as a souvenir. I only threw it out a few years ago. Although she never missed her brothers playing, my mother only ever saw me play three times. I was small as a kid, and the first time she saw me play she was afraid I would be killed. When I became an international she would turn on the radio from time to time during the game to see if my name was mentioned. When it was she knew at least I was still alive. That was really all she was concerned about.

Rugby was in Campbell's genes. His maternal uncles had won Leinster Cups with Belvedere College.

> My uncle Michael was captain of the Belvo winning team of 1946, so my maternal grandmother is the only mother in the history of Belvedere to have presented the Senior Cup twice: to her eldest son, Seamus Henry, my uncle and godfather – captain of the 1938 cup-winning team – and again eight years later to her youngest son.

Seamus captained Suttonians to their last Metro Cup win in 1947, when they were only a minor club. Campbell's father was also on that team as prop. His father played minor football with Louth, but after he left school he went to live in Howth and joined Suttonians, where he met his wife, Joan. It was his father who bought Campbell his first leather ball.

Cian Healy of Belvedere, 2005.

I was only five or six and he said, 'If you can catch this you can keep it.' I did! He only missed one international between Ireland and Scotland in over forty years. The gap was caused by the birth of my sister. I always thought it was a very weak excuse! My father was hugely supportive right through my career. It was he who taught me the skill of tackling.

At school not only was I not a kicker in terms of kicking for goal but I hardly kicked in play at all and was not even responsible for 25-yard drop-outs or kick-offs or restarts. Times change! When I played my first game for Old Belvedere firsts after I left school and we scored a try, the captain assumed that, because I was playing fly-half, I was a kicker. So I just did what other fly-halves do, and it sailed through. And that's how it started. After that it became something of an obsession to perfect the art of place-kicking, and I practised endlessly. I figured everybody else had been taking place-kicks right through their school days, so I had to make up for ten years' lost ground.

Schools rugby also gave Campbell much of his philosophy of life, as is evident in the frequency with which he quotes his main coach in Belvedere, Jim Moran: 'Rugby is like having an international passport and an international language. It is not an end in itself but a means to an end, the end being the people we meet and the friends that we make', 'After every shipwreck there is enough wood to build a raft' and 'The meaning of life comes from the meaning we put into it.'

RIVALRIES

The Leinster Cup has generated rivalries such as that between Belvedere and Blackrock. One of the most important iterations came on 17 March 1954, when a Blackrock team captained by Niall Brophy, one of the greatest Irish wingers, came up against Tony O'Reilly's Belvo.

Belvedere also provided a nursery for O'Reilly's entrepreneurial skills. When he was seven he was the only boy in his class to make Holy Communion. To mark the occasion, a priest gave him an orange – a luxury during the war years. Like most of his friends, O'Reilly had never seen an orange. He later claimed: 'After I ate the centre I sold the peel for one penny per piece, thereby showing a propensity for commercial deception which has not left me since!'

Coached at Belvedere College by the legendary Karl Mullen, O'Reilly played his first match when he was six. His mother asked a priest what he thought of the young players on show. The priest had no idea who she was and answered: 'The red fellow's the best.' She glowed with pride: that red fellow was her son. Such was his impact that when he played in an under-nines match, with the team leading 30–6 at half-time, the coach told him to give the opposition a chance and pass the ball more. The young O'Reilly answered, 'Ah, Father, you're only wasting your time. If I pass it they'll just knock it on or drop it.'

In his last year in Belvedere, O'Reilly scored 42 tries in 21 matches – a school record. He captained the school to the Leinster Cup final only to see his side lose 11–3. He claimed it was the biggest disappointment of his life at that time – and 'almost since'!

Blackrock College players celebrate winning the Schools Rugby Cup, 2006.

O'Reilly likes to quote a conversation he once had with the surgeon Bob O'Connell: 'You always know Blackrock boys. They rattle.'

'With what?' O'Reilly asked.

'With medals,' he was told. 'Big boys, small boys, fat boys and tall boys – they all have medals.'

There was further drama after that losing match for O'Reilly: 'My mother refused to speak to me for nine months after the event, because she had bought a new hat and didn't get the chance to present the Cup.'

STEPPING STONES

Joseph James Barnett was capped 12 times in the centre for Ireland between 1899 and 1903. He has the distinction of being Ireland's first scorer in the twentieth century: he dropped a goal against England in 1900 – Ireland's only score that season. At the tender age of 18 he won his first cap for Ireland while still at Campbell College in Belfast. Ireland went on to win the Triple Crown that season – though he was forced to miss the final match against Wales because of mumps. He died at the age of 26 in 1907.

Barnett is one of many examples showing that the schools have generated a pathway for many players to the Irish team. The former Ireland captain Phillip Matthews was born in Gloucester and had his first introduction to rugby at lunchtime at school when he was eight. He left his mark on proceedings by scoring a try – at the wrong end! Soccer was in his family tree: his father, Mike, had a trial with Stoke City. In 1969 his English father and Irish mother took the family to Newtownards at a time when the Troubles were starting in Northern Ireland.

Matthews was educated at Regent House Grammar School in Newtownards, Co. Down. There he would meet two

Christian Brothers College huddle

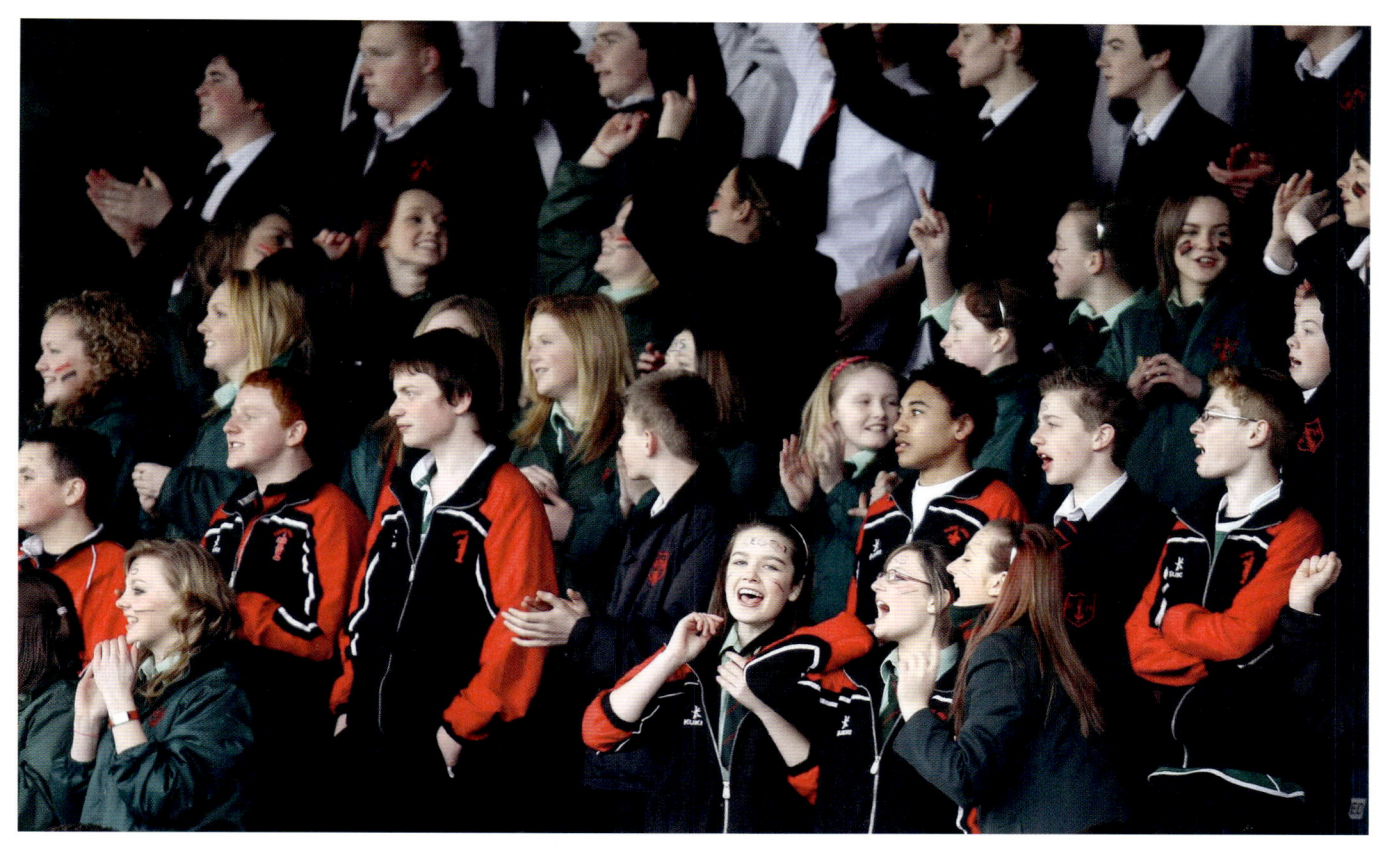

Regent House supporters, 2006.

people – one a teacher, Dave McMaster; the other a student, Nigel Carr – who would play a prominent role in his life. The fruits of McMaster's success as a coach were plain to see in the fact that Matthews played on the Irish schoolboys' side for two seasons, captaining the team in his second year against an Australian side that included the Ella Brothers and Tony Melrose. In 1985 Matthews would become a key member of the Irish team that won the Triple Crown.

Another former Irish captain, Donal Lenihan, cuts an imposing figure. As was so often the case his rugby career owes a huge amount to his school, CBC Cork, and to the influence of one man, Br Philip O'Reilly, who put a string of internationals through his hands. After captaining his school to Munster Junior and Senior Schools titles, Lenihan was capped for the Irish Schools. He would follow this up with caps at under-23, B and full level.

> I never lost a Cup match at school. My parents had never been at a rugby match until I started playing, but they got swept away by the fanaticism of the schools final in Musgrave Park. For my first Irish schools match my teammates included Hugo MacNeill, Paul Dean, Brian McCall and Phillip Matthews. My father told me nothing could top his feeling of pride that day seeing me walk out in my Irish jersey.

In 1963 the former Tánaiste Dick Spring began his secondary education as a boarder in Cistercian College, Roscrea. There he was introduced to rugby, but his love affair with the game was not immediate.

> For the first two-and-a-half years I only played Gaelic football and hurling. I couldn't understand what those mad fellas were doing playing rugby, especially with all that wallowing in the muck. In my third year, though, I discovered that the rugby guys got good grub, hot showers and trips to Dublin.

> I was getting disillusioned with playing Gaelic games, especially after a match in Abbeyleix, where the pitch was also used for grazing sheep and cattle. You can imagine what I was covered in at the end of the match! As if that wasn't bad

Sligo Grammar players celebrate after the Senior A Cup semi-final, 2020.

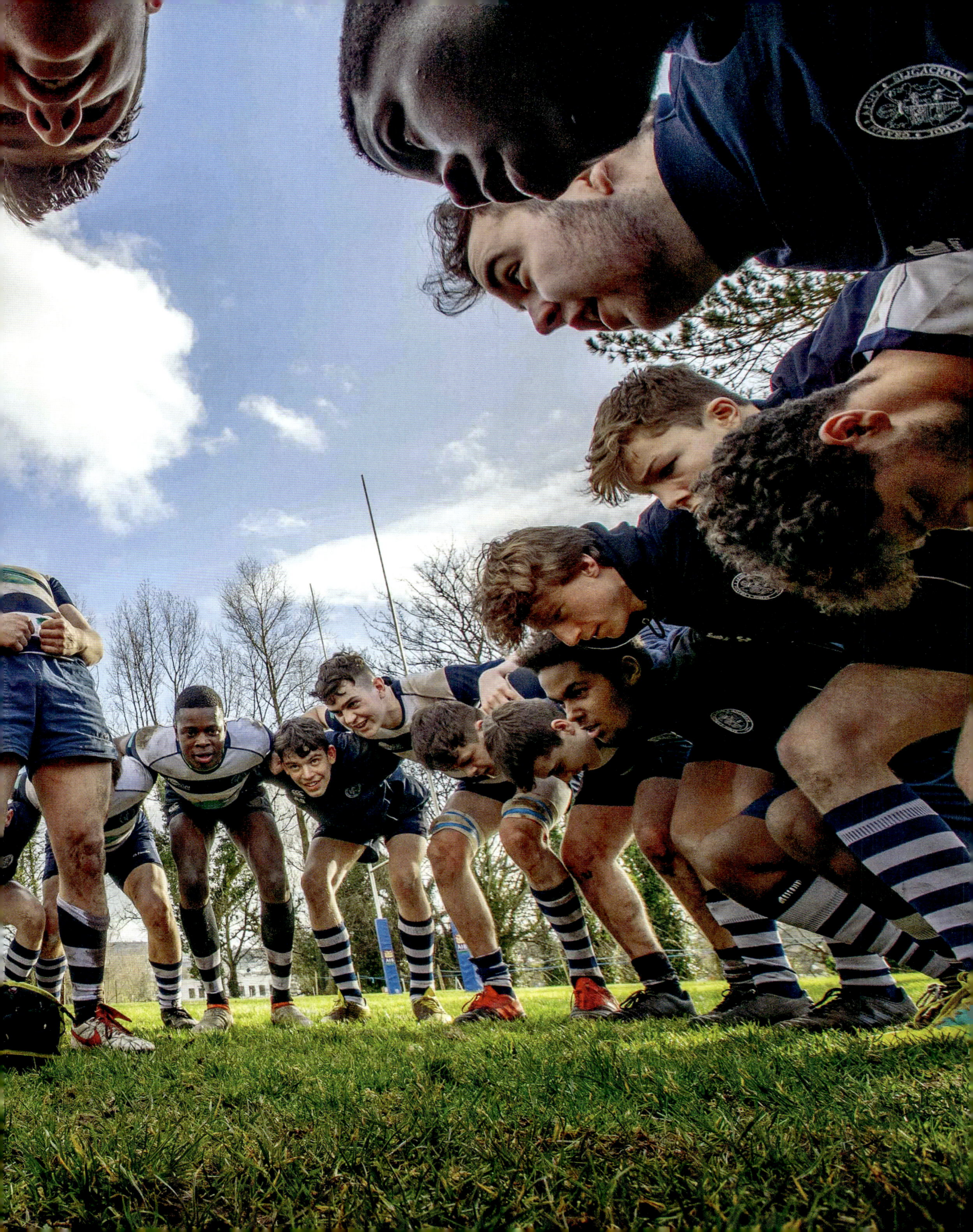

enough, all we had in the way of washing facilities afterwards was one cold tap for the entire team.

My schoolboy memories are mainly of the matches we lost. I remember losing a quarter-final of the Junior Cup to De La Salle, Churchtown, in a high-scoring game for them, 3–0! Coincidentally, a generation later they beat my son's Roscrea side 5–3. Some things never change.

We also lost a Cup quarter-final to Newbridge. Their side featured two players who would later be my teammates at Lansdowne: the one and only – thank God – Mick Quinn, who was only up to my navel at the time; and Paddy Boylan, who later became one of the great stalwarts of Lansdowne.

Spring's brother Donal also played with Cistercian Roscrea and captained Ireland Schools in their first international in Lansdowne Road.

Ciaran Fitzgerald, John Muldoon, Noel Mannion and Ray McLoughlin are just some of the former Irish internationals who attended Garbally College in Ballinasloe. The 'voice of rugby', Bill McLaren, described McLoughlin as 'one of the greatest prop-forwards in the history of the game' and 'one of its finest minds'. McLoughlin won 40 Irish caps, toured twice with the Lions and captained Ireland in the mid-1960s. Although he was well known in professional circles for his business activities, he got a first-class honours degree in chemical engineering. He applied scientific principles to his time as Ireland captain. What is often forgotten is that he coached the forwards during part of Tom Kiernan's reign. He did it in a low-profile way and kept well out of the limelight.

At Garbally, McLoughlin came under the influence of a wonderful coach and educationalist, Fr Kevin Ryle, who was a brilliant judge of character and potential. He coached both athletics and rugby and got athletes to play rugby and vice versa. At one stage he persuaded Harold Connolly, an Irish American who was then the world champion hammer thrower, to come to the school to give the students a demonstration. Another time he persuaded no less a player than the Welsh legend Cliff Morgan to give the team a coaching lesson. Such was Fr Ryle's desire to learn that he was constantly seeking new ideas. He got permission from his bishop to attend the 1960 Olympics, but the bishop attached a condition: Fr Ryle was forbidden from watching the women swimming in case his morals were corrupted!

As a PE teacher at Holy Faith Clontarf, Fiona Coghlan is keenly aware of the importance of schools to the development of the women's game.

> I moved a few years ago from a mixed school to an all-girls' school. I introduced rugby to the school, and it has really taken off. If we are to get more girls playing the game, the schools have a huge part to play … It is great to see the way the game is spreading into new schools all round the country. The fee-paying schools in the past made a huge contribution to the spread of the men's game, and the new schools today have a huge role in spreading the women's game.

Fiona Steed has a similar view.

> It won't be like what schools like Blackrock College or St Michael's have done for the men's game in terms of providing an assembly line of talent for the national team, but the schools are a wonderful opportunity for us to grow the game for girls. It is beginning to happen already, but this trend will accelerate in the coming years.

> Even for girls in the smaller schools they can now dream of putting on the green jersey. And that was one of the great things about the fact that now Ireland's Six Nations games are on free-to-air television, so everyone can watch them. When Ireland won the Grand Slam, girls could turn on the TV or go to the games and see women that looked like them and so many strong women out there doing amazing, incredible things.

ALL THINGS BEING EQUAL

The tennis legend Arthur Ashe once said, 'You learn about equality in history and civics, but you find out life is not really like that.' Tony Ward understood this sentiment. He juxtaposed his rugby career with his role as a teacher.

> In my first season playing for Ireland I was also doing my teaching practice in Ballyfermot Vocational School. I remember the Monday morning after an international going to school on

the 18 bus. I had to bring a group to the swimming pool, and there was a supervisor waiting for me. I was still struggling with the aches and pains of the previous Saturday, and the last thing I needed was that kind of pressure.

The Ballyfermot experience was as much an education for Ward as for the pupils he taught. It was a real eye-opener for him to be in daily contact with kids who came to school without any breakfast. It was one thing to read about it in the papers; it was quite another to see its human faces. One incident encapsulated the harsh lessons Ward had to learn about the inequalities that bedevil Irish life.

Every Friday evening I had a geography class in one of the prefabs. Out of the corner of my eye I noticed a paper bag at the back of the class, and it was moving. Suddenly it started clucking. I naturally asked what a hen was doing in my class, to be told that the principal had given permission for it to be there. I discovered that the daily egg from this hen played a crucial part in the family's diet, and on Fridays there was no one in the family home to mind the hen, so one of the children brought it into school in case it would be stolen. The idea of a hen in the class seemed funny at first, but it was very, very sad, though real, to hear that people had to eke out an existence in this way.

It was a great lesson to learn so early on about what life is really like for so many people. That boy could have had the skills of Brian O'Driscoll or Paul O'Connell, but he would not have played rugby. Why? He was preconditioned to think of the game as being for the wealthy elite who attended fee-pay schools and 'not for the likes of him'.

One of the most positive developments in my lifetime has been the way rugby has spread out to so-called 'non-traditional rugby schools'. In recent years Irish rugby has been massively enriched by sourcing players such as Seán O'Brien and Tadhg Furlong from the non-traditional areas. Schools have a crucial role to play in bringing rugby to all girls and boys today, and the better we do that, the more success both our national teams will have.

LIFE COACH

What is sometimes forgotten is the number of coaches who have cut their teeth in schools rugby, such as Eddie O'Sullivan and Declan Kidney.

When Joe Schmidt was 24 he opted to take a year overseas. He and his wife, Kellie, moved to Mullingar, Co.

Declan Kidney and Eddie O'Sullivan.

Westmeath. He played for the local club and was persuaded to do some coaching at Wilson's Hospital school. That year Wilson's Hospital made the A final of the Schools Cup for the first time. They won and scored five tries, 'throwing the ball around'. Schmidt can still remember the names of the lads who got them. His briefs to the players are the stuff of legend, including the instruction to one aspiring star : 'Don't smoke in the showers.'

Schmidt believes coaches are like magpies: they take 'shiny bits from wherever they've been and keep adding to the nest. I have no doubt some of the things I believe in now come from the time I spent in Westmeath'.

UNIVERSITY CHALLENGE

While being hugely appreciative of the role of the schools in the development of Irish rugby, the IRFU has always recognised that there was a need to have bridges between the schools and the senior international team. In 1975 Ireland played its first B international against France B in Lansdowne Road in a 9–6 win. The match was memorable for the fact that four players were sent off. In the 1992/3 season, B internationals were designated as A.

The universities were, and are, one thread of the tapestry. Andy Courtney, who was born in Nenagh and graduated from UCD, became the first person from UCD to represent Ireland in rugby when he finished on the losing side against the Scots in the Edinburgh suburb of Inverleith back in 1920. He had republican leanings and, according to legend, threw a military motorbike into the Liffey while being pursued by the Black and Tans after the funeral of Thomas Ashe, who had died on hunger strike in 1917. On another occasion he gave a British platoon the slip while they surrounded the field where he was playing in College Park. He casually jogged past the cordon with his fellow players and promptly made his escape via the Turkish baths in Dawson Street.

James 'Jammie' Clinch's father, Andrew, was a wing-forward and won 10 caps for Ireland between 1892 and 1897, playing in all the 1896 matches, which saw Ireland win the championship for the first time, and in all four

UCD women's team, 1993.

BRICKS IN THE RUGBY WALL | 223

Tests against South Africa during the 1896 Lions tour. Jammie spent seven years at Trinity, though he never graduated, and his father famously said that he had sent his son to university for the rugby, not the education. In response, Jammie replied, 'What a wonderful father to have.' He won 30 caps for Ireland. In 1926 he played a prominent role on the team, which was narrowly beaten by Wales for the Triple Crown, and he toured with the Lions to South Africa in 1924, making the Clinches the first Irish father and son to tour with the Lions.

The Irish Universities played their first international against Scottish Universities in Ravenhill in March 1954 and had their first tour to New Zealand in 1978. In 1990 the Irish Students, a cross-fertilisation of colleges and university players, played Argentina and Scotland.

Brian O'Driscoll is one of the many players to have benefited from a rugby university education.

> One of the best pieces of advice I've ever been given was from my old coach in UCD, Lee Smith. Lee always wrote out a couple of sentences on a piece of paper for each player before a match telling you what he wanted you to do and what your role on the team was. But when he came round to me he said, 'Just go out and play your own game.' Such a small thing made a big difference and inspired me and gave me a lot of confidence to go out and play well because I thought very highly of Lee, and I still do.

It helps that the universities have had the benefit of great coaches. The former Ireland coach Roland 'Roly' Meates, a noted scrum guru, was interviewed for the position of

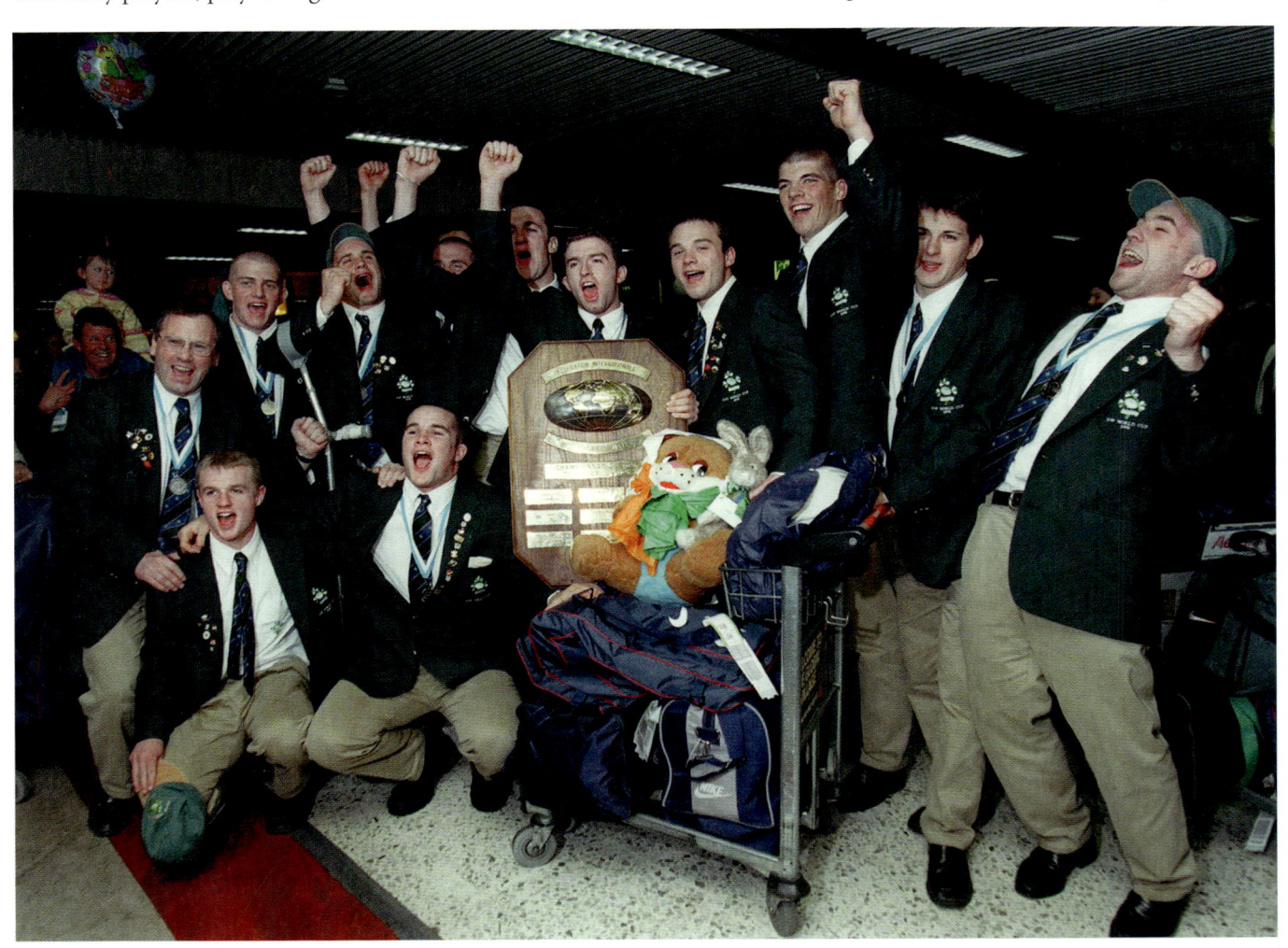

Ireland's Under-19s team, 1998.

Lions coach for their historic tour to New Zealand in 1971, only to lose out to the legendary Welsh coach Carwyn James. A former prop at the college, Meates coached Trinity for 30 years from 1966 to 1996.

BUILDING BRIDGES

Underage teams are crucial links between the schools scene and the senior side. In 1980 it was decided to initiate an under-20s interprovincial series later that decade. Youth interprovincials for under-18s were also introduced. On 11 April 1992 Ireland played Scotland at the Sports Ground in Galway in their first youth international. In 1988 they had their first under-21 international in Lansdowne Road in a 22–13 win over Italy. A milestone came in 1989 when Ireland under-21s drew 13–13 against the All Blacks. In 1995/6 the Irish team, coached by Eddie O'Sullivan, won their first Triple Crown at the under-21 level.

Ireland's first under-23 match came in October 1979 against a full Holland side in Hilversum. Ireland won 31–3, with Moss Finn contributing 15 points.

The first under-25 Irish international came in a 50–25 victory over Canada in September 1986. Ireland Youths (Under 18) played their first international in a 4–0 defeat to Scotland in 1992 in the Sports Ground.

At under-19 level Ireland had their first international in a 39–20 win over Portugal in 1997. Ireland competed in the World Youths Cup (under-19s) for the first time in 1997 and, with Declan Kidney in charge, won the World Cup in 1998 in France. The winning squad was:

BACKS

Kieran Campbell	London Irish
Aidan Considine	Bective Rangers
Matthew Cupitt	Instonians
Darragh Holt	UCC
David Mescal	Ballina/UCG
Shane Moore (capt.)	UCD
Barry McCracken	CIYMS
Brian O'Driscoll	UCD
John Reynolds	Watsonians
Brendan Ronan	CBC Cork
Donovan Rossi	Clontarf
Paddy Wallace	Campbell College

FORWARDS

Damien Broughall	UCD
Brian Cahill	UCC
Neil Coughlan	UCD
Conor Fitzgerald	Garryowen
Adrian Flavin	London Irish
Aidan Kearney	St Michael's College
Chris McCarey	Ballymena
Andy O'Brien	UCD
Donncha O'Callaghan	Cork Con
Frank Roche	Bohemians
Chris Schofield	Bangor
Joey Sheahan	PBC Cork
Ben Urquhart	Methodist College
Chris Good	RBAI

The Ireland national under-20 rugby team was formed in 2006, having previously been known as the under-21 team. They have won the Grand Slam five times, in 2007, 2010, 2019, 2022 and 2023. They won a Grand Slam title for the second year running under head coach Richie Murphy in 2023. They followed the lead of their senior counterparts in completing the clean sweep by edging England in front of a sold-out Musgrave Park. It was a special weekend for the Sexton family: a day after his older brother, Johnny, captained Ireland to the country's fourth senior Grand Slam, Mark was part of the under-20s coaching team.

The team was peppered with potential stars of the future. Keith Wood, a man noted for his aversion to hyping young players prematurely, went public with his suggestion that the team's playmaker and fly-half, Sam Prendergast, ought to be considered for selection on the senior team's World Cup squad that autumn. Quite the compliment.

In July 2023 Ireland again reached the Under-20s Rugby World Cup final in South Africa, only to lose to France. Despite the defeat, the future is bright for many of the players.

The tournament was overshadowed by tragedy. Before Ireland's 47–27 victory over Fiji, the team wore black armbands as a mark of respect after the deaths of two Irish teenagers in Greece who were known to a number of the squad. Then, the day before the game, it emerged that the Munster Rugby elite performance officer, Greig Oliver, father of squad member Jack Oliver, had passed away after an accident in Cape Town, where he had been supporting his son.

A potent example of the importance of the underage structure to the development of Irish rugby is the Irish side that reached the 2016 Under-20s World Cup final, which beat New Zealand in the process. Although they lost the final to a powerful English team, the squad featured such future Irish internationals as Jacob Stockdale, Shane Daly, Hugo Keenan, Andrew Porter, James Ryan, Max Deegan, Jimmy O'Brien and Will Connors. The side also included the 2022 World Sevens Player of the Year, Terry Kennedy.

While the 2019 team did not have the same impact at the World Rugby Under-20s Championships, it nonetheless brought such players as Ryan Baird, Craig Casey and Niall Murray to the fore. Matt Williams contends that Ireland now has the best pathway in world rugby from the underage structure to the senior side.

Sam Prendergast scores a try at the World Rugby Under-20 Championships, South Africa, 2023.

Ollie Campbell has sung a hymn of praise to the underage success.

> The IRFU deserve great credit for the effectiveness of the system set up to nurture young Irish talent in the professional era. It is a fantastic system in place. When they came out of the schools, very talented players were put into foundation and academy programmes. In my day we did lose an awful lot of young players.
>
> The IRFU have had the foresight not just to develop the talented players in terms of skills and fitness but to look after them and give them the right advice towards getting their careers up and running.
>
> When I was a player, beating the All Blacks seemed like an impossible dream: they were the gold standard. Since 2016, though, it has happened with a frequency that I find dizzying. Ireland have spent many weeks as the world's number one ranked team in the world. This is a momentous change and it has not happened by accident. It reflects the great work that has been done by so many wonderful coaches throughout the underage system.

Tony Ward agrees:

> Ireland have always been pretty successful at underage level, but since professionalism has come in, players have come through more at a hugely impressive rate. In the case of Leinster it's almost been breathtaking – a bit like an assembly line.
>
> When professionalism came in, the IRFU had two options: take the long-term view or the short-term approach. Scotland are an example of a country that tried to take short cuts by scouring the southern hemisphere for what some people call 'rugby mercenaries' that could play for them. Just look and wince at what good that did them.
>
> Ireland have taken the long-term view and have reaped the harvest they deserved from those seeds they sowed so lovingly. The provincial academies have been critical in that respect. Take the example of the U19s World Cup–winning side from 1998 and the players that came through on the Irish senior side from them, like Paddy Wallace and Donncha O'Callaghan and, of course, he who walked on water: Brian O'Driscoll.

For his part, O'Driscoll sees the underage system as having been pivotal to Ireland's success in recent years.

> In the 1990s Ireland lost more games than we won. That situation was reversed in the noughties. A big reason for that was the number of great players like Ronan O'Gara and Peter Stringer, who came through the ranks from the underage teams and had tasted success with the schoolboys, under-19s and under-21s. They expected to beat teams like England and France when they played for the senior team because they had done so often at underage level, and they brought that confidence with them, which previous Irish teams did not have. They also brought the benefits of years of good coaching and physical conditioning. So the underage structures have to take huge credit for the upturn in Ireland's fortunes in recent times.

These young players will safeguard Irish rugby history.

An Ireland fan at the third Test match against New Zealand, 2022.

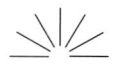

10

THE BEST IS YET TO COME

LOOKING BACK

Irish rugby can look back on the last 150 years with pride.

From its humble beginnings in Trinity College in 1874, its small acorns have grown into a great oak. Of course, there have been many setbacks on the journey, but even in the most turbulent times there have been great characters – and none more so than Willie Duggan. He will always be celebrated for both his talent and his bravery. Phil Bennett, as captain of the Lions team that toured New Zealand in 1977, needed players willing to shed blood for the cause. He found one in Duggan. During one match Duggan was so battered and bloodied that he went off for stitches just before half-time. When the rest of the team came into the dressing room, they saw him sitting there with a fag in one hand and a bottle of beer in the other as they stitched up his face. 'Bad luck, Willie. Well played,' Bennett said.

'What do you mean?' Willie demanded. 'As soon as the f**ker sorts my face out I'll be back on.'

On the tour Duggan played for the Lions against a Māori team in a very physical contest. At one stage he was trapped at the bottom of a ruck when a few players kicked him on his head. True to form, he got up and carried on. After the game Bennett asked him whether he remembered the pounding on his head. His reply was vintage Duggan: 'I do. I heard it.'

*

Irish rugby has produced many comic moments off the pitch. In 1974 Ireland had what was then a rare Five Nations Championship success. The highlight was unquestionably against England in Twickenham in 1974. Although Ireland won 26–21, they faced England as underdogs.

The Irish players were about to run onto the pitch when they were stopped in the tunnel by an official in a blazer who had the archetypal RAF moustache. He said, 'Tally ho, boys. Tally ho. The BBC cameras are not ready for you yet.'

The Irish lads were just itching to get on the pitch and found the waiting a pain, particularly when they were joined in the tunnel by the English team. Their opponents were led by their captain, John Pullin, who was shouting at his team about Waterloo. The Irish players could not understand what Waterloo had to do with them. They were studiously trying to avoid eye contact with their opposition. However, Tony Neary of England went over and tapped Moss Keane on the shoulder and said, 'Moss, best of luck. May the best team win.'

Keane growled back, 'I f***ing hope not!'

MOVING FORWARD

A recurring feature of Irish rugby is its capacity to look ahead and become a crucible of innovation, as in its imaginative recalibration of its use of the provincial structures. Few rugby nations can match Ireland when it comes to underage structures. In 2023 the Irish under-20s won the Grand Slam for the second successive year and reached the World Cup final. There are therefore solid reasons to be hopeful that many more good days will follow. Ireland's love affair with rugby will continue.

Above all, the great constant of Irish rugby has been its capacity to produce great players. Willie John McBride. Ciaran Fitzgerald. Fiona Coghlan. Paul O'Connell. They watched history. They made history. They became history.

*

Trophies are one measure of success, but there are others that are less easy to quantify. Many former players judge their careers not only in terms of caps or trophies but also of friendships.

Fiona Steed is keenly aware of this.

> I was very privileged to play for Munster and Ireland. The reward for me was not money but in the many great friends I made. I fell in love with rugby. I fell in love through rugby.

In the past, Irish rugby was seen to be a bastion of male privilege. Rugby games today are much more likely to be family outings. Inclusion and diversity are actually lived on Irish rugby pitches and terraces and not are not just empty phrases.

The evolving Irish rugby story continues to navigate to new shores and is increasingly responding to the wider issues in Irish society. Such internationals as Hannah Tyrrell, Jack McGrath, Tadhg Furlong and James Lowe have shown leadership in Ireland's mental health crisis through their involvement in the Tackle Your Feelings campaign and talking publicly, with incredible honesty and bravery, of their own struggles.

There are countless examples of players getting involved in charity work. In 2023 the former Irish captain Rory Best did a 10-day walk across Ireland to raise €2 million for a child cancer charity. Andrew Porter is an ambassador for the Cancer Society, Garry Ringrose supports the LauraLynn Children's Hospice and Andrew Trimble is an Oxfam Ireland Ambassador. Linda Djougang's advocacy for the Black Lives Matter movement is powerful, and Kathryn Dane is leading the way in tackling safety issues in the women's game.

NO THEM AND US

Perhaps the greatest service that Irish rugby has given the country in the past 150 years is being a rare unifying force. In a county in which a 'them' and 'us' mentality has been a recurring feature, rugby has offered an alternative vision and showcased a different path. Long before the word 'inclusive' entered the vernacular, Irish rugby was sculpting a model of unity in diversity and of diversity in unity. In the process it offered a symbol of hope and fellowship across borders and through conflicts. In the landscape of Irish rugby, the divisions of nation and rank – the oppressions of dogma and tradition – are swept aside, and all band together in solidarity.

For better or worse, international sport is shrouded in symbols of nationalism: the badge, the emblem, the flag, the anthem. In 1995 the IRFU sought to transcend this by commissioning the songwriter Phil Coulter to write 'Ireland's Call', which focused on the harmony of 'the four proud provinces of Ireland'.

Irish rugby has never produced a more loved character than Moss Keane, whose defining characteristic was his keen intelligence, evident in the speed with which he could complete the *Irish Times* crossword. He spent most of his life trying to disguise his intelligence, but there were times when the mask slipped. Once he was asked what it was like to share a dressing room with players from a unionist tradition and with a British passport. Quick as a flash Moss replied, 'There are no borders in the Irish dressing room.'

Like a rowing boat, Irish rugby moves forward while looking back. Though we cannot predict what will happen in the next generations, we can hope that in the coming years the rich legacy of Irish rugby will continue to reach towards something profound.

What can be said with confidence is that Irish rugby heads into its next 150 years in a position of strength and with the necessary components to create a vibrant, dynamic and flourishing future.

The late Tony O'Reilly claims that rugby is a 'great template for life, and anyone involved in the game should have a commitment to excellence and a commitment to the beauty of the game.' Irish rugby needs constantly to strive to preserve and even enhance everything that is worthwhile in the game and everything good the game has stood for.

Jack Kyle's last words to me encapsulate this feeling: 'I played with some great players, great teams and great coaches. We all should be grateful for the past, enthusiastic about the present and confident about the future.'

The last 150 years were great.

The next 150 will be even better.

vodafone
#TEAM OF US
AVIVA
AVIVA STADIUM
CAR INSURANCE
vodafone
vodafone
vodafone
canterbury
IRFU

The Ireland team stand for the national anthem ahead of their 2024 Six Nations clash with Scotland.

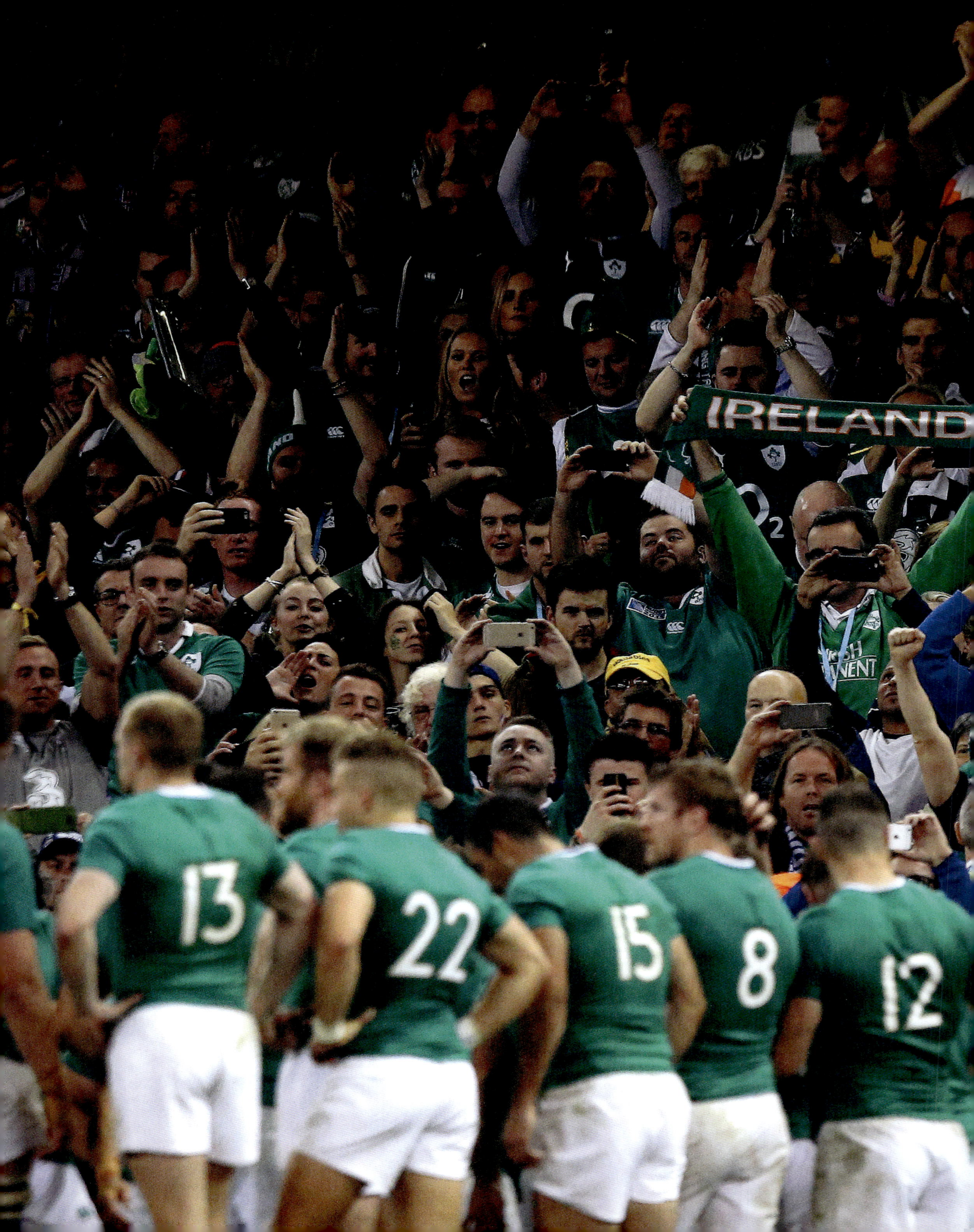
IRELAND
13
22
15
8
12

EXTRA TIME

I was honoured to be asked to write this book. But, equally, I was aware that it came with an enormous responsibility.

It is said that it takes a village to raise a child. It takes something similar to write a book like this.

Teresa Daly of Gill Books made the approach to me to write this book. She and her talented and dedicated team have been models of professionalism and a trove of advice.

Peter Breen of the IRFU has played an invaluable role and has been the glue between all the relevant parties.

Billy Stickland is a national treasure and his brilliance – and that of his photographers in Inpho – is magnificently showcased in this book.

I am deeply honoured that the legendary Paul O'Connell kindly agreed to write the foreword for this book.

I am grateful to Feargal O'Rourke for placing his vast reservoir of knowledge about Irish rugby at my disposal.

According to the author Eckhart Tolle, 'acknowledging the good you already have in your life is the foundation for all abundance.' The greatest giving is thanksgiving. I am profoundly grateful for the opportunity to work with such extraordinary rugby legends.

My own interest in rugby can be traced back to just two words: Tony Ward. I am very appreciative of his support.

As always, I am grateful to the person Tony O'Reilly has called the 'great gentleman of rugby', Ollie Campbell.

A very particular thanks to Joe Schmidt for his many kindnesses.

I am delighted that this special year in Irish rugby sees Mick Quinn restored to good health and doing what he does like nobody else: creating mischief and mayhem everywhere!

Rugby thrives on storytelling. I am grateful to some great storytellers, including the many players, past and present, who generously shared their stories and thoughts with me and who made this book possible.

Special thanks to one of the great warriors of Irish rugby, Jack McGrath, for his support.

One of the most inspirational experiences I had while writing this book was an evening immersing myself in the story of Clogher Valley RFC. Thanks to my educators: Bob Beatty, Stephen Hetherington and Gordon Montgomery.

Thanks to Shannon's Katie McCloskey for her practical assistance.

Anyone writing the story of Irish rugby follows the trail blazed by Ned Van Esbeck. I am grateful to him for welcoming me into his home and for his willingness to support this project.

Over the past 12 years, one of the biggest inspirations in my life has been Emma Spence. I want the last words in this book to be hers. Her personal motto can serve as the motto of Irish rugby for the next 150 years: 'Keep looking up.'

INDEX

A

Abrahams, Harold 140
Adeolokun, Niyi 169, *169*
Afrika Korps 19
Aki, Adrienna 172, *172*
Aki, Bundee *125*, 127, 135, 169, 172–3, *172*
Alexander, Bob 20
All Blacks 1, *37*, 44, 48, 54, 73, 86, 94, 106, 110, 203
    Barbarians vs All Blacks (1973) 47
    Britain and Ireland, tour of (1905) 9
    Chicago (2016) 111, *112–13*, 114, 114–15, 116
    Dublin (2018) 120, *121*
    Lions (2021) 124–5, *125*
    Lions (2022) 127, *128–9*
    Munster vs All Blacks (1978) 185–7
    World Cup (1995) *80*, 81–2
    World Cup (2023) 135
    World Cups 157
All-Ireland League, launch of 205
All-Ireland League (1992) 86
All-Ireland League (2014) *213*
All-Ireland League (2023) 208
Allen, J. 7
Am, Lukhanyo 131
Anderson, Henry J. 168
Anderson, Willie 73, *76–7*, 202–3
Andrews, Eamonn, *This Is Your Life* 47
Andrews, G. 7
Anglo-American Cable Company 6
anti-apartheid movement 41, 61
apartheid 58–9, 61
Argentina 33, *34–5*, 41, 74, 90, 95, 100, 110, 124
    players, imprisonment of 202–3
Aristotle 183
Ash, W. 7
Ashe, Arthur 220
Ashe, Thomas 222
Ashton, Brian 86, *87*, 88
Asmal, Kader 41
Aucklinleck, General Claude 19
Australian Open 11
Autumn Nations Cup 122, 124
Aviva Minis Festivals 206
Aviva Stadium 8, 122, *122–3*, 132, 184

B

Bagot, John Christopher 10
Baird, Ryan 226

Baker, Kathy 160
Ballinasloe RFC 6, 168
Ballymena 133, 198, 225
Baloucoune, Robert *126*
Bancroft, William James 8
Bandon RFC 205
Barbarians vs All Blacks (1973) 47
Barbarians vs Ireland (1996) 176, *177*
Barlow, M. 7
Barnes, Stuart 86
Barnett, Joseph James 215
Barrett, Beauden 120
Barrett, Greg 186
Barrett, Kevin (Smiley) 120
Barry, Kevin 212, *212*
Bateman Cup 204
Batty, Grant 47
Baxter, Ashleigh *147*, 151
Beatty, Bob 209
Beaumont, Bill 59, 62
Beckett, Samuel 14, 139
Beckham, David 92
Bective Rangers 36, 37, 133, 225
Beirne, Tadhg 132
Belfast Harlequins 6, 86, 151
Bell, Jonathan 176, *177*
Bell, R. 7
Belton, Jack 133
Belvedere College, Dublin 212–14
Bennett, Phil 47, 230
Bentley, John (Bentos), *Living with Lions* 88
Berkery, P.J. 36
Best, Rory 106, 122, 133, 206, 231
Birch, John 133
BKT United Rugby Championship (2023) 184
Black Ferns 150, 154, 157
Blackrock College, Dublin 41, 151, 160, 196, 198, 212, 214, *215*
Bohemians 37, 187, 196, 225
Boland, Eavan 141
Boles, Claire 160
Boss, Isaac 99
Bourke, Gillian 151, *155*
Bowe, Tommy 104, 106
Bowen, Bleddyn 73
Bowen, Jimmy 186
Boyle, Charles Vesey 20
Boyle, Peter 20
Bradley, Michael 69, 75, 198
Brady, Rab 133
Brazier, Kelly 150
Bresnihan, Barry 39, 199

Briggs, Niamh *147*, 150, 151, *152–3*, 154, 161, 162
British Army 8, 14, 19
Brophy, Niall 33, 37
Broughall, Damien 225
Browning, Frederick 14
Bruff RFC 201, 202
Bulger, Larry 9
Bulger, Michael 9
Burns, Megan 160
Butt, Nicky 92

C

Cahill, Brian 225
Cahill, Des 75
Callan, Colm 26
Campbell College, Belfast 215, 225
Campbell, Sir James 212
Campbell, Kieran 225
Campbell, Ollie *48–9*, 55, 61, 62, 64, 154
    Australia (1979) 53, 54, 58
    Belvedere College 212–14
    Charitable Trust 68
    Old Belvedere 212–13
    underage system 227
Campese, David 74, 176
Canniffe, Donal 186
Cantillon, Christy 186
Cantona, Eric 92
Cantrell, John *200*
Cantwell, Lynne 151, 154, *155*
caps
    awarded (1946-89) 133
    awarded to female players 158
Carbery, Joey 110, 125
Cardiff Arms Park 39, *39*, *40*, 54, 70
Carlow County 6
Carmichael, Sandy 200
Carr, Nigel 173, 174, *174*, 175, 217
Casement, B. 7
Casey, Craig 226
Casey, Pat 39
Castleisland RFC 204
Catholic University School, Dublin 19
Catt, Mike 86
CBC Cork *216*, 217, 225
Celtic Challenge competition 160
Celtic League (2006) 176, *178–9*
Celtic League (2011) 191
Charitable Trust 68
charities, support for 231
Charles, Prince 39, *39*, 41

Cheika, Michael 180, 182
Chicago (2016) 111, *112–13*, 114, 120
Chicago Cubs 114, 116
Chile *34–5*
Cistercian College, Roscrea 217, 220
CIYMS Rugby Club 36, 225
Clarke, Jack 74
Clifford, Tom *25*, 30, 185
Clinch, Andrew 222, 224
Clinch, James (Jammie) 222, 224
Clinch, Paul 133
Clogher Valley Rugby Club 208–9, 235
Clohessy, Peter (The Claw) 86, 93, 184, 191, 198
Clongowes Wood College, Kildare 196
Clovers, The 160
clubs 195–209
    competitions 204–5
    in Limerick 195–8
    mini rugby 205–8
Coghlan, Fiona 144–7, *145*, 154, 155, 161, 206, 220
Cogley, Fred 155
Collegians 6, 26, 36, 133
Combe, A. 7
Concerned Citizens 59
Connacht 7, 168
    European Challenge Cup (1998) 88
    Friends of Connacht 169
    Gatland as coach 203
    Guinness Pro-12 title (2016) 169, *170–1*
Connacht Schools Cup (1913) 211
Connacht Senior Cup (1896) 204
Connolly, Harold 220
Conners, Will 226
Considine, Aidan 225
Contepomi, Felipe 180
Conway, Andrew *126*
Cooke 151
Coolican, Edward (Teddy) 133
Corcoran, Michael 155
Cork Constitution 36, 186, 187, 195, 198, 199, *204*, 205, 225
Cork Constitution (newspaper) 198
Costello, Victor 81
Coughlan, Neil 225
Coulter, Phil 231
Court, Tom 106
Courtney, Andy 223
Coveney, Terry 133
COVID-19 pandemic 122, *122–3*, 124, 127
Cox, H.L. 7
Crawford, Ernie 14, 19
Crean, Tom 10

Croke Park 54, 99–100, 104
Cronyn, A.P. 7
Crossan, Keith 62, 69, 70
Crotty, Ryan *111*
Crowe, Amee-Leigh Murphy 160
Crowley, Jack 135, 184, 205
Cruyff, Johan 39
Cullen, Leo 184
Cupitt, Matthew 225
Curry, Revd Austin 133
Cussen, Denis 14

D

Daly, Jack 26
Daly, Shane 198, 226
Dalymount Park 41, 54
Dane, Kathryn 231
D'Arcy, Gordon 99, 106
Dave Gallaher Memorial Park 9
Davidson, Jeremy 86, *87*
Davidson, Jimmy 73, 74
Davies, Gareth 58, 64
Davis Cup 11
Davitt, Grace 151, 155
Davy, Eugene 14
Dawes, John 47
Dawson, Matt 96
Dawson, Ronnie 33, 36, 41, 74
De La Salle, Churchtown 220
Dean, Paul 62, 69, 73–4, 217
Deegan, Max 226
Deering, Shay 54
Dempsey, Girvan 96, *96–7*, 98, 99
Dennison, Seamus 185–6, 187
Dinnen, Revd John 176
Dolan, Hugh 133
Dolphin Rugby Club 26, 36, 187, 201
Donaldson, J.A. 36
Donohoe, Paschal 124
Doris, Caelan 125, *126*, 135
Dowling, Stephanie *142*
Doyle, Mick 52, 68–9, *69*, 70–1, 73, *73*
Doyle, Philip 145, 150
Dublin Hospitals Cup 10
Dublin Hospitals Football Union 10
Dublin University Football Club 6, 7, 133, 204
Dudgeon, Hugh (Gordon) 133
Duggan, Willie 23, 48, *48–9*, 62, 64, 68, 114, 230
Dungannon Royal School 6
Dungannon Rugby Club 6, 203
Dunlop, Henry Wallace 8

Dunnes Stores workers 61
Dupont, Antoine 131

E

Earley, Dermot 41, 43
Earls, Keith 116, 127, 133, *134*
Easter Rising (1916) 11, 14
Easterby, Simon 92, 117
Edwards, Ben 31
Edwards, Gareth 23, 41, 47
Egan, Ailis 151
Ella Brothers 217
Elwood, Eric 81
English, Mick 33, 196
English Rugby Union 6, 168
Ensor, Tony 44
European Challenge Cup (1998) 88
European Cup (1999) 86, 176, *177*
European Player of the Year (1978) 54
European Player of the Year (1979) 54
Exiles vs Munster (1992) 168

F

Farrell, Andy 86, 122, 124, *124*, 135
Farrell, Chris 117
Feighery, Con 39
Feighery, Tom 39
Ferris, Stephen 106
Fiennes, Sir Ranulph 95
15-a-side, first match (1877) 7
Finn, Moss 62, 186, 198, 225
First International Ireland squad *4*
First World War 10, 11, 14, 204
Fitzgerald, Ciaran 62, 64, 68, 71, 74, 75, 220
Fitzgerald, Conor 225
Fitzgerald, Des 74
Fitzgerald, Luke 106
Fitzpatrick, Paula 151
Fitzpatrick, Sean 81, 203
Five Nations Championship 168
Five Nations Championship (1926) 14
Five Nations Championship (1972) 43
Five Nations Championship (1974) 44, 230
Five Nations Championship (1978) 54
Five Nations Championship (1980) 58
Five Nations Championship (1981) 61
Five Nations Championship (1991) 74
Five Nations Championship (1996) 86
Five Nations Championship (1998) 88
Five Nations Championship (1999) 88
Flannery, Jerry 106

Flavin, Adrian 225
Fleming, Siobhan 151
Flood, Stacey 160
Flutey, Riki 104
Flynn, Kevin 39, 43, *43*
Foley, Anthony (Axel) 47, 93, 111, *112–13*, 114, 144
Foley, Brendan 47, 58, 111, 114, 151, 154, 186, 200, *200*
Foley, Rosie 144, 151, *154*
Football Association Council 140
Foster, Ian 127
Friends of Connacht 169
Furlong, Tadhg 132, 135, 221, 231

G

Gaelic Athletic Association (GAA) 6, 41, 43, 99, 140, 144
Gaffikin, W. 7
Gaffney, Alan 184
Galbraith, E. 7
Gallaher, Dave 9
Galvin, Leo 133
Galway Town 204
Galwegians RFC 144, 203
Galwey, Mick 75, 81, *92*, 93, 184, 191
Garbally College, Ballinasloe 220
Garryowen 26, 36, 86, 186, 196, 198, 205, 225
Gatland, Warren 90, 92, *93*, 110, 124
    Connacht coach 88, 203
    O'Sullivan, Eddie and 94
    Welsh team and 106
Gavin, Revd Tom 30
Geoghegan, Simon 14, 74, 75, 81, *82–3*
Gibson, Lady Cecily 173
Gibson, Lord Justice 173, 174
Gibson, Mike *40*, 44, 48, 199, 200
Gibson-Park, Jamison 135
Giggs, Ryan 92
Glennon, Jim 169
Glynn, Billy 203
Good, Chris 225
Goodall, Ken 199
Goodhue, Jack 127
Grace, Tom 44, 47
Grand Slam (1948) 23, 25–6, 133, 184
Grand Slam (2009) 23, *104–5*, 106, 133, 198
Grand Slam (2018) 116–17, 133
Grand Slam (2023) 132–3, 225
Greer, Hugh 133
Griffin, Ciara 155
Guest, Laura 151
Guiney, Jack 133
Guinness Pro12 (2016) 169, *170–1*
Guinness Six Nations (2024) *232–3*
Guscott, Jeremy 86
Guy's Hospital Football Club 6

H

Hagler, Marvin 95
Halpin, Gary *80*, 81, 82
Hamilton, Gordon 74, *78–9*
Hanna family 175–6
Hanna, James 175
Hanna, Maureen 175
Hanna, Robert 175
Hannon, Neil 139
Hansen, Mack *126*, 127, *134*, 135
Harvey, George and Frederick 10
Harvey, Thomas Arnold, Bishop of Cashel 10
Havili, David 127
Hayes, Bill 201, 202
Hayes, Fiona 151, 155
Hayes, John 92, 99, *100–1*, 106, 133, 135, 144, 201–2
Hayes, Dr John 6
Hayes, Róisín 201
Hayes, Sally 201
Healy, Cian 120, 133, *214*
Heaney, Seamus 20, 155
Heaslip, Jamie 106
Heffernan, Katie 160
Heineken Cup (2006) 187, 190, *192–3*
Heineken Cup (2008) 187, 190
Heineken Cup (2009) 180, *180–1*
Heineken Cup (2012) 182–3, *182*
Henderson, Iain 116
Henderson, Jill 141
Henderson, Noel 30, 33, 36
Henderson, Rob 86, *88–9*
Henshaw, Robbie *114–15*, 117, 124, 127, 132
Herring, Rob 131, 132
Hewitt, David 33, 36, 37
Hewson, F.T. 7
Hickie, Denis 200
Higgins, Dudley 26
Higgins, Sir Eoin 175
Higgins, Eve 160
Highfield Rugby Club 69, 151
Hogan, Niall 81
Holt, Darragh 225
Home Nations Championship (1887) 7–8
Home Nations women's competition 141
Horan, Marcus 106
Horan, Tim 74
Horgan, Shane 92, 99, 110

INDEX | 239

Horrocks-Taylor, Phil 196
Houlihan, Con 155, 204
Humphreys, David 135, 176, *177*
Hurley, Gerry 187
Hyde, Douglas 41

I

Instonians 36, 225
International Women's Day (2013) 146
Interprovincial Championship
    Exiles vs Munster (1992) 168
    Ulster vs Leinster (1875) 173
Ireland team (1914) *12–13*
Ireland team (1949) *32*
Ireland team (1968) *50–1*
Ireland team (1982) *66–7*
Ireland vs All Blacks (2016) 111, *112–13*, 114, 120
Ireland vs All Blacks (2018) 120, *121*
Ireland vs All Blacks (2021) 124–5
Ireland vs All Blacks (2022) 127, *127, 128–9*, 131
Ireland vs Australia (1958) 36
Ireland vs Barbarians (1996) 176
Ireland vs England (1886) *8*
Ireland vs England (1887) 8
Ireland vs England (1939) 19
Ireland vs England (1946), ticket *20–1*
Ireland vs England (1948) 25
Ireland vs England (1969) 39
Ireland vs England (1972) 43
Ireland vs England (1973), ticket and programme *45*
Ireland vs Fiji, Rugby Sevens Series (2023) *157*
Ireland vs France (1909) 10
Ireland vs France (1947) 19
Ireland vs France (1948) 24
Ireland vs France (1949) 30
Ireland vs France (2000) 90, 92
Ireland vs Italy (2020) *122–3*
Ireland vs New Zealand (1905) 9, *9*
Ireland vs New Zealand (1935), programme *15*
Ireland vs Scotland (2004) *98*
Ireland vs South Africa (1912) 10
Ireland vs Wales (1926) 14
Ireland vs Wales (1948) 25–6
Ireland vs Wales (1969) 39, 41
Ireland vs Wales (1980) 114
Ireland Women's squad (2014) *150*
'Ireland's Call' 147, 172, 201, 231
Irish Anti-Apartheid Movement 41
Irish Football Union 7
Irish Republican Army (IRA) 43, 173, 175, 176

Irish Rugby Football Union (IRFU)
    amalgamation of two unions (1879) 7
    branches 7
    Centenary 47
    Committee, first female member 157
    Connacht branch 7, 168
    first elected president 10
    flag 168
    four provincial sides 7, 168
    Head of Equity, Diversity and Inclusivity 161
    Head of Women's Performance and Pathways 161
    Irish Exiles committee 168
    Leinster branch 7
    Long Term Player Development 206
    Munster branch 7
    professionalism and 82, 167, 168–9
    Safeguarding 206
    Spirit of Rugby 206
    Ulster branch 7
    Women's Sub-Committee 162
    women's under-20s programme 161
Irish Times/Irish Sports Council Sportswoman of the Year 147
Irish Universities vs Scottish Universities (1954) 224
Irish Women's Rugby Football Union 141
Irish women's team, first international 1
Irvine, Andy 44, 47
Irwin, David 62, 64, 173–5, 202

J

Japan 71, 120, 122, 124, 141
Jennings, Shane 183
John Paul II, Pope 54
Johnson, Martin 94
Jones, Alun Wyn 124
Jones, Eddie 117
Jones, Stephen 103, 104

K

Kavanagh, J.R. 36
Kavanagh, Niamh *155*
Keane, Moss 23, 44, 48, 61, 68, 92–3, 204, 230, 231
    Munster vs All Blacks (1978) 186, 187
    Triple Crown and 62, *63*, 64, 69
Keane, Roy 54, 92
Kearney, Aidan 225
Kearney, Rob 106
Keenan, Hugo *126*, 127, 226
Kelleher, Olann 187
Kelleher, Rónan 124, 125
Kelly, Jimmy 200
Kelly, John *185*

Kennedy, Ken 41, 44, 86
Kennedy, Terry 226
Kennington Oval 7
Kent, Charlie 187
Kerry County 6
Keyes, Ralph 74, 198
Kidd, Murray 86
Kidney, Declan 100, 106, *107*, 110, 187, 190, 191, *221*, 225
Kiernan, Michael 64, 69, *70*, 71
Kiernan, Tom 37, 61, 62, 64, 168, 186, 198–9, *199*
Killorglin Rugby Club 6
King, Billie Jean 154
King, Erin 160
Kingstown (Dún Laoghaire) Regatta (1898) 155
Kirkpatrick, Ian 59
Kyle, Jack 20, 23, 24–7, *24, 27*, 30, 31, 36, 54, 103, 231

L

Ladies' Land League 140
Lam, Pat 169, 172
Lambie, Pat 111
Lancaster, Stuart 184
Lane, Emily 160
Lane, Michael 30
Lansdowne FC 6, 14
Lansdowne Road Stadium 8, 10, 11, 14, 99, 176
Lapasset, Bernard 157–8
Laune Rangers Gaelic Football team 6
Laura Lynn Children's Hospice 231
Lawler, Paddy 33
Lawrence, John, Handbook of Cricket in Ireland 6
Leamy, Denis 106
Leinster 7
    Champions Cup and League double (2018) 184
    Great War volunteers *15–16*
    Heineken Cup (2009) 180, *180–1*
    Heineken Cup (2012) 182–3, *182*
    Heineken Cups 110
    volunteers *16–17*
Leinster Cup 213, 214
Leinster Cup (1969) 200
Leinster Schools Cup (1887) 211
Leinster Schools Rugby 196
Leinster Schools Rugby Junior Cup (1917) 212
Leinster Senior Cup (1882) 204
Leinster vs Ulster (1916) 11, 14
Lenihan, Donal 62, 64, 68, *72, 73*, 217
Letterkenny Rugby Football Club 9
Limerick 10, 195–8
Limerick Leader 196

Lions 9
    Australia (1979) 53, 54, 58
    Australia (1989) 73–4
    Australia (1991) *78–9*
    Australia (1994) 81
    Australia (2001) 93–4
    Australia (2013) 110
    Australia/New Zealand (1950) 24, 30
    Australia/New Zealand (1959) 33, *37*
    Australia/New Zealand (1966) 39
    New Zealand (1971) 199–200, 225
    New Zealand (1976) 47–8
    New Zealand (1977) 230
    New Zealand (1983) 64
    New Zealand (1991) 74–5
    New Zealand (1997) 86
    New Zealand (2005) 99, 106
    New Zealand (2012) 108
    New Zealand (2021) 124–5, *125*
    New Zealand (2022) 127, *127, 128–9*
    South Africa (1896) 9
    South Africa (1938) 19
    South Africa (1955) 33
    South Africa (1962) 23, 37
    South Africa (1968) 39
    South Africa (1974) 47
    South Africa (1980) 58–9, 61
    South Africa (1997) *87*, 88, 93
    South Africa (2009) 106
    South Africa (2016) 111
    South Africa (2021) 124
Little, Jason 74
Lomu, Jonah 81, 82, 172
London Irish 26, 36, 74, 186, 187, 225
Lowe, James 125, *126, 127*, 231
Lowry, Mike *126*
Lynagh, Michael 74
Lynch, Seán 199–200
Lynch, Sharon 151

M

McAleese, Mary 94
Macaulay, John 1
McBride, Willie John 23, 37, *46*, 47, 199
McCabe, Edward, Archbishop of Dublin 140
McCabe, Kate Farrell 160
McCall, Brian 217
McCall, Mark 176
McCarey, Chris 225
McCarthy, Jim 26, 27, *27*, 30, 31, 33, 36, 173, 185
McCarthy, Joe 135

McCarthy, Mick 54
McCaw, Richie 157
McConnell, Albert 26
McCracken, Barry 225
MacDonald, J. 7
McFadden, Fergus 116–17
McGann, Anna 160
McGann, Barry 39, 43, 44, 187, 198
McGinn, Vikki 151
McGrath, Jack 110, 114, 231, 235
McGrath, Pat 198–9
McGrath, Robbie 62, 64
McIlwaine, E. 7
McKay, Bill *25*, 26, 27, 30, 33
McKee, William 26
McKeowan, Ruth *141*
McKibbin, Harry 19
McKinley, Ian 182
McKinney, Stewart 44
McLaren, Bill 41, 220
McLeod, Hugh 47
McLeod, Scott 127
McLoughlin, Gerry (Ginger) 62, 186
McLoughlin, Ray 44, 200, 220
McMaster, Dave 217
McNaughton, Paul 54, *56–7*
MacNeice, Louis 32
MacNeill, Hugo 61, 62, 69, 70–1, 176, 217
McQuaid, John Charles, Archbishop of Dublin 140
MacSwiney, Terence 212
McVerry, Fr Peter 212
Magennis, J. 7
Malone 14, 26, 205
Manchester United 92
Mandela, Nelson 61, 82
Mannion, Noel 73, 220
Mason, Simon 176
Matthews, Mike 215
Matthews, Philip 74, 215, 217
Mayne, Lt-Col. Robert Blair *18*, 19
Mealamu, Keven 99
Meates, Roland (Roly) 224–5
Melrose, Tony 217
Mescal, David 225
Methodist College 14
Millar, Syd 33, 36, 37, 58, 199
Miller, Alison 145, 146, 150
Miller, Eric 86
Milliken, Dick 44
mini rugby 205–8
Molloy, Claire 151

Moloney, Johnny 44, 74
Moloney, Larry 186
Montgomery, Lieutenant-General Bernard 19
Montgomery, Gordon 209, 235
Moore, Shane 225
Moore, Terry 44
Morgan, Cliff 220
Morgan, Dermot 58
Morgan, George 20
Moriarty, Eoghan 201
Mulcahy, Bill (Wiggs) (W.A.) 33, 36, 37, *38*, 39
Mulcahy, Ted 187
Muldoon, John 169, 220
Muldoon, Larissa 151, 161
Mulhall, Lucy 160
Mullan, Barney 24–5
Mullen, Karl *25*, 26, *27*, 30, 199, 201, 214
Mulligan, Andy 33
Mullin, Brendan 69, 73, 74
Munster 7, 86, 184–7
    BKT United Rugby Championship (2023) 184
    first players chosen (1879) 7
    Heineken Cup (2006) 187
    Heineken Cup (2008) 187, 190
    miracle match (2003) 184
Munster Cup (1886) 204
Munster Cup (1958) 196
Munster Cup (1962) 37, 196
Munster Schools Cup (1909) 211
Munster Senior Cup (1886) 6
Munster vs All Blacks (1978) 185–7
Munster vs Gloucester (2003) 184, *185*
Munster vs Leinster (2006) 187, 190
Munster vs Wallabies (1948) 185
Murphy, Con 19, 20
Murphy, Geordan 95, 106
Murphy, Gerry, RTÉ interview 75
Murphy, Jenny 151, 155
Murphy, Ken 74
Murphy, Noel A. 33, 36, 39, 41, 74
Murphy, Noel F. 74
Murphy, Richie 225
Murray, Conor *114–15*, 124, 125, 133
Murray, Jenny *146*
Murray, Niall 226
Murrayfield 14, 33, 69, 169
Myles, J. 7

N

Nacewa, Isa 180, 182
Neary, Tony 230

Nelson, Jimmy 26, 30
Neville, Gary 92
Neville, Joy 145, *145*, 151, 154, *155*, *156*, 157, 160
Neville, Phil 92
Neville, William Cox 10
Nevin Spence Memorial Stand 108
New Zealand Herald 120
NIFC (North of Ireland FC) 6, 7, 26, 36, 133, 204
Norley, J. *25*
Northern Football Union 6, 7
Norton, George 30, 31, 33, 200
Ntamack, Émile 92

O

O'Beirne, Mary 141
O'Brien, Andy 225
O'Brien, Des 26, 27, 30, 31-3
O'Brien, Heather 150, 151
O'Brien, Jimmy 226
O'Brien, Seán *107*, 221
O'Callaghan, Donncha 106, 225, 227
O'Callaghan, Phil 48, 201
O'Connell, Paul 104, 122, 133
    Heineken Cup (2008) 187, 190
    Lions and 106, 110
    Munster jersey 191-2
    World Cup (2003) 95-6, *95*
O'Donnell, Rodney 58
O'Donoghue, P.J. 36
O'Driscoll, Billy 206
O'Driscoll, Brian 88, 95, 96, 100, *100-1*, 133, 157
    Australia (2001) 24, 93
    Grand Slam (2009) 104, *104-5*, 106
    Heineken Cup (2009) 180
    Heineken Cup (2012) *182*
    Lions Test (2013) 110
    mini rugby 206
    Paris (2000) 90, *91*
    Triple Crown (2004) 98-9
    underage system 227
    university rugby 224
    World Youths Cup (1998) 225
O'Driscoll, Frank 94, *132*, 133
O'Driscoll, Geraldine 94
O'Driscoll, John 58, 61, 62, 64, 69
O'Driscoll, Mick 106, 191
O'Flanagan, Michael *27*
O'Gara, Ronan 92, *92*, 93, *102*, 132, 133, 135, 227
    Celtic League (2011) 191
    Cork Constitution 195, 198
    Grand Slam (2009) 104, *104-5*, 106, 116, 184

    Heineken Cup (2006) *192-3*
O'Halloran, Clodagh 162, *163*
O'Hanlon, Bertie 25, 26
O'Kelly, Malcolm **90**, **95**
Old Belvedere 26, 36, 133, 151, 154, 160, 199, 212, 214
Old Wesley 133, 205
O'Leary, Anthony 187
O'Leary, Tomás 106
Oliver, Greig 226
Oliver, Jack 226
O'Loughlin, Dave 25-6
Olympic Games (1928) 14
Olympic Games (1960) 220
Olympic Games (1992) 81
Olympic Games (2024) *161*
O'Mahony, Peter 120, 131, 135, 198
O'Meara, John 27, 30, 36
O'Rafferty, Emmet 133
O'Reilly, Br Philip 217
O'Reilly, Tony 23, 33, 36, **36**, 37, 176, 196
    Belvedere College 214-15
    schools rugby 211
Originals 9
O'Rourke, Feargal 167
Orr, Phil 48, *48-9*, 58, 62
O'Sullivan, Eddie 94, **94**, 95, 96, 100, 106, *221*
O'Sullivan, Joanne *145*
O'Sullivan, Mickey 187

P

Parke, J.C. 11
Parsons, Béighinn 160
Patterson, Colin 58, 59
Paul, Gregor 120
Payne, Shaun *192-3*
Peace International (1996) 176
Pearse, Chloe 162, *163*
Peat, Lindsay 155
Pedlow, Cecil 33, 36
Perón, Eva (Evita) 33
Phillips, Mike 106
Pienaar, Francois 176
Plumtree, John 127
Popplewell, Nick 81
Porter, Andrew 127, 226, 231
Portora Royal School 6, 139
Prendergast, Sam 226
Price, Brian 39, 41
professionalism 82, 167, 168-9, 227
Pullin, John 43, 47, 230
Purcell, Mai 196

Q

Queen's College Cork (later UCC) 6, 198
Queen's University Belfast 6, 24, 26, 33, 36
Quinlan, Alan 95, *192–3*
Quinn, Gerry 133
Quinn, Mary 157
Quinn, Mick 44, *44*, 47, 169, 220, 235

R

Railway Union 160
Rainey, Philip (Chipper) 173, 175
Ramsbottom, Sue 144
Ravenhill Stadium 14, 19, 25, 26, 133, 143, 224
RBS Women's Six Nations Championship (2015) *138*
referee of the year (2017) 157
Reid, Paddy 25, 26
Reid, Tom 33, 36
Reilly, Marie Louise 151
Retallick, Brodie *127*
Reynolds, John 225
Ringland, Trevor 64, 69, 70, *72*, 176
Ringrose, Garry 117, 127, 135, 231
Ritchie, Jim 14, 74
Robbie, John 58, 59
Robinson, Mary 140–1
Roche, Frank 225
Rockwell College 8
Roe, Robin 33
Rommel, Field Marshal Erwin 19
Ronan, Brendan 225
Rooney, Tom 155
Rosser, Tania 150, 151
Rossi, Donovan 225
Royal Humane Society 10
Royal Inniskilling Fusiliers 20
RTÉ 75, 147, 155
rugby
    development in Ireland 10
    oldest rugby club 6
    social class and 10, 196, 198
Rugby Football Union (RFU) 6, 117
Rugby School 5
Rugby Sevens Series
    Ireland Sevens players (2024) *161*
    Ireland squad (2023) 160
    Ireland vs Fiji (2023) *157*
Ryan, Donnacha 86
Ryan, Jack 8
Ryan, James 120, 226
Ryan, Mick 8
Ryle, Fr Kevin 220

S

St Mary's College 44, 60, 74, 133, 151, 186, 199–200, 212
St Michael's College 220, 225
St Munchin's College 37
Saint-André, Philippe 201
Saracens 190–1
Saunders, Rob 74
Schmidt, Joe 86, 110–11, 120, *120*, 122, 124, 127
    Grand Slam (2018) 116–17
    Heineken Cup (2012), Leinster and 182–3
    Leinster head coach 182–4
    schools rugby, coaching 221–2
    World Coach of the Year (2018) 116
Schofield, Chris 225
Scholes, Paul 92
schools rugby 211–3
Schools Rugby Cup (2006) *215*
Scown, Alastair 47
Second World War 11, 19, 20, 204
Sella, Philippe 176, *177*
Sexton, Johnny 116–17, 120, 124, 131, 132, 133, 150
    career points 135
    Grand Slam (2023) 225
    Heineken Cup (2012) 182–3
    mini rugby 206
    World Cup (2023) 135, *136–7*
    World Rugby Men's Player of the Year (2018) 116, 131
Sexton, Luca 135, 206
Sexton, Mark 225
Shankly, Bill 185
Shannon 143, 144, 186, *197*, 198, 200, *201*
Sheahan, Joey 225
Sheehan, Dan 125, 132, 135
Shehadie, Nick 185
Six Nations Championship 7, 88, 90
Six Nations Championship (2001) 93, 94
Six Nations Championship (2009) 103, 104
Six Nations Championship (2011) *107*
Six Nations Championship (2012) 108
Six Nations Championship (2013) 110
Six Nations Championship (2014) 110
Six Nations Championship (2015) 110
Six Nations Championship (2018) 117, 120
Six Nations Championship (2019) 120
Six Nations Championship (2021) 124
Six Nations Championship (2022) 125
Six Nations Championship (2023) *131*, 132
Six Nations Championship (2024) *130*, 135, *232–4*
Skibbereen Eagle 198
Slattery, Fergus 41, *42*, 44, 62, 64, 68, 200
Sligo Grammar *218–19*

Smith, Brian 73
Smith, Declan 187
Smith, John 33, 73
Smith, Lee 224
Smith, Marcus 135
Smith, Steve 73
Smith, Zadie 162
Smyth, Tommy 10
social class, rugby and 10, 196, 198
Spence, Emma 108, 235
Spence, Graham 108
Spence, Nevin 108
Spence, Noel 108
Spence, Sophie 151, 154
Spillane, Brian 70–1
Spirit of Rugby 206
sports commentators 155
Spring, Dick 54, 217, 219
Spring, Donal 61, 187, 220
Sprinkboks 10, 33, 41, 59
Stack, George H. 7
Stander, C.J. 111
Staples, Jim 74
Stapleton, Nora *147*, 151, *158–9*
Staunton, Cora 144
Steed, Fiona 142–4, *143*, 161–2, 201–2, 220, 230
Stevenson, J.B. 36
Stockdale, Jacob 117, *118–19*, 120, *121*, 226
Stoker, Ernest 10
Stoker, Frank 10
Stokes, Paddy 10
Strathdee, Ernie 26, 30
Stringer, Peter 92, *92*, 93, 106, *191*, 195, 198, 227
Sugden, Mark 14
Sundays Well RFC 86, 187, 196
Suttonians 160, 213
Sweden 203

T

Tackle Your Feelings 231
Tanner, Haydn 26
Te Whata, Mikaera 100
Temple-Jones, Allan 160
Thomond Park, Limerick 144, 184, 186, 196
Thorpe, Des 133
Thrift, Harry 14
Tierney, Tom *90*
Toner, Devin 120
Tralee Rugby Club 6, 151
Traynor, Paul 133
Trimble, Andrew 231

Trinity College Dublin (TCD) 6, 7
　　see also Dublin University Football Club
Triple Crown (1894) 8, 10
Triple Crown (1899) 8
Triple Crown (1926) 224
Triple Crown (1939) 19
Triple Crown (1948) *28–9*
Triple Crown (1949) 30
Triple Crown (1982) 1, 52, 61–2, 64
Triple Crown (1983) 68
Triple Crown (1985) 1, 68, 69–71, *70*, 173
Triple Crown (1987) 71, *72*, 73
Triple Crown (2004) 98
Triple Crown (2006) 99
Triple Crown (2007) 100
Triple Crown (2009) 104, 106
Triple Crown (2022) 125, *126*
Triple Crown (2023) *131*
Tucker, Colm 58, 186
Twickenham 14, 25, 37, 43, 47, 62, 73, 74, 81, 96, 99, 117, 125, 132, 135, 230
Tyrrell, Hannah 231

U

UL Bohemians 144, 151
Ulster 7, 14, 108, *108–9*, 176
Ulster Schools Cup (1876) 211
Ulster Senior Cup 204
Ulster vs Colombiers (1999) 176
Ulster vs Leinster (1875) 173
Umaga, Tana 99, 172
underage teams 225–7
　　first under-19 match (1997) 225
　　first under-23 match (1979) 225
　　first under-25 match (1986) 225
　　Grand Slams, under-20 team 225
　　under-12 European tournament (1990) 198
　　under-19s team (1998) *224*
　　under-20s (2019) 226
　　under-20s team (2016) 226
　　World Cup (1998), winning squad 225
Underwood, Rory 176
University College Cork (UCC) 6
University College Dublin (UCD) 37, 158, 222, *222–3*
university teams 222–5
University of Ulster 176
Urquhart, Ben 225

V

Valentine, Emily 139
Valentine, William 139
Valentine, William and John 139

van der Flier, Josh 127, *130*, 131, 132
Van Esbeck, Ned 155, 235
Vermeulen, Elvis 99

W

Wales XV vs English Civil Service FC 10
Walker, Sam 19–20
Walkington, R.B. 7
Wallace, David 94, 99, 106
Wallace, Paddy 106, 225
Wallace, Paul 86, *87*, 94
Wallace, Richard 81, 94
Wallace, Thomas 10
Walsh, H.D. 7
Walsh, Jerry 39, 198–9
Wanderers 6, 7, 36, 133, 205
Ward, Tony 58, 59, *60*, 61, 68–9, 82, 157
    European Player of the Year 53, 54
    first season playing for Ireland 220–1
    Garryowen 196, 198
    Munster vs All Blacks (1978) 186
    teaching post 220–1
    underage system 227
Watson, Cheeky 59, 61
Watson, Gavin 59
Watson, Ronnie 59
Watson, Valence 59
Webb Ellis Cup 96
Webb Ellis, William 5, 139, 199
Wheel, Geoff 48
Whelan, Pat 186
White, Les 186
Wild Geese 41
Wilkinson, Jonny 98
Williams, Bryan 47
Williams, John 47
Williams, J.P.R. 54
Williams, Matt 99, 226
Williams, Rhys 37
Wills's Cigarettes cards *11*
Wilson, Frank 202
Wilson, Stu 185–6
Wilson's Hospital School 222
Wimbledon 10, 11, 31
Winiata, Selica 150
Wolfhounds, The 160, 196
women
    caps awarded to 158
    GAA and 140, 144
    Ladies' Land League 140
    marriage bar 140
    role models 154–5, 157
    rugby and 1, 139–62
Women's Five Nations Championship (1999) *143*
Women's Grand Slam (2013) 160
Women's Rugby World Cup (1991), Inaugural 141
Women's Rugby World Cup (2014) 147, *147*, 150–1
Women's Rugby World Cup (2017) 157–8, 160
Women's Sevens squad (2023) 160
Women's Six Nations (2013) 145–6, *146*, *148–9*
Women's Six Nations (2023) 158
Wood, Gordon (B.G.M.) 33, 36
Wood, Keith 86, *87*, 93, 131, 168, 192, 226
Woodward, Sir Clive 96
World Cup (1987) 52, 71, 73, 173
World Cup (1991) 52, 73, 74
World Cup (1995) 81–2
World Cup (1999) 90
World Cup (2003) 94–6, *95*
World Cup (2011) 106
World Cup (2015) 110
World Cup (2019) 120, 122
World Cup (2021) 160
World Cup (2023) 1, 133, 135, *136–7*, 160
World Player of the Year (2018) 116, 120
World Player of the Year (2022) 131
World Rugby awards (2018) 116
World Rugby Coach of the Year (2023) 135
World Rugby Men's 15s Dream Team of the Year 132
World Rugby Men's Player of the Year (2018) 116, 131
World Rugby Men's Player of the Year (2022) 131
World Rugby Player of the Year (2023) 169
World Rugby Sevens Series 160
World Rugby Team of the Year (2023) 135
World Team of the Year (2018) 116
World Youths Cup (under-19s) (1997) 225
World Youths Cup (under-19s) (1998) 225

Y

Young Munster 30, 196, 198, 205
Young, Roger 41, 59, 199

Z

Zebo, Simon 198